Fresh Fields

Fresh Fields

More Writing from Out of Town

Edited by John Gordon

SHOAL BAY PRESS

First published in 2001 by
Shoal Bay Press Ltd
Box 17661, Christchurch

Cover painting: 'Trimmed Pines' by Dick Frizzell 2000
Private collection, Auckland
Reproduced with the kind permission of the artist

'Down the Hall on Saturday Night' (Peter Cape) Kiwi Music
reproduced courtesy Kiwi Pacific Records Intnl Ltd

ISBN 1 877251 11 9

Printed by Rainbow Print Ltd, Christchurch

For my mother, Muriel,
who always encouraged us to read good stuff.

Contents

Acknowledgements   11

Harvest William Hart-Smith   12

Introduction   13
With the Musterers William Langton   20
Ao Tea Roa Vernice Wineera   22
High Country Yva Momatuik and John Eastcott   23
Love at First Sight Bridget Musters   24

Beginnings   25
Between Earth and Sky Patricia Grace   29
The Constant Help Field Candy   32
Twilight Eileen Duggan   35
Birth Joy Cowley   36
Spring Patricia Grace   41
The Farm-Boy Rides a Yamaha Vernice Wineera   42
Off to School Noel Hilliard   43
Blood Poisoning John Newton   48
The Fifteenth Day J.H. Sutherland   49
The Water-Joey Mona Anderson   54
Fondest Memories Gordon Lucas   57
Poles Apart Nancy Patulski   59
My Landlord Peter Jackson Webb   61
Shaping Up Neroli Cottam   64
Quite a Lot of Bull Elizabeth Underwood   66
The Rise and Fall of H.G.-S. and A.M.C. W.H Guthrie-Smith   69

Animals   71
The old way of learning to ride Rod Campbell   75
Accident Prone Nora Sanderson   77
Harsh Mistress Amanda Jackson   80
Rajah Jim Morris   82
Uncle Wally's Pacer Barry Crump   84

O'Reilly's Pig Glynellen Slater   86

Sausages for Tea Heather Browning   88

Cats Pat White   89

My New Heifer Frank S. Anthony   90

Texas Longhorns John Dawson   95

Bulls' Horns Nelson L. Cooper   98

Bart and the Cows Ormond Burton   101

Sheep Fiona Farrell   103

Drama at the Yard John Gordon   104

Baa, baa, baa Millicent Bennett   106

Au Revoir Joy Cowley   107

Uncle Trev and the Howling Dog Service Jack Lasenby   110

The Commentators   113

The Farmer's Wife Anne Earncliff Brown   117

Rounding up Recalcitrant Cattle 'J.J.'   119

Age-Old Right of Farmers For the *New Zealand Free Lance*   121

A Shepherd's Calendar Oliver Duff   123

The Cold Shoulder 'Whim Wham' (Allen Curnow)   125

High Country Diary 'Tussock Jumper' (Sean Pennycook)   126

Sheepmen and their Dogs Peter Newton   129

Toprail Talk H.N. Munro   131

The Month Down South 'Nor'wester' (Roland Clarke)   133

The EEC Anon.   138

The View From Our Hill Bob Linton   139

Follow Fellow M. Weatherall   141

Bloody Friday June Slee   142

The Land John Kneebone   148

Sustainability Jim Morris   151

People Heather McCrostie Little   152

Make a poem of this Pat White   154

Tourist venture earns more aggro than EBIT Tim Gilbertson   156

Local farmers seek assistance Pat White   158

At First Hand   159

The Khaki Pit Field Candy   163

Milking before Dawn Ruth Dallas   165

Life on the Farm Amiria Stirling and Anne Salmond   166

A Day in the Life of a Farmer Becchi Watt   171

Busy Katie Pye   172

The Dipping Mary Scott   173

Love Poem to a Farmer Karalyn Joyce   176

The Hired Man Brian Turner   177

Of Cooks Philip Kenway   178

'Killing a Bit of Beef in the Morning' For the *New Zealand Free Lance*   180

Yes, to the Very End 'Augustus' (R.A. Copland)   182

Getting to Know You Joan MacIntosh   185

The Snow Down South 'Nor'wester' (Roland Clarke)   189

A Rural Experience of the Napier Earthquake E.J.V. Barry and Jane Foster   192

Pastimes and Occasions   195

The Wrath of God Tommy Cowan and Valerie Cowan   199

The Honey Tree M.H. Linscott   201

'Hey! The Mill's Coming!' Peter Dunbar   204

Calf Club Day John Gordon   206

The Battle for the Nodding Thistle Shield Field Candy   208

Representative Cricket Ralph Lowry   211

Country Member Dawn Hayes   212

Down the Hall on Saturday Night Peter Cape   213

The Young Farmers' Club Experiences a Blackout Fiona Farrell   214

The Last of the Barn Dances Jack Lasenby   216

The Opener May Williamson   219

The Women's Division of Farmers' Union Alice Mackenzie   222

The Good Old Days Peter Newton   223

One Trial After Another John Gordon   225

The Single Shepherd David Geary   228

Nga Puke (The Hills) John Broughton   229

Boys will be Boys Louisa Herd   235

Reality   237

Different Worlds Jim Morris   241

Isolation Joan MacIntosh   242

The Winner May Williamson   245

All for Ayrshire M.L. Allan   246

Lambing Beat John Foster   247

Bobby Calf Barry Mitcalfe   248

Sweet Dieseline Tom Landreth   249

Scientific Management David Ray   250

Loading the Bulls William Owen   251

The Hydatids Officer Michael Henderson   255

Death in the Hayfield Maureen Doherty   258

The Initiation Brian Turner   260

Ferreting About Dan Davin   261

Pioneer Woman with Ferrets Ruth Dallas   265

Nor'wester C. Evans   266

The Dam Elizabeth Hill   267

So easy Pat White   270

The Past and the Passing   271

Mutton John Newton   275

Boots Field Candy   276

When Jean Deans Raced the Train 'Blue Jeans' (Ross McMillan)   277

One of Our Aircraft Failed to Return Patricia M. Saunders   280

The Old Kitchen Table Jim Henderson   281

Squatters' Rites John Gordon   283

38 Years J.M. Kerwin   285

Mapiu, Remembered Roses Nancy Fox   286

Farewell Prickly, Luscious Blackberry 'Grammaticus' (E.M. Blaiklock)   287

Clarence Pack Team Frances Blunt   290

We Mustered Sheep Together 'Blue Jeans' (Ross McMillan)   290

A Bitch Called Fly Peter Stewart   291

A Glass of Prosek Amelia Batistich   296

Journey Barry Crump   299

Requiem in a Town House Owen Marshall   300

Abandoned Homestead Brian Turner   304

Contributors and Sources   307

Acknowledgements

My grateful thanks to all the contributors to this collection. Finding their work was a lot of fun and making contact with them was a pleasure, thanks to their friendly and totally supportive replies to my permission-seeking letters. Long may they continue to write about life out of town and may others join them in describing farming and its folk.

Much of the required research and reading was carried out at the Alexander Turnbull Library. Without its existence, gathering material for anthologies such as this would be extremely difficult. As with *Out of Town*, my first rural collection, I am indebted to the friendly, helpful and knowledgeable staff in the New Zealand Collection research library, along with those who helped me negotiate both the newspaper and manuscript collections.

My thanks also to those who made suggestions for directions I should look in and material I should read. Special mention should be made of fellow Turnbull reader/researcher of the time, Lydia Wevers, and my sister Fay.

To David Elworthy and Ros Henry of Shoal Bay Press, thank you for being prepared to publish more words and works about the country.

I have been fortunate that Anna Rogers, a professional to the tip of her discerning red pen, has edited all the books I have worked on. I am deeply grateful for her expertise and forbearance.

For her unfailing support and interest in the project, as with those preceding it, my grateful thanks to my partner Kereyn.

Harvest

Look what has happened to the sun
the power we intercept. It falls
in a singing torrent of little hard grains.

A man wades knee-deep on the
slopes of a sharp-peaked mountain
digging shovel-fulls of sunshine into sacks.

William Hart-Smith, *Harvest*, 1945

Introduction

When researching and compiling the rural anthology, *Out of Town*, I never intended it to have a companion volume. Once Glover's 'The Magpies', Baxter's 'Farmhand', Anthony's 'Winter Feeding the Herd', Ihimaera's 'One Summer Morning' and Ruth Dallas's 'Photographs of Pioneer Women' had been placed between two covers the task seemed complete, especially when those pieces were accompanied by a hundred other works by the likes of Amelia Batistich, Dan Davin, W.H. Guthrie-Smith and many lesser-known writers and poets whose lives were steeped in matters rural. No, with what I thought was a well-rounded combination of the so-called heavyweights and practically inclined journeymen, a second collection would never go past the first round.

The first to lay down the challenge of round two was Jim (*Open Country*) Henderson. Ever pastoral New Zealand's most positive and persuasive supporter, he wrote, 'Thank you for your beautiful *Out of Town*, New Zealand breathing. Masterly selection, (Southland Knowse!)…' and signed off with, 'Onward to book two.'

'Silly, marvellous man,' I thought, 'how can there be two?'

Reasonably easily, once you make your mind up to do it and reflect on the content of the first volume. In the collected words of a diverse group of writers, it was very much the sum of what we would expect to celebrate about our rural history. In the introduction I explained that the collection would follow, 'by means of my convenient idealism', a logical, rural chronology that began with childhood, moved through settlement and development and ended in a reflective mood. In the main, the chosen tales and verses described the years between the First and Second World Wars and the rapid expansion of both farming and its community that followed 1945.

The inference could have been taken that farming and rural life as we knew it was finished, and that the will to observe and celebrate it in poetry and prose was also fading. At a personal level, I did feel a need to gather what I could before at least some of it was forgotten or, worse still, lost. This is because in a traditional and emotional sense, statements that the old-style country life has disappeared are true: it's called progress. Equally correct, though, is the fact that farming is not dead, and nor are those who people it. There are fewer of them, sure, and the units they manage are gaining in size and employ smaller staffs. In addition, those with ancillary skills – drivers, mechanics, contractors, storekeepers and schoolteachers – now live in centralised communities which, if they're lucky, service a 'rural hinterland' that is no longer hinter as once it was.

Both volumes are personal selections. In the first I concentrated on the rural New Zealand of my immediate ancestors and my youth. In this volume, with the exception of a few pieces from earlier times that I've recently discovered and cannot overlook, I want to recognise the farmers, creators and commentators of my adulthood. Some of them are friends or acquaintances – even a former employer – and all describe the way life out of town is now or was not so long ago. They prove that the art of writing about our countryside and its occupants – two- and four-legged – has not been lost, nor the will to describe it diminished. In fact, published work by rural dwellers has increased and now has a sharper tone, challenging the formerly accepted status quo. Politicians, bureaucrats, unions and industry are now all fair game for the rural pen.

The introduction to *Out of Town* said it was a celebration of those who 'cut scrub, drained swamps, sowed swedes and strangled teats'. This volume is about those who, either directly or indirectly, inherited that land and suffered seasons of drought, saw traders leave and fly-by-nighters hover, watched prices drop as costs rose. Some, in the spirit of the old lottery winner's joke, had no option but to farm on until all the money had gone. Governments weren't much chop either, imposing policy changes at short-term cost to the individual and long-term cost to the nation.

The community that has withstood the 1980s and 1990s is leaner, meaner and, in some respects, greener than the generations that preceded it. This is apparent in much of what has been written and, very often, in who wrote it. This volume has many more women writers, a reflection of economic reality, as there are now even more female farming partners involved in full-time, day-to-day farm work. Where once a sheep and beef property employed a staff of two, now there's likely to be a very busy woman working long hours in the paddock, stock yards and sheds. And husbands, after kicking off their boots, have found themselves preparing the meal as well. None would be more used to doing so than the scores of men whose wives literally saved the farm by returning to their old careers in nearby schools, hospitals or offices. Others turned their hand to occupations as varied as school bus driver or knife hand at a meat-packing plant. Home or away, during the drought-ridden, cost-plus or -minus years, rural women contributed as much to the family's on-farm survival as their more land-based partners.

Another factor that has broadened the written record of the last two decades and, therefore, this book, has been the proliferation of creative writing groups throughout provincial New Zealand. From Hokianga to Matamata, Taihape to Hokitika, Nelson to Cromwell, all have produced small books or booklets on an annual or occasional basis. Going by these publications, the greater percentage of the membership are women and many of them use writing as an outlet from their total involvement at home. A good example is one of my favourites, 'Busy', by Katie Pye. It may not be one of the great rural ballads, but as a relief valve from farm work, it's a beaut.

> I inspected the dam while drenching the lambs
> and mended the gate between breaths
> and while sharpening a scythe-blade, I thought, I'm glad I'm not paid
> or I'd think I was being worked to death.

Participation in day-to-day farming is a feature of both this collection and of many of the contributors. Among these is Jim Morris of Ben Avon Station in the Omarama district. One of the South Island high country's characters, Jim wears size 14 hobnailed boots with ease and, at the drop of a musterer's hill pole, can deliver a back country ballad of his own making. Some of these celebrate his beloved backblocks, others are wry observations and then there's Jim's 'occasion material', written for special gatherings, such as the toast to the daughter of a friend at her wedding.

> But the things that seem to make it work,
> With help from Him above,
> Are the good old twins of the mountains,
> Hard work, and lots of love.

Poet Pat White has always been a farmer and, for most of the time, a provincial librarian as well. The damp West Coast dairy lands he hails from, and the drought-prone hills of the Wairarapa, where he now lives, are very much part of his poetry. So too are governments who don't help farmers or farming: of all the rural writers featured here, Pat is the most direct with, at times, an extremely acerbic edge. And he has good reason, as nature turns nasty in tandem with the politicos. Typical is this extract from 'The hills aren't dying':

> there's a joke going round the valley
> 'get back at your kids, leave
> them the bloody farm.'

Perhaps the greatest pleasure of being the musterer of two anthologies of rural stories and verse has been finding tales that are new to me but also being able to admire and imagine the creators of those works. Field Candy, once a Bay of Plenty dairy farmer, is one of those. After coming across a story of his about a country cricket match in the *New Zealand Farmer*, I fired his name into the Alexander Turnbull Library's computerised catalogue. Instantly the screen came up with *Every Living Thing*, a collection of his short stories published by his wife, Mona, in 1988, four years after his death. A generation older than Morris and White, and farming during slightly easier times, Candy threw few challenges at those who lived beyond the farm gate. His gentle yet enquiring prose enshrined both his farm and the family who grew up on it, and all of this with a reflective tone that allowed him to celebrate objects that symbolise spring on a dairy farm, but would make the uninitiated take a step backwards.

> Four fresh placenta gleamed in the grass. Collapsed capsules, newly abandoned after nine months faultless service within the universe of the womb.

Rural life, independence, solitude and respect for the natural world mean that country folk mull over a wide range of topics and some have been able to air their thoughts in print as regular columnists in papers and periodicals. Their brand of considered honesty and criticism, and wonderful mix of other attitudes, observations and humour, are to be found in the section, 'The Commentators'. The other categories are 'Beginnings', 'Animals, At First Hand', 'Pastimes and Occasions', 'Reality' and 'The Past and the Passing'.

Grouping material under those headings has ensured that I have collected a different range of material. Some is written by people who had probably always dreamed of living in the countryside but didn't expect to be able to long before they retired. I'm referring to the new country folk, those who maintain an urban-based or Internet-connected professional life, but live beyond the suburbs. Many of them are creative people and their influence has been felt in many areas.

And this book contains work from more recent contributors to this country's literature. Novelist and poet Fiona Farrell lives and writes on a Banks Peninsula farm. Poet and editor Bridget Musters lives in countryside she describes as '…the brown muscle of Tahuna hills' and Gordon Lucas still farms Nine Mile, below the shoulder of the Lindis. Michael Henderson had the same rural Takaka background as his uncle, Jim, but only Michael could unite, as he did in 'The Hydatids Officer', English, Pidgin and flat-voweled new-zild – spelt as she is spoke – with both aplomb and sinister meaning. Patricia Grace's word pictures of rural Maori, Jack Lasenby's knowledge of life in the lee of the Kaimais during the 1930s and the images of rural fact in Joy Cowley's fiction, all ring with credibility.

Even so, Lydia Wevers was quite correct when, in her editor's introduction to the fourth in the Oxford series, *New Zealand Short Stories*, she noted the passing of the rural voice from stories published during the decade (1974-84) her collection encompassed. 'The laconic farm labourer familiar from the work of Sargeson, Middleton and Finlayson, scarcely exists.' Reading that early in my research I nearly threw in the towel, but she was right – although others were writing in new ways, their work often lurking within publications that few bookstores would ever shelve. Unearthed, their poems and stories continue a New Zealand tradition of describing life on the land. Moreover, their words and thoughts are more direct than the laconic voices of the past. That is how it should be. Once, farming was about settlement and development – realising a dream. Recently many have found that it's about survival, and survive they have. Theirs is a new agriculture, both socially and economically – fresh fields that are satisfying to write of and to read about.

With the Musterers

William Langton

The run to which they were going to muster the sheep, preparatory to shearing them, lay at some distance from Hilton, and comprised about 30,000 acres of wild, hilly country, remote from public road or dwelling. The way to it was by a winding sheep track which led along and up the slopes of the intervening ridges, and when the horsemen reached the top of the first ascent – nearly 2000 feet above sea level – Mark halted to survey the prospect in their rear. Far away in the dim horizon, across the vast plains, he distinguished the hazy outline of Flagstaff and Maungatua, frowning on the Taieri flats, and forming, as it were, a Northern barrier; while eastwards the Pacific spread its glittering waters, and fringed the shore with an edging of foaming surf. In the west the Blue Mountains reared their hoary peaks and completed the rampart of hills, which immured wide, open downs, falling and heaving like a troubled lake. And bearing on their crests homesteads, white as surf, looking all the brighter for the background of blue-gums by which most of them were half surrounded and wholly sheltered.

Here and there he could follow the course of streams as with the shiny trail of a serpent they crept along, past farmyards and townships, until swallowed in the muddy waters of the Molyneux, which rolled along a valley green with the richness of a southern Goshen. Descending the other side of the ridge by a steep, circuitous track, which led to a stream whose watershed they had just surmounted, they crossed the creek by a rough wooden bridge. They then rode for some miles up a glen hemmed in on either side by swelling, bracken-breasted hills, and followed the windings of the stream as they went. Passing through a narrow gorge and turning an abrupt angle, they came unexpectedly on a wide valley, almost Alpine in its loveliness and rugged grandeur, at the mouth of which stood the yards and hut of Mr Turnbull's station....

The country to be mustered consisted of two long, winding, parallel valleys, whose dividing ridges issued like ribs from a backbone of lofty hills, which formed the main range and the southern boundary of the run. It was not an easy country to muster, or, rather, it was not a safe one. For let the sheep get a sudden fright, or suppose them to be over-driven by a careless shepherd or unmanageable dog, then at the foot of every rock or precipice, or at the ford of every land-locked creek, there would be found numerous fleecy carcasses, to tell a tale of recklessness and disaster.

The four men left the hut before daybreak, and for some miles rode together up a

1889, *Mark Anderson*

glen which in the grey dawn of morning looked so wild and solitary that as Mark looked on the fantastic rocks that broke the sky-line, and the jagged peaks that rose like huge stakes against the horizon, he could not help exclaiming to Ross, who rode by his side –

'This beats the Highlands!'

But the patriotic Celt fired up at the artless remark, and almost shrieked –

'What is tat you say? Peats ta Hielants! Haf you lost your senses, Mr. Anderson? – or wass you soper? Where is ta heather or ta hazel or ta pirch? To you hear ta scream o' ta eagle, ta whirr o' ta muir-cock, or ta plast o' ta paag-pipes? Can you show her a clansman's cairn, or a corry where a chief was kilt in a creagh, or ta plue reek o' ta still, or a trop o' ta mountain tew, Mr. Anderson?–

Put, Mr. Anderson, she'll no call tem hills, whatefer, put only heaps o' ruppish trown up, maype, when ta earth wass sick?'

Ao Tea Roa

Vernice Wineera

She is a tidy country,
manicured hourly
by her millions of sheep.
The earth's golf course.
'God's Own Country'
her natives sheepishly call her,
as if self-consciously aware
of some obscure ambiguity in the phrase.
The real natives called her
Ao Tea Roa,
the long white cloud.
The land has changed since then.
The tangled forests have been cut,
and bulldozed and burned.
The land has been settled,
and civilized,
and the neat and tidy,
orderly arrangement
of a well-kept golf course
has replaced the unproductive virginity
of the land before the pakeha.
Perhaps because I am not entirely pakeha,
I think I would have preferred
her former state,
for my Walden is her lakes,
her mountains, her wild beaches,
and her dark and secret forests
which offer sanctuary
to the lost and tangled thoughts
of my mind.

1978, *Mahanga: Pacific Poems*

High Country

Yva Momatuik and John Eastcott

Seasons unfold. Farm life in the high country stirs up in spring, with late, wet snow, floods and feeding of winter-weary stock. Then shearers come with a clamour of blades to peel thousands of fleeces in a furious rush of work, hurried by threatening rain, until the last bale of wool leaves for the market. Lambs arrive, but these mountain-raised ewes, light-footed and packed with muscles, need no help with lambing and must be left undisturbed, for they are seldom handled and remain half-wild.

When the air warms up, the sheep are sent back into the mountains to graze and follow the retreating snowline; cattle scatter to browse on swampy river flats, spring vegetables sprout in gardens and children bound around their enormous playground on long-haired ponies. Summer comes with afternoons baking in the sun oven. It is the time for haystacks, fence mending, machinery repairs, races, horse shows and sheep dog trials.

Autumn means arduous foot musters, starting before dawn, often ending in pouring rain and a howling nor'wester. And then comes winter … Families huddle together, sometimes snowbound for days. People keep a watchful eye on the weather, feed struggling stock and shovel thick logs onto the hearth. The homestead becomes the whole world where without tolerance, mutual liking and ability to find something to do, life would be miserable. The spring comes slowly, pouring tall clouds and warm winds into valleys. The seasons unfold again into another year.

What *is* the high country then?

It is air so clear that the eyes hurt from looking into a 50-kilometre corridor of a valley, a cradle of the glacier, with rolling boulders for toys and silver ribbons of a river, entwined and gurgling under shimmering beech forests. It is an abyss of scree so steep that stones seem glued to their rocky bed. It is a sudden sight of sheep, strung like a necklace on an invisible thread, little white beads following one another, heads into the wind, suspended high among yellow strands of tussock just below the blue of the sky. It is the time when you try to reach them across the steep ravine, first thundering down, sliding in your thick, nail-studded boots, then climbing quickly among rocky spurs, feeling your muscles strain and lungs gasp sharp gulps of air with the quickening of the heart. It is the country where a confident breed of people came to terms with their place under the sun.

1980, *High Country*

Love at First Sight

Bridget Musters

They told me to expect
the polka dots of sheep
that blew away as the plane came in to land
and they said there'd be
outside dunnies
earthquakes
attitudes that went with the ark
and a moon that waxed and waned
the Other Way

But no-one told me of
the Kodak blue
the light that made my forehead ache
the rumpled bedsheet of the country's spine
and the brown muscle of Tahuna hills

Nor warned me I was coming home

1994, *Ten*

Beginnings

It's a start, I suppose – a beginning, introduction or initiation that is looked back on with the fondness or humour that hindsight and the passing years allow. Sometimes, though, there's disbelief, 'Did we really do that? Don't know how we got away with it …certainly wouldn't try it now!' Many of the incidents described in this section are childhood experiences, often made more vivid by the shapes and shadows of adolescent imagination. Sometimes, a single episode points to a new direction and a life on the land. Patricia Grace's 'Between Earth and Sky' began a new life – in one of those marvellous, small maternity hospitals that, alongside a general store, post office, hall, garage, tennis court, footie field and three- or four-teacher school, were once dotted around the country in virtually self-sufficient communities. Those days are over, and not just 'The Home', as it was always known, but probably the store, the garage, the post office, the bank and maybe the school have gone too. Alas, the downhill journey towards what bureaucrats call 'rationalisation' starts with subtraction. Thanks to Patricia Grace, this section begins with an addition.

In earlier days, when farming here was about initial settlement and development, quite a number of those who 'started out' were people whose inclination to become New Zealand farmers or run-holders was completely contrary to their backgrounds. In print the best known of these was W.H. Guthrie-Smith, a Scottish-born grandson, son and brother of Edinburgh doctors. He came to New Zealand in his late teens to become a farmer. At first, he was in partnership with his cousin, and the two had less than four years' practical experience between them. This was of little matter to Guthrie-Smith: his university was the land itself and he became New Zealand's most able landowning observer/naturalist and communicator. To read his 'The Rise and Fall of H. G.-S. and A.M.C.' is to share the joy of experiencing and observing new things, a trait that he never lost in the 58 years he farmed and described his property, Tutira.

Other beginnings can be very different: a first impression leading to sunken stomached dismay. I well remember going to a new job late on a southern midwinter's night and parking the car almost on the doorstep of the hut I had hoped to call home. This was to avoid tracking mud from the ankle-deep mire that surrounded the car into what was once an old teamster's abode. All but buried beneath as tall a row of sou'westerly blasted macrocarpas as has ever stayed rooted to the spot, it was, to put it mildly, damp. Adding to the hut's moisture content was the wet wallpaper my new boss had finished hanging onto the scrim-lined walls only an hour or so before. And to complete the picture, the night was successfully laying the foundations for a day that would dawn with a -25°F frost. At that dark and dismal hour I did not have a good feeling about that farm and my future on it.

Monday dawned crisp, clear and icy. On my first trip to the nearby village I saw two cars parked against telegraph poles, one of them driven by a sidestepping rugby winger and idol of my childhood who, I had always thought, could avoid anything. On reflection I realised that I hadn't come out of the night too badly after all. After a cautious return journey at the wheel of an ultra-basic, 1944 US Army two-ton truck, I went back to the hut to deal with the dismal damp. In the brick and corrugated iron fireplace I created a bigger blaze than any teamster would have cooked his tea on (I ate at the house) and nearly straightened the hooks and hob a succession of old-timers hadn't threatened. The walls were soon dry and I and that ancient hob and hearth began a warm and lasting friendship. In the months to come many a Young Farmers' Club committee meeting was attracted to that fireside's glow. Tea from the old black kettle that hung above embers which quickly converted bread into crisp, butter-dripping squares were added attractions. In fact, those open fire tuck-ins were the envy of many a youth who worked on the home farm, with mothers who supervised orderly tea-and-cake-on-a-tablecloth suppers for committee members.

I liked that job, which goes to show that though first impressions may be lasting – I will never forget how bloody cold I was that night – they are not always an accurate portent of what is to come.

Between Earth and Sky

Patricia Grace

I walked out of the house this morning and stretched my arms out wide. Look, I said to myself. Because I was alone except for you. I don't think you heard me.

Look at the sky, I said.

Look at the green earth.

How could it be that I felt so good? So free? So full of the sort of day it was? How?

And at that moment, when I stepped from my house, there was no sound. No sound at all. No bird call, or tractor grind. No fire crackle or twig snap. As though the moment had been held quiet, for me only, as I stepped out into the morning. Why the good feeling, with a lightness in me causing my arms to stretch out and out? How blue, how green, I said into the quiet of the moment. But why, with the sharp nick of bone deep in my back and the band of flesh tightening across my belly?

All alone. Julie and Tamati behind me in the house, asleep, and the others over at the swamp catching eels. Riki two paddocks away cutting up a tree he'd felled last autumn.

I started over the paddocks towards him then, slowly, on these heavy knotted legs. Hugely across the paddocks I went almost singing. Not singing because of needing every breath, but with the feeling of singing. Why, with the deep twist and pull far down in my back and cramping between the legs? Why the feeling of singing?

How strong and well he looked. How alive and strong, stooping over the trunk steadying the saw. I'd hated him for days, and now suddenly I loved him again but didn't know why. The saw cracked through the tree setting little splinters of warm wood hopping. Balls of mauve smoke lifted into the air. When he looked up I put my hands to my back and saw him understand me over the skirl of the saw. He switched off, the sound fluttered away.

I'll get them, he said.

We could see them from there, leaning into the swamp, feeling for eel holes. Three long whistles and they looked up and started towards us, wondering why, walking reluctantly.

Mummy's going, he said.

We nearly got one, Turei said. Ay Jimmy, ay Patsy, ay Reuben?

Yes, they said.

Where? said Danny.

1980, *The Dream Sleepers*

I began to tell him again, but he skipped away after the others. It was good to watch them running and shouting through the grass. Yesterday their activity and noise had angered me, but today I was happy to see them leaping and shouting through the long grass with the swamp mud drying and caking on their legs and arms.

Let Dad get it out, Reuben turned, was calling. He can get the lambs out. Bang! Ay Mum, ay?

Julie and Tamati had woken. They were coming to meet us, dragging a rug.

Not you again, they said taking my bag from his hand.

Not you two again, I said. Rawhiti and Jones.

Don't you have it at two o'clock. We go off at two.

Your boyfriends can wait.

Our sleep can't.

I put my cheek to his and felt his arm about my shoulders.

Look after my wife, he was grinning at them.

Course, what else.

Go on. Get home and milk your cows, next time you see her she'll be in two pieces.

I kissed all the faces poking from the car windows then stood back on the step waving. Waving till they'd gone. Then turning felt the rush of water.

Quick, I said. The water.

Water my foot; that's piddle.

What you want to piddle in our neat corridor for? Sit down. Have a ride.

Helped into a wheelchair and away, careering over the brown lino.

Stop. I'll be good. Stop. I'll tell Sister.

Sister's busy.

No wonder you two are getting smart. Stop ... .

That's it missus, you'll be back in your bikini by summer. Dr McIndoe.

And we'll go water-skiing together. Me.

Right you are. Well, see you both in the morning.

The doors bump and swing.

Sister follows.

Finish off girls. Maitland'll be over soon.

All right Sister.

Yes Sister. Reverently.

The doors bump and swing.

You are at the end of the table, wet and grey. Blood stains your pulsing head. Your arms flail in these new dimensions and your mouth is a circle that opens and closes as you scream for air. All head and shoulders and wide mouth screaming. They have clamped the few inches of cord which is all that is left of your old life now. They draw mucus and bathe your head.

Leave it alone and give it here, I say.

What for? Haven't you got enough kids already?

Course. Doesn't mean you can boss that one around.

We should let you clean your own kid up?

Think she'd be pleased after that neat ride we gave her. Look at the little hoha. God he can scream.

They wrap you in linen and put you here with me.

Well anyway, here you are. He's all fixed, you're all done. We'll blow. And we'll get them to bring you a cuppa. Be good.

The doors swing open.

She's ready for a cuppa Freeman.

The doors bump shut.

Now. You and I. I'll tell you. I went out this morning. Look, I said, but didn't know why. Why the good feeling. Why, with the nick and press of bone deep inside. But now I know. Now I'll tell you and I don't think you'll mind. It wasn't the thought of knowing you, and having you here close to me that gave me this glad feeling, that made me look upwards and all about as I stepped out this morning. The gladness was because at last I was to be free. Free from that great hump that was you, free from the aching limbs and swelling that was you. That was why this morning each stretching of flesh made me glad.

And freedom from the envy I'd felt, watching him these past days, stepping over the paddocks whole and strong. Unable to match his step. Envying his bright striding. But I could love him again this morning.

These were the reasons each gnarling of flesh made me glad as I came out into that cradled moment. Look at the sky, look at the earth, I said. See how blue, how green. But I gave no thought to you.

And now. You sleep. How quickly you have learned this quiet and rhythmic breathing. Soon they'll come and put a cup in my hand and take you away.

You sleep, and I too am tired, after our work. We worked hard you and I and now we'll sleep. Be close. We'll sleep a little while ay, you and I.

The Constant Help

Field Candy

(1)

We are nearly half a mile from the house and I have only an hour's battening to finish the new fence. Then I'm all set to hang the new gate, except that I've forgotten the gudgeons with which to hang it. I contemplate my workmate with a speculative eye. I've not used him as a messenger before, but it's worth a try. Accordingly I hand him this note, written on a page torn from the crumpled memo book I habitually carry.

'Dear Mo, would you please give Hugh the gudgeons I left on the back step.'

With the message clutched tightly in his hand, the diminutive courier sets off down the hill on winged feet. Since running is one of his favourite things, he is soon out of sight. Hazards aplenty confront him on his journey, but he is equipped to deal with them all. He must climb over some fences and crawl under others that are electrified. He is wise in the ways of the latter and knows from experience what it's like to be fully charged by a 'shocking wire'. He must pass several water troughs, but I feel no concern for him. He doesn't fall in by accident but climbs in on purpose for a swim, when the spirit and the season move him. He'll make it all right, but can he be persuaded to make the long climb back up the hill?

An hour later, I hammer the last staple into the final batten and start towards home. But what is this? The tip of his head comes into view over the brow of the hill. You little beaut! As he approaches I see the galvanised gudgeons flashing in the sunlight. I can only praise him and say thank you. He is content. He has discovered another resource within himself and proved his reliability.

(3)

'Me yelp Dad?'

'Yes, you can help Hugh.'

I am building gates in the woolshed on a wet day. I hand over my hammer and a box of bolts to my three-year-old apprentice. He applies himself eagerly to the task of driving bolts into their tight-fitting holes. I know from experience that he will see the job through. It will be a long time before my hammer is returned, but I'm a poor fellow if I can't find other work in the interim. So I measure and cut another gate, I'm not redundant yet.

1988, *Every Living Thing*

At last he looks up from his labours. There is achievement in his attitude and in his voice.

'Finned Dad.'

He has indeed finished; every bolt has been driven clean through the three-inch bulk of timber.

I congratulate him on the quality of his workmanship.

Flipping the gate over I start fitting washers and screwing on nuts.

'Me do 'at Dad?'

Deposed again. I hand over the spanner and go back to the other gate. He begins by twirling the spanner in the wrong direction.

'You're undoing it, Hugh.'

'Uzzer way Dad?'

He rearranges his work forces.

'Is way Dad?'

'Yes. That's better.'

The project requires his total application. Except for a periodic, 'Is way Dad?', we work in easy silence. Later, as he comes to terms with the gentle art of tightening bolts, conversation is resumed.

Outside the rain sluices down. On my own I might have noticed the gloom, but not today. Not with this small presence glowing gladly beside me.

(5)

When Hugh weighed into the world at only four pounds we were advised to rear him on goats milk. So Neila was introduced to the farm. Pure white in colour and golden-eyed, Neila nourished the child for three years in one prodigious, non-stop lactation.

Hugh grew into a happy, fleet-footed boy, whose greatest friend and playmate was Neila. She was still producing a foaming billyfull of milk a day when she suddenly became ill. We called the vet, but she continued into a swift and mortal decline.

We laid her on the verandah, wrapped her up in blankets, and told Hugh she was dying. He was not especially concerned but we could see that he did not really comprehend. Death was something outside his experience.

But the instant the light left the golden eyes, his attitude changed dramatically. Intuitively he knew his friend had passed beyond his reach.

Then the floodgates opened. The tears began to roll. For two days he was inconsolable.

(6)

And here is this sprite coming to terms with a spade. I am bewitched by the enquiry and the application of the small hands.

The fencing proceeds apace. My assistant is digging a hole of his very own. The morning spins by recklessly.

The inner man calls for attention. The smoko basket beckons. Using the hub of the trailer as a step he hauls himself up the sides onto the deck amidst sundry tools and fencing gear. Leaning over at full stretch he lowers the basket gently to the ground. Much more casually, he flings himself after it with an easy nonchalance.

On the vast evergreen, ever-clean tablecloth of rye grass and clover, he sets out my thermos and his bottle of lemon drink. He unwraps mother's miraculous scones. I pretend not to have seen any of these catering arrangements. When he is satisfied that everything is ready he announces, 'Moke moke red' Dad.'

'That's very nice of you, Hugh.'

We sit side by side, our backs against the tractor's rear wheel. This is no smoko. This is a banquet.

(7)

We are grubbing Scotch thistles. The day is hot and arid. I confront the big ones with my favourite spade. He assaults the little ones with a light hoe.

Without thinking I moisten my hands in the traditional manner. Immediately there follows the most horrendous hawking noises. My workmate rubs slobbered hands together before taking up his grubber and advancing matter-of-factly upon the next thistle.

(10)

After a prodigious performance, Summer has handed over the baton to Autumn and departed the scene with typical grace and dignity. We are back in the potato patch, garnering gratefully.

We both have forks. There have been some casualties. He is somewhat downcast because of the various wounds he has inflicted on this mysterious subterranean vegetable. So I promote him to chief bagger and grader. Now he pounces delightedly upon the smooth-skinned miracles as I expose them to the light.

An earthworm attracts his attention. Handled with care it insinuates itself across the juvenile palm, taking no harm in its travels. I am glad, for where there is no respect for an earthworm or any other creature, there can be no respect or hope for anything.

Twilight

Eileen Duggan

I was driving the cows and the frogs were soothsaying,
'Woe, land and water! All, all is lost!'
It was winter full grown and my bones were black in me.
The tussocks were brittling from dew into frost.

The earth looked at me, ears up in a stillness.
I was nine at the time and a coward by fate:
The willow-trees humped into cringing old swaggers,
And the cows lunged up unicorns, passing the gate.

A sudden wind clouted the nose of our chimney,
It rumbled and bellowsed its sparks in a spray;
I took to my heels in the terrible twilight,
For I thought that the sky was blowing away.

1937, *Poems*

Birth

Joy Cowley

Tassy peered up at the dark hole under the cow's tail. 'I can see its feets, Daddy. I can see its two little feets.'

'Out of the road,' said Eric. 'If she breaks the chain she'll bowl you for six.'

He put an empty bucket upside down in the next bail, picked up his daughter and set her on it with a clatter that made the cow jump and roll its eyes. Ripples passed across the animal's flanks. She stretched her neck and bellowed over her tongue, a low sound, mostly steam.

'Stay there,' Eric said.

'I can't see!' Tassy turned on the bucket, scraping it over the concrete. 'Daddy? I want to see the calf.'

'You'll see it soon enough,' he said. 'Keep still and be quiet or I'll send you back to the house.'

The cow's ears twitched. She shivered again and tried to turn in the bail, nostrils dilated, sniffing for the rest of the herd which was now far away in the night paddock, udders empty.

Her own udder was springing hard and square as an overstuffed cushion, big teats for a heifer, and every now and then her back would arch, raising her tail. She didn't know what was happening to her, only that the security of the herd had gone at a time when she most needed it. She was alone, chained into a bail in an empty yard still awash from the afternoon milking. At the noise of the bucket she tried to kick her way out and when that failed, she charged the door in front of her with her sawn-off horns, slicing upwards against the bars. Finally she settled again, quivering and defeated.

Eric rolled up his sleeves as far as they would go and washed in a bucket of disinfectant and water, closing his breath against the smell that foamed on his clothing. It was a strong antiseptic and they'd been using it for so long on the farm that its smell immediately brought images of sickness and decay. Sometimes he could even smell it in his dreams.

The cow made a belching, grunting noise. With curved back, she strained against the chain.

'Doing it again, Daddy,' Tassy said, easing the bucket closer.

1984, *Two of a Kind*

The hole opened like a mouth, spilling a thread of water and mucus, and Eric reached inside. Legs were through all right, one behind the other, but the head was twisted back. No good trying to turn it. No room. Young heifer not much bigger in there than a ewe, and a whacking great calf.

'Can you feel its feets?' said Tassy.

The calf was still alive. As he tried to push it round, a quiver answered his hand. Too bad. When you got one this size, all you could do was cut it up and take it out piece by piece.

The contraction went and as the muscle tightened against his arm, he withdrew his hand. The cow kicked him. He hit her on the rump. 'You stupid – so-and-so!'

Tassy grinned. 'She's stupid, isn't she, Daddy?'

'Mind your own business,' he said.

He remembered how his father had once told him he had no feeling for animals He leaned forward to rub the heifer's back.

'She's having a bad time,' he said to Tassy. 'That's why she's behaving stupid. All right, easy girl, easy does it. Just you relax and you'll be okay.'

Tassy frowned. 'What you say that for? She's not people, she's a cow.'

'She understands.'

'She doesn't, Daddy. Cows don't know people talk. Uncle Dave told me. They don't know about words and things like we do. And Uncle Dave says it's not swearing when we say bloody to the cows because the cows think it's something else. That's true, Daddy. Uncle Dave says cross his heart and hope to die.'

'You talk too much,' said Eric. 'So does Uncle Dave.'

'It's not swearing when you say it to cows.' She moved her bucket close to the railing that separated her from the heifer. 'Bloody, bloody, bloody,' she sang. 'Bloody cows. Bloody ears and bloody mouth and bloody legs and bloody tits – '

'Shut up, Tassy!' said Eric.

'Tits isn't swearing. Cows' tits isn't a bad – '

'Be quiet! I told you you could watch if you weren't a nuisance.'

At once she closed her mouth, swung her knees together and sat forward, chin in hands.

'I think you'd better go back to Mum,' he said.

She was silent.

'It's going to take a long time. Tell Mum to put my dinner in the oven.'

She bent her head and her lip trembled. 'I won't talk. I won't do anything.'

He hesitated, then he looked through the door to the veterinary supply cupboard and he felt the meanness of the saw with its loop of serrated wire. You never knew how a thing like that might affect a kid.

'Do as you're told,' he said.

She started to bawl. 'You promised. You said – you did, Daddy. You said I could.'

'You can watch next time. Okay?'

'That's what you said before. You told me – '

The heifer crashed against the door of the bail. Her legs trembled, she hit her head again and again on the pipes, trying to escape, then she backed until she was half-sitting on the chain behind her tail. The contraction overpowered her. Her spine humped as her womb tried again to expel its load. The flesh round the hole pouted and dribbled. A pink hoof appeared like a forked tongue.

Eric put his hand in and leaned forward, his gumboots sliding on the concrete as he forced his weight against the calf. It moved. He might turn it yet. His hand spread blind over the slippery body, felt the neck shaped into a U. He tried to grip it, the neck, the bony bulge of the head; and then suddenly, the whole calf seemed to slide round. The pressure had eased. He could bring the head forward now. As he drew it to the cervix, he felt the nose wrinkle against his fingers. It was still very much alive.

'Get the rope, Tassy,' he yelled. 'Hurry!'

She brought it to him and held it ready.

'Put it in the bucket. The bucket full of that yellow stuff.'

As the contraction weakened, the cow closed tight on his wrist. He withdrew his hand. 'That's right. Good. Now give it to me.'

He cleared the calf's hooves and tied them together, then he stood to one side, holding the rope loosely. 'Got to wait till the next time,' he said. 'Can't pull now or I'll hurt her insides.'

Tassy was all eyes. 'Is that the way you do it, Daddy?'

'Yep.'

She bounced up and down on her bucket. 'It's time. It's time. Pull the calf!'

He stepped back and took up the strain, then he pulled away from the calf. It wasn't coming. He took the rope in both hands and leaned backwards. His hands slipped. A second later he was sitting in a mess on the concrete, manure and water seeping cold through his jeans.

Tassy put her hand over her mouth. He stood up and grinned at her. She took her hand away and laughed out loud, six year old, a mouth like a moulting hen. 'You got dirty pants. Ha, ha, Daddy, you got dirty poos all over your pants!'

'Bet you can't wait to tell your mother.'

The heifer was quiet and trembling with fatigue, her eyes half-closed, mouth agape, legs splayed outwards barely strong enough to support her. When she blinked, water ran down her face and stained the brown hair on her muzzle. Her breathing was fast. He picked up the rope.

'What's it take so long for, Daddy?'

'It's her first calf. Next year she'll be all right. A whole lot bigger.' He wound the rope twice round his hand. 'Come on, girl, let's make this the last one, eh? All you've got now, come on, push!'

Hard back against the chain, the heifer bellowed and fought to stay on her feet. He pulled the rope until his entire weight was against it. The chain cut into her withers. Her rump hung over it, wet and distorted.

He pulled, and again she bellowed.

He pulled. And the calf came.

There it was at last, two legs and a nose under her tail, lips drawn back from teeth strung with mucus. He untied the rope.

'Here, Tassy, you can do the rest. Get the legs, one in each hand, and give a long steady pull.'

Her fists closed round the knobs of wet hair and she gave a tentative tug.

'That's no good. Put some muscle into it.'

She screwed her face into lines of determination and struggled backwards, trying to keep a grip on the legs which were almost as thick as her arms. 'It's slippery, Daddy. It won't come. It's stuck.'

'It's coming, all right. Keep at it.'

Relieved of pain, the heifer was now trying to see what was happening behind her tail. She turned her head as far as she could and sniffed, her ears pricked forward.

'I can't, Daddy.'

'You can. Pull!'

It came away with a wet sound and fell awkwardly to the concrete, lay there blinking and mouthing the air while Tassy knelt over it. 'I did it, Daddy. I borned it. Look, it's got ginger eyelashes. I borned it all by myself, didn't I? Yuk! It's got stuff on it!'

He shrugged. He might have known it'd be a bull. A heifer wouldn't have survived. Well, that's the way it went, all that trouble for a hide and a dozen cans of dog meat. He unhooked the chain and put his hand in front of the cow. 'You can come out now, girl. It's finished.'

She backed out slowly, her legs still weak, and tried to sniff her tail where a strand of afterbirth hung down nearly as far as her udder.

Tassy looked up. 'It's a boy calf. It's got whiskers on its tummy.'

'That's right.'

She touched the limp pink umbilical cord. 'It was tied in the cow. That's why it was stuck, wasn't it, Daddy?'

Already the calf was threshing about and trying to lift its head. It was a big fellow all right, aggressive jaw, thick neck, plenty of energy in spite of the long struggle.

He said to Tassy, 'Leave it to its mother. She won't go near it with you there.'

Tassy wiped her hands on her dress. 'Can I think up a name for him?'

'I suppose so. Come on, hop up on my shoulders and I'll give you a ride over to the house.'

'What about the calf?'

'It'll be all right, if we leave them alone.'

She wriggled onto his shoulders and wrapped her arms round his neck. 'You're a nice father,' she said.

The sky was now dark with a flush of green over the hills and a pale bit of moon above them. The mud on the race had dried into the pockmarks of hooves. He tried to walk in a straight line, treading on the strips flattened by the tractor tyres. Branches of macrocarpa hung overhead, thickening the darkness, and through the smells of leaves and pollen and cows, he kept getting the whiff of honeysuckle. It was blooming early this year.

Tassy squirmed on his shoulders. 'I know! I know!'

'Know what?'

'I'm going to call him Christopher Robin. That's a good name. Isn't it a good name, Daddy? You think he'll like Christopher Robin? Let me down!'

She slid down his back, dropped to the ground, then ran ahead of him to the house, calling long before she reached the back porch, 'I borned it, Mum. Mum? I borned the calf all by myself.'

Spring

Patricia Grace

The children know about spring.
    Grass grows.
    Flowers come up.
    Lambs drop out.
    Cows have big bags swinging.
    And fat tits.
    And new calves.
    Trees have blossoms.
    And boy calves go away to the works on the trucks and get their heads chopped off.

1975, *A Way of Talking*

The Farm-Boy Rides a Yamaha

Vernice Wineera Pere

Skinny shoulders blistered by the sun,
freckles prominent across his serious face,
the ten-year-old herds slow cows
towards the milking-shed.
Back and forth behind them
the eager dogs bound and skip
watching for a sign
but he gives none.
 – He is wearing blue and gold,
silk and leather,
numbered helmet that glitters in the sun.
The guttural lowing of the cows
are roars from great excited crowds
of watching people.
These tufts of tussock
veering his machine aside
are hillocks on his dangerous
and lonesome victory ride,
when, the gate ahead a chequered flag,
he guns into the cloud of dust
to roar across the finish line
bettering the record time.

Then,
wiping his face
on his scarf of silk,
he bails the cows
and prepares to milk.

1978, *Mahanga: Pacific Poems*

42

Off to School

Noel Hilliard

Dad told Paikea he could spend his last morning at home in bed for an extra sleep-in to be ready for the long bus journey to the city; but Paikea surprised everyone by saying he wanted to go to the cowshed as usual – on his own. Dad kidded him and Bubby teased, but he stuck to it; and at last Dad said all right, if that was what he wanted, but what was Dad to do? – hang around the house getting in Mum's road? Paikea told him he could sleep in, seeing he thought it such a good idea. Dad laughed and said it might get him into lazy habits, but he didn't mind just this once.

Paikea was awakened, as usual, by the sound of Mac scratching the corrugated-iron wall under his window. He put his head out and whispered, 'Way back out, Mac.' The dog took off over the damp paddock. Paikea chewed an apple as he tramped into his gumboots on the back step. The clouds were starting to clear in the east and a part of the sky was faint blue. Mist hung in wisps and shreds over the bush.

Now that he was going away, it seemed strangely as if he had never been in the shed before. Every part of it that he knew so well took on an extraordinary new significance; what he saw now seemed to be a part of him: the spare set of cups hanging on a nail; the brushes, the shed-sheet stained and blurred with creamy fingermarks; Dad's receipts stuck on a wire; buckets, the broken car-pump, a chisel, heaps of rusty nails, empty tins of yellow teat-salve; the old .22 hanging in a corner under cobwebs.

He put the separator together, set up the vat, put out the buckets and rags, and started the engine. The old belt with the rough join idled slowly round. One morning they'd had trouble with that belt; milk had filled the vacuum-tank and was spilling over the floor by the time they'd found out what the trouble was.

The cows were in the yard, stomping the slush, trying to stand on the stones Dad had piled there last winter: dripping from the mouth, heads weaving from side to side, now and then giving a low stomach-grumble, a half-hearted moo, chewing the cud with a triangular movement of lean jaws. He opened the gate and they blundered in, idly swishing their tails. He filled the three bails and sat on a stool listening intently to the sounds of the shed, as if he had never heard them before: the clack of hoofs on concrete, the machine's exhaust puttering outside, the splash of bubbly milk into the vat. He put a spanner in the loop at the top of the cups for extra weight to force out the last creamy bit of milk, and leaned his face against the cow's warm flank.

1963, *A Piece of Land*

People look at a herd of cows and think, There they all are, just a big clump of them, they're milked twice a day and that's all there is to it. But it wasn't, at all. A herd of cows is like a big family, he reflected. Every cow in the shed has a name and a character and a history. After they're born you feed them the skim and keep them away from the mother; and if Dad isn't looking you sneak some cream from the shed to feed your pet for the Calf Club. You brush its coat smooth and glossy, and when it's to be exhibited you even polish its hoofs. You nurse the calves through their illnesses and worry about their troubles when they tear their udder on barbed wire or get bitten on the heels by the new dog. You get them used to the machine; you know after a while how much milk each gives and can guess exactly when to take the cups off. You can tell the hard-case ones from the placid and easy-going, the ones you have to leg-rope and the ones you needn't bother about. You see them growing older and slowing down, and when they're sold you're sorry. But there are always heifers coming in, for you to get to know and take an interest in. There were the cows in some way different, too: a twisted horn, or born without a tail, or small and pushed around by the others for you to pet and protect and stick up for. They'd once had a cow called Queenie, she was a peculiar colour of green, and you couldn't see her even in the smallest and most open paddocks unless you were right up next to her.

He poured skim into cans and when the last cow had been milked he filled the calf-buckets. He liked the calves, skinny-legged, frisky, eager, waiting keen and restless for the gate to open: the rush for the buckets, the jostling, jamming noses into the foamy skim, kicking: driving them out, tapping the holding-back ones on the nose with a stick, chasing out the ones that wanted to clean up what was left in the other buckets. Then the second lot, the smaller ones, jamming around, guzzling fast, like children eating ice cream at a birthday party. Their eyes were more alert than their mothers': they knew nothing yet of the cow-yard and the swamp-paddock, of bloat or foot-rot, of breaking legs on log bridges over drains, of trying to feed in paddocks scorched brown and crisp in late summer; of the fright of topdressing aeroplanes zooming low over the hills. They were like little kids. Some even had their favourite part of the calf-paddock, where they always went to graze or lie down – just like the tiny-tots at lunchtime at school.

Starting a new calf on the bucket was a real technique. You let her suck your finger for a while, and gradually draw her mouth down into the milk. Sometimes you'd lose patience, get mad and jam her head in.

It seemed very cruel to take the calf away from its mother and put it in a paddock so far away. When you saw the calves in the yard, crushed together and swinging in a big circle, furiously nuzzling and sucking and biting each other, you realized how much they wanted to run with their mothers. And the poor little bobby-calves, locked in the pen at the gate waiting to be taken off in the truck to the slaughter-house – how the mothers looked down the hill towards the pen, and stamped and bellowed and carried on. Yes, it was cruel, all right; but you couldn't run a dairy farm without doing it. Perhaps that was why the grown cows looked sad and suspicious and bad-tempered.

He remembered a mother cow once that was mad on its calf, couldn't bear to be separated from it. She bellowed for it all day and all night, tried to jump the fence every chance she got, and at last fell and hurt herself so badly that Dad had to shoot her. It was lucky they weren't all like that.

You knew all the cows by name, and their different ways; and of course you got to know the dogs, too, and the old horse. You know what each dog could do, what job it was best for; you trained it, taught it a bit and let it pick up the rest. It was great how a dog would find out how to do new jobs on its own after you'd helped it up to a certain point. They'd had a dog once that could take the horse's reins in its mouth and lead it right down to the front gate with the sledge.

And the bull, sitting alone, solid and unmoving, in his own big paddock of dock and *wiwi*: what was he thinking?

What a waste, Paikea thought as he dipped the cups in hot water, what a sheer waste to learn all about the farm and the herd, and then have to go away to boarding-school and forget all about it. Whatever you knew about farming could be of no use there. He knew the herd now; but in a season or two they'd change, and when he came back he'd have to learn them all over again. They'd laugh at you, down there, because you couldn't do algebra; but how many of them could take a tractor engine to pieces and put it together again properly? Still, that wouldn't count, with them. You'd have to do precis-writing and paraphrasing and all that. Why wouldn't Dad let him stay? Perhaps, when Dad realized how much they would miss him, he might change his mind even yet.

Washing the separator parts, he looked down the valley. Green paddocks for miles, with cows scattered over them like pepper on a lettuce leaf. The first thin sunlight was touching the battens along the ridge fence, and mist lay in little hollows of the bush.

When Dad had first said about sending him away to school in the city, he'd thought it would be great to get away from this place for a while. Now he didn't want to go...

Paikea had a thorough wash after breakfast and put on a collar and tie. Looking in the mirror, he was irritated by the black fuzz on his cheeks and upper lip. It'd have to come off before the year was out. The big boys said that if you cut it once it'd grow again quickly, bigger this time, and before you knew where you were you'd be shaving regularly. That'd be good. He'd write to Dad for a razor-set for his birthday. Then, when he came home for his holidays all the schoolkids would look at his whiskers and be jealous. Later on he might grow a moustache. One of those long thin ones, a line along the lip, like the crooks in the pictures.

He had a last check-through of his bag: a pocket diary, his Bible and Maori prayerbook (Christmas presents from Mum and Dad), his pencil-case, and the new fountain-pen that Grandpa and Grandma had given him when he won the scholarship. That had been a real thrill for them; they'd thought it something really marvellous.

He combed his hair with special care and stood on the front veranda with his bags while Mum took his photograph. Then, while Mum and Bubby tidied themselves, Dad brought the car up to the house and loaded the bags into the back.

Paikea had his last look around, said good-bye to the dogs, and climbed in. Bubby hoped the car would break down again, like it did that Christmas, so that Paikea would miss his bus. As they jolted down the hill over the sledge-tracks, she reached out and held his hand. He was going to knock it away and tell her not to be silly, it only made him feel worse; but when he looked at her large sad eyes staring up at him, he let her hand stay on his.

He looked out at the things that had made him angry so many times: the track, so greasy in winter rains; the rickety old cream-stand – how often had the can nearly fallen back on top of him when he was hoisting it up? – the *ngaio* where they'd smoked out a swarm of bees last summer and found nothing, not even an old comb. This was his place: here he should stay. Would Dad change his mind? Should he refuse to go? – what could they do then? Never mind the school! His thoughts of meeting new boys, having adventures like you read about in school-comics, new excitements and discoveries, disappeared as he looked through the window. All he wanted now was to saddle the horse and go galloping over the hills, the wind singing in his ears…

They pulled up at the turn-off to the main road, where the mail-boxes were propped on poles, and unloaded the bags. Dad made a great show of being busy, stacking the cases where he figured the rear door would be when the bus stopped.

Mum gave Paikea a shoe-box of sandwiches and cakes, a bar of chocolate, chewing-gum, a bottle of soft-drink, and a comic to read. He stood awkwardly in the dusty grass, his raincoat over his arm, not knowing what to say.

'Cheer up, son,' Dad said, looking far from cheerful. 'You'll be all right when you can't see us any more.'

Paikea felt a curious hollowness in his stomach. He glanced over the bank. A cow was standing in the middle of the creek, motionless, looking at its own reflection. The poplars, willow, *puriri*, wattle… the purple hills in the distance – he'd never been past them before except with his family. George Fowler's herd moving slowly into the hill-paddock… The cow in the creek was leaning forward to drink, now. A cloud of blue smoke from Kingis down the road – they must have started that *manuka* burn today, while the weather holds…

The bus roared tooting around the corner and stopped in a cloud of dust. The driver climbed down. 'Gidday, Matt!' Dad said.

'Boy off, eh? How far's he going?' The driver knew very well how far he was going; but he looked at the labels and threw the bags in. He was making out he wasn't interested. But all the passengers, people from town who didn't know them, were staring through the windows with an angry look, as if they thought these roadside stops a nuisance.

Dad held out his hand. 'Good-bye, Paikea,' he said, lips tight, eyelids damp at the corners. 'All the best, son.'

Mum put her arms around him and sobbed; he could feel her tears warm against his cheek.

He stooped to kiss Bubby.

'You have to write to me!' he said fiercely.

'You too!'

'Every day you write to me!'

The tightness in her throat stopped the words coming. She nodded hard, shaking tears from her eyes.

He climbed into the bus, found a seat by himself and put his coat and sandwich-box on the rack. The driver revved up. Mum was holding Bubby on her arm, now, and they were all looking at him with wet faces.

The bus started. He spread his fingers and waved, a small twist of the wrist that he hoped the other passengers would not see. Bubby waved her hanky, and Dad stood with an arm high above his head. Then the bus turned a corner and he couldn't see them any more.

They passed the church, the school. It seemed no time since he'd been in the primers, wandering around on his own, afraid the big boys would hit him. Then he'd been a big boy himself, swaggering around showing off, trying to slog the cricket-ball out of the playground...

He settled back in his seat and was surprised how good he felt. He'd always enjoyed a journey; now he could look forward to a really long one! He saw some of the schoolkids hanging around outside the store, but couldn't be bothered waving. Dad was right: it made a lot of difference when you couldn't see the home folks any more.

The bus was in top gear, hurtling around bends and joggling over culverts. In no time they were at the coast, driving along the road above the sea. He could see men on launches putting out set-lines with milk-tin buoys. They were well past the purple hills, now, turning inland, pointing towards a new lot of purple hills.

No more cows! He could hardly believe it. No more four-in-the-morning! No more cream-cans, sledges, rainstorms, frosts!

This was beauty!

He opened the packet of chocolate.

Blood Poisoning

John Newton

Cold-start mornings   tractor coughing blue smoke
a child's landscape blanketed in frost

Trailer   rocking
haybale, chainsaw, two-stroke fuel in a Gordon's bottle;
animals in blithe
possession of their element, the way that sheepdogs
sidle out of the path of a moving vehicle

Tractorbox:
rubber rings, long handled pliers,
penicillin, pocket-knife, amyl nitrate, Park Drive

Hot greasy naked
skin of a ewe's armpit:
blunt needle, angry purple udder

A child's landscape: forest of frost
Seagull sideways at a safe distance   head cocked

Watchfulness, hunger, bloodlust,
greed: percussion in a dog's throat
gulping   afterbirth

1989, *Landfall,* No.169

The Fifteenth Day

J.H. Sutherland

I'm sure the Welfare Officer didn't mean me to overhear – but I'm pretty cunning at listening to what concerns me. He said to Uncle Andrew that if I stayed fifteen days on the farm it would be a breakthrough, a fortnight was my best time yet. I'd run away from all my foster homes. But this was my last chance. Next time it would be Kingseat …

I could tell you things about those homes you wouldn't believe. They'd look so good to *you*. But what's the use? …

Right from the start it *seemed* different at the farm. As soon as I met him the man told me to call him Uncle Andrew, and his wife Aunt Mary.

On my very first day he'd given me a wonderful pair of workboots – King Leos. He told me they were half a size too small for him. The Farmers' Co-op had made a mistake sending them out to him, and if I hadn't turned up they would have gone back for a refund. But when I pulled them on they fitted me as snug as lambswool slippers.

There's only three things a man needs in life, Uncle Andrew said, and good boots is one of them. I kept meaning to ask him what the other two things were.

Perhaps the horse and dog. That's the next he did for me. Gave me Brumby, my own pony; and Sniff, the old eye dog, to work for me …

It was only just the fifteenth day, still early, when Uncle Andrew shook me: wakey, wakey, boy! Feet on the floor! Rise and shine!

I didn't need much shaking. The uncertainty about my new life had got into my dreams and I was having a nightmare. Don't ask me what about. Five minutes after I'd woken the breathless feeling was all that was left of it.

I could hear roosters crowing and the voice of a ewe from the hill behind the homestead, calling and calling for her lost lamb. But it was still dark outside.

Last night I'd told Uncle Andrew that I wanted to go mustering with him, I didn't want to help with the shearing; but he'd just laughed. 'There'll be plenty of time for tearing round the hills on the horse. They're going to be shorthanded in the shed. That's where you'll be most use tomorrow, Douglas.'

But I thought he might be in a better mood this morning, so I tried again. 'Can't I come with you? I won't be much use to them. I don't know anything about shearing …'

'Enough of that, Douglas! Just do your best, that's all anyone can ask.' Uncle Andrew looked as if he might do his block if I kept on. 'Go up to the quarters and wake the

1977, *This Earth and Other Stories*

shearers. By the time you get back here I'll have the water boiled and you can take the billy of tea and the sandwiches over to the woolshed. You can have your morning tea with the shearers. Try to make yourself useful, don't sulk. Do whatever Bill Dooley tells you …'

I sat on the kitchen step thinking that if I took the billy over, and waited till Uncle Andrew was well away to the back paddock I'd have a good start. I'd make sure they didn't catch me this time.

As I clumped off in the new hobnails Uncle Andrew told me off for not lacing them properly. He claimed he could always judge a man by his feet. If he stopped around with his laces undone his work would be sloppy, too.

All right man. I don't owe you anything … Just for that I'll take the car when I go …

When I reached the shearers' quarters the men seemed to be sleeping so soundly it was my turn to put on the reveille act, 'Wakey, wakey! Rise and shine!'

I should have realised they weren't sleeping as soundly as all that. The thud of my boots along the wooden verandah floor would have boomed through the quarters.

A sandshoe whizzed past my ear. So that was all right. The shearers were awake.

I still had to go to the end room to call the two Maori girls, Hera and Wiki.

'They sleep pretty sound. You'll have to go in and shake them,' said Bill Dooley.

My fourteen-year-old shyness would have made that something of an ordeal. But Bill was having me on, I think. They answered when I knocked on the door.

I went back to the house for the billy of tea and the sandwiches. By now the sky in the east was a pale yellow, most of the stars had faded, and the birds over in the bush were in full voice. As I went over to the woolshed I could tell Uncle Andrew was catching the horse because the dogs over at the kennels were barking like mad, jerking at their chains, begging to be let off.

The noise disturbed the sheep who had been penned in the woolshed overnight. As they moved, their hooves clattered on the slats. Some of them coughed, some bleated.

Just before I reached the woolshed with the tea and sandwiches I saw Uncle Andrew, a dark shape on Rata, riding over the hilltop into the dawn … He'd be sorry he hadn't taken me with him, sending me over to a stinking woolshed when I should've been riding, too, with Sniff tagging along at heel. I liked mustering, and Uncle Andrew said I was good for a beginner…

When I got there Bill Dooley was the only one at the woolshed. He was sewing sacking round his feet.

'You can't clump about the shed in those clodhoppers,' he said. 'Hang on till I finish my moccasins, and I'll sew a pair for you.'

He explained that the board gets very slippery, and sacking seems to grip better than anything. It's cheap, too.

But, being a shearer, he couldn't resist the practical joke. He got me to sit down on a sack of dags with my stockinged feet out. He diverted my attention by asking me to reach him down a hank of twine. While I was turned away he sewed the moccasins together, and the end of the twine to the sack of dags.

As I got up to walk away I took a tumble, and for a moment or two I was like a cast ewe, rolling around in the spilling dags, trying to regain my feet. In the end I reached the footrot shears hanging from the stud, and I managed to snip through the twine. I had to resew the moccasins, though.

I don't know if you'll miss me, mate, I thought; but I certainly won't break my heart if I never see you again …

Sandy McLeod was next to the shed. He was the learner; and I soon found out this was his first day shearing. Last year he'd been shed-hand. Uncle Andrew's was the gang's first shed of the season. That's why they were short-handed. The shed-hands were still at their winter job.

When Pete Anderson and Mick Storey came to the shed Bill sent Pete and Sandy up to the grinder to do the experting.

'Sandy's been moping over that Wellington judy long enough,' said Bill. 'Let's sool Hera on to him, eh?'

Mick would kid Sandy along that Hera liked him – and try to get him to ask her to the R.S.A. dance on Saturday. See what happens, and play it from there, they decided.

But Mick said it would be a good idea for me to do the same with Hera – tell Hera that Sandy had said that he liked her. I was too young to realise all the implications of their plan. I was proud of being considered one of the gang, taken into their confidence; and for a while I forgot my grievance with the world.

As I poured her tea and offered the sandwiches I somehow managed to mumble the message to Hera. I couldn't help it that Wiki overheard.

Even at that age I wished I was pleading on my own behalf. Hera had a glowing Maori beauty, dark eyes like pools in the forest, soft black hair with coppery glints in it, and girlish plumpness. And she'd have been only three or four years older than me, at the most.

Wiki seemed peeved that Hera was getting the attention. She sang 'It Makes No Difference Now' in an aggressive way as she went about her work. Since it was a favourite of mine I joined in, but my voice wasn't anywhere near good enough to keep in tune with hers. I gave up in confusion.

Wiki was the fleeco, and Hera did the skirting and rolled and binned the fleeces. My first job was to help the fleeco by sweeping up little pieces of wool. When I got used to the noise – the whine of the electric motors and the clatter of the machines – I found I had time to watch the shearing and notice what was going on in the shed.

'How about filling my oil can, Wiki?' asked Sandy, vainly trying to get a squirt of oil into his handpiece.

'I'm busy. Fill your own oil can,' said Wiki sulkily, probably still upset by his supposed interest in Hera. She deftly rolled up the fleece and flounced off down the board.

'I'll fill it,' I offered.

'No, no! Don't bother, son,' said Sandy. 'It's Wiki's job. Just quietly change my can with Bill's will you? Don't let anyone see you.'

He winked when he saw I'd effected the exchange secretly.

A little later when Bill tried for a squirt of oil he said, 'Oil, Wiki!'

Without a word Wiki took the oil can and refilled it. She didn't guess the trick that had been played on her. Sandy smiled at me – it was a joke between us all morning.

Bill, acting as timekeeper with the boss not in the shed, bonged the axle with the hammer to signal the end of the first run – time for breakfast.

I took my boots from the top of the bale of oddments in the end bin and sat on the loading ramp to put them on. When I held up the right boot a couple of rusty cutters and a broken comb rolled out. I looked up into Bill's twinkling eye. 'You won't catch me like that,' I said. 'I always shake my boots before I put them on.'

'That's interesting,' said Bill. 'Do you shake your head before you put your hat on, too?'

With Uncle Andrew's instruction firmly in mind, I carefully laced the boots, even though it was little more than a step to the kitchen. Already I cared what these men thought of me. I didn't want to seem sloppy to them.

Sandy and Hera had lingered, too. I overheard Sandy gently ask if she'd like to come to the dance with him on Saturday.

'Yes. That'd be lovely. I'd like to. Where can I meet you?'

They went off to breakfast with Hera leaning towards Sandy in the way women do to show a man they've taken a shine to him. She was so close her hair brushed his cheek. So it looked as if Bill's scheme was working out well. As I watched them, something new, some insight into the meaning of life, was trying to get born in me. Whatever it was it didn't quite make it.

Because I began planning my escape. Morning smoko would be the time to light out, I decided. I'd take off on the way back after returning the billy and the cups to the kitchen.

Up the old formed road recommended for four-wheel drive only. Through the bush to the 'possum-trapper's hut. They'd never think of looking for me there. And I wouldn't be stupid and take the horse or the car or anything.

By smoko I'd learned how to pick up and throw a fleece, and I was able to help Wiki if two shearers happened to finish their sheep at the same time. Wiki was helpful and friendly to me; and I was ashamed of the joke I'd played on her with the oil cans.

As it happened Hera was sent for the smoko and I didn't get a chance to try my plan. Never mind, there was still afternoon smoko.

When his railway watch hanging by its chain on the stud beside his stand said smoko

Bill had just caught a sheep. Instead of putting it back in the catching pen he said, 'Like to learn to shear, Doug?'

Bill opened the fleece, shore the belly and the crutch and then handed the sheep over to me. He showed me the correct position for my legs and how to hold the sheep in a firm but relaxed way. Fill the comb, keep it flat on the skin, don't rush, just follow the handpiece – he brought over his cup of tea and scone and stood beside me, talking me through the blows, but letting me get a feel of the job for myself.

I didn't find shearing as easy as it looked. The hinged steel arms kept swinging the wrong way. The handpiece vibrated and tried to twist from my grip. The sheep kicked.

The sheep looked ragged when I finished. But Bill said not to mind, they didn't do second cuts in his gang, they'd get the wool I'd left next season. It was shorn and I hadn't cut it, that was the main thing. And he said yes, sure, when I asked him if I could have another go during the lunch hour …

By now it was really hot in the woolshed. The red corrugated iron held the heat from the sun, and the packed sheep made the atmosphere steamy and smelly.

I ran backwards and forwards along the board making hard work of helping Wiki with the fleeces, sweeping up the pieces and bagging them.

That last run before lunch seemed interminable. But, in my own mind anyway, I had become part of the gang, racing one another and the clock as well, laughing and joking and singing as we worked …

'Cripes, Bill, cut his throat and put him out of his agony,' said Mick as I joined in with the song about Bill Brink, a tiger for work and a devil for drink, who'd shear his three hundred a day without fear, and drink without winking four gallons of beer …

Uncle Andrew had finished yarding the back paddock mob, and it was him who bonged the axle for lunch.

'You've done a good job in the shed, Douglas,' he said. 'You can give a hand taking the shorn sheep back to the paddocks, after lunch, if you like.'

'I don't mind staying in the shed if they need me,' I said.

'Good lad,' said Bill Dooley. 'You'll shear your three hundred some day.'

I was so happy I couldn't speak …

Even though I'd hidden the King Leos in the corner behind the woolpress one of the shearers had found them and stuffed the toes with wool. For quite a while I wondered why I couldn't get them on …

As I walked with Uncle Andrew to the house for lunch I remembered something. 'What's the other two things, Uncle Andrew?'

'Huh?'

'That a man needs in life?'

'Oh, good bed and good tucker,' he said.

The Water-Joey

Mona Anderson

'Where's that blasted water-joey? Me boilers are nearly dry.' The engine driver bellowed like a bull caught in a barbed-wire fence.

Then the cook, who spoke with r's broad enough to span the Rakaia River, came to the galley door and roared: 'No warter for the tea. Where's that damn joey?'

It sounded through the water-joey's half-sleep, like peals of distant thunder. He turned in his bed. He wished the noise would stop, but now the voices grew suddenly quite close. 'Hey, boy!' someone called in a powerful bass. 'You going to sleep all day?'

The boy, who was thirteen years old with a peach-fuzz on his upper lip and an unpredictable croak in his voice, was only an inch or so higher than the wheat stooks in the paddock. He jumped from his bunk, hurriedly pulled on his clothes, then tore away to catch the horse and yoke it to the dray.

The mill boss, a big redfaced man with freckles, sandy hair and clear blue eyes, had a worried scowl on his smooth face. 'I knew the young devil was no good when I gave him the job last night,' he said to himself.

A choice of water-joeys was a choice between the devil and the deep blue sea. The old ones were usually boozers who would often drive the water-cart to the nearest pub and leave the horse standing for hours while they quenched their thirst. Sometimes they worked well and almost saw the season out before their skin started cracking. Then they took off to the pub and forgot to return to the mill. Occasionally the older joey was a man who had been such an embarrassment to his family that they had paid him to live in a faraway land. The trouble there usually lay with the bottle too.

One thing about the young water-joeys, they didn't dash off to the boozer, but they were irresponsible little devils. To be fair, some were really good boys, but others couldn't care less about consequences. Others again were always tired, and like the present one fell into such a depth of sleep that not even a full-scale pipe band could waken them in the mornings.

And then there were those who'd scarcely given up baby food when they fell in love with some girl and were reduced to a state of idiocy. The symptoms of their being in love, like the symptoms of the common cold, could be confused with many other conditions, but once the seizure was recognised as love, the water-joey became the butt of the mill-hands' jokes.

1976, *The Water-Joey*

At harvest-time men from all over the country, tinkers and tailors, swaggers and vagabonds, responded to the call for labour. Honest men who worked the clock round to get the crops cut, stooked, and stacked before the fields of ripe corn became alive with plagues of hungry sparrows or the dry nor-west winds whipped across the country and shook half the grain to the ground.

Later, when the threshing mills came along to thresh the grain from the straw, they too had to recruit some of their crews off the roads.

Last night the boy had come to the mill asking for work. 'Well, I need a water-joey,' said the boss, then went on to explain that the water-joey's first job in the morning was to catch the draught-horse, yoke it to a dray which carried a 200-gallon square water-tank, then drive to the nearest water-race or pond and fill the tank by hand-pump. The dray must then be on hand to take the first load of straw to the back of the mill to make a bed or stand, for the bags of wheat. The bags held 200 pounds of grain and were stacked in a neat pile, then the last loads of straw were used to cover the stacked bags. (In the early days the bags held 240 pounds (4 bushels). Later they were reduced to 200 pounds, and in the late 1930s came the Chapman sacks which held 180 pounds (3 bushels).)

'You'll soon get the hang of it,' said the boss. 'Just remember to close everything behind you. Leave a gate open and you'll have the farmer roaring like his prize bull that's got boxed with his maiden heifers.' Then, looking at the boy's blank face, he said: 'Now, what's the first thing you'll do in the morning?'

'Oh, I suppose I'll widdle up against the dray wheel,' was the prompt reply.

But on this, his first morning, the water-joey had been in too much of a hurry to even look at the dray wheel. As he drove along he met a farmer, who enquired where he was going.

'I'm not quite sure,' replied the joey, 'I'm following some tracks.'

'What're you looking for?'

'Water,' the boy answered, biting at a wart on his thumb.

The farmer pointed. 'Well, there's a pond over to your left.'

He found the pond. A paradise drake with its black head glossed with green had it all to himself. Maybe the duck wasn't far away thought the joey, as he backed the dray towards the water's edge. The drake called a guttural glink, glink and paddled off to the opposite shore, stretched its wings, and then inquisitively, and in half circles, began flying towards the dray, but suddenly changed its mind and swooped down by some rushes nearby.

Now, one hour, five blisters and an aching back later, the tank was full ...

He climbed up on to the front of the dray, took hold of the reins and whacked the horse across its rump, 'Giddup, you lazy old cow. Gee-up!' But the lazy old cow, who had greasy heels, refused to pull the loaded dray and instead of geeing-up it geeed back.

It backed the dray into the pond then sat down on its haunches like a dog, and no amount of pulling and coaxing would budge it.

Now too excited to think clearly, the water-joey left the horse sitting in the pond and ran all the way back to the mill yelling: 'Help, Help, Help!' The mill boss hurried off the engine and men came running from all directions.

'Where's the dray? What's happened?' said the worried boss.

'The dray's in the pond,' panted the boy.

It was some time before the men could get a coherent account of what had happened. Finally, when they learned that the horse and dray were still in the pond they drove the big traction engine down and pulled them both out.

'How in God's name did you get into this tangle?' the boss said then stopped, for the soft face confronting him had started to pucker.

'When I said "gee-up" the horse just went back and back,' the boy answered in a small, shaky voice.

'All right, all right,' said the boss as he straightened the wet harness. 'Now get on up the road. Might as well fill up while we're here.' The steerer jumped down off the engine and undid the hose then put it in the water.

The water-joey hadn't cried for a long time, but he cried when the engine had gone and he was left to drive the dray back to the mill. Then, wiping his eyes on his coat sleeve, he turned on to the track and, screwing up his sardonic face, he called to the horse: 'Everything's gone wrong today. This must be Black Tuesday.'

Fondest Memories

Gordon Lucas

The stand out year of my life was 1960. I was 18 years of age and had been brought up on a farm halfway between Luggate and Wanaka. I spent my early teenage years sitting on a tractor gazing at the surrounding mountains and always wondering what was over the tops and in the valleys beyond – much as I used to wonder what was beyond a woman's cleavage.

The former, I was about to find out about in a big way. I'd had the cheek to apply to go on the local [Hawea-Wanaka] mustering run as Dingle Burn Station's man, and I'd been accepted. Wow! Eight months work guaranteed, seven days a week at £3 a day. Johnnie Sargeson's man on the run – unbelievable! There was a nervous wait for a month or so, until the season started. Makarora and Dingle Burn were going to pre-lamb shear that year, so we were to start in mid-August, which was earlier than usual.

I made a cunning looking dog box out of old cupboards, various bits of wood and some netting. It fitted roughly on the back of an Austin A55 truck that Dad had bought. I loaded my gear and headed off up past the Ben Wevis homestead to meet Sarge and his whaling boat. I hadn't really met Sarge before, but I can say that I lived in awe of this man and his brothers. They were in their real prime when I was a boy and the stories we heard put them into true-life folklore. Sarge certainly didn't disappoint me on that score. He was larger than life and seemingly indestructible, as he was to prove some days later.

The old wooden whaleboat was the lifeline to Dingle Burn Station, as everything had to come in and go out on it, including the wool clip. It was powered by a Fordson Dexta diesel motor, with a few tarpaulins tied over to provide some shelter. Often it was loaded up with six musterers, 30 dogs and a week's rations, to head up the lake – frequently, with a blustery nor'westerly blowing. We would huddle under the covers with the stink of diesel and dogs, while Sarge would sit up the back, out in all weathers. I can't ever remember seeing a life jacket, but I do remember one dark night coming down the lake towards Dingle Burn Bay. Before the boat got to the shore it became tangled in some manuka bushes and wouldn't shift. Lake Hawea had recently been raised by about 60 feet and the manuka had not been removed beforehand, making the shoreline very hazardous. Anyway, over the side went Sarge, the lake well over his waist. He pushed the boat out of its entanglement, pulled it to shore and then drove the

1998, *On the Run*

tractor to the homestead a couple of miles away. He was soaking wet and it was a freezing night – he never mentioned the cold.

The homestead, when I was there, was a little corrugated iron house where Peg, Sarge's wife, was raising their children. There was a range for cooking that used a never-ending supply of manuka wood, and enough electricity from a small generator for two or three light bulbs, but not much else. Peg also had to put up with all the men on the place sharing her bathroom. That wouldn't have been easy – and then there was the isolation.

During that summer, when things were a bit quieter, Sarge would send me up the narrow spur to hunt wethers out or sometimes he sent me to muster woollies off the Waterfall block. They were long days in the bluffs and scrub, and not always successful. But what a great way to get the boy out of your hair for the day. When Sarge said 'Put another chop in your bag,' you knew this to translate to an extra long day or even a night under a beech tree or in the fern.

Once, Sarge, Allan May and I brought the first mob of sale sheep out of the Dingle; previously surplus stock was killed on the property. We drove the mob towards Rocky Point the first day and camped in the fern that night. At daybreak we took the mob straight up the face, through a few chutes, and straight back down again. We camped in the fern again that night before going on to Timaru Creek the next day.

That was a memorable year and I would like to thank all the run-holders – on the run – who employed me. It was like a great Outward Bound course, and a privilege to have been there before the advent of tracks, roads and helicopters – the end of an era.

Poles Apart

Nancy Patulski

After a few days of marriage my worst fears had been realised: my husband was quite mad. Who but an idiot would end up living in the back of beyond, no neighbours, no electricity and no access except on horseback? I had met him briefly before leaving to start my nursing training in the South Island. A few letters had been exchanged in the first year, certainly no words of love. One flying visit and the gift of a ring (that it was diamond-studded had no significance). There was no bended knee, no flowers.

He had been a refugee, forced from his homeland at the age of four and with his mother, brothers and sisters transported to Siberia. His mother died there of typhoid, so in the care of his elder brother he came across the world to settle in New Zealand. He was alive because of his strength of will, his ability to fight and steal, but the good qualities in him that survived made him unique, not typical.

Our wedding ceremony staggered the guests. The 40 boys who lived those first years in camps and hostels with my husband drank their way through a week of tears, laughter and reminiscences. I made the mistake of expecting the traditional wedding trappings of a honeymoon.

'Honeymoon, what's that?'

He'd had enough time off and had to get back to work. We loaded up the wedding spoils and set off to meet the boss. We were going to work on a farm in the country. Visions of frilly aprons, hot scones and fat woolly lambs – oh dear.

We met the boss, a lovely, gnarled old fellow, who took one look at me and started to laugh. Poor old chap, a bit queer I thought, as I swirled to the Land Rover in my full skirt and stilettos. Some kind person had spread a manure sack on the back seat; the nightmare had started. We banged, thumped, swayed and skidded for hours and hours. My husband ignored my distress and talked of docking, cattle hunts, wild boars and other topics that bewildered me.

We stopped at last to spend the night with Ron, the single shepherd, whose hut was just one room. The night dragged, and the blankets were prickly and smelt of sheep. My new husband slept by the fire, alternately snoring and talking the night away; things would look better in the morning. A cold wash and indeed, I did feel better in new slacks, jersey and bright lipstick. We would soon be in our own home, the new

---

1980, *Top Yarns from the New Zealand Farmer*

linen waiting for a new bride. Lace cloths, embroidered slips, I'd show this rough husband of mine.

The morning sun was bright and enticing, the view breathtaking. A hundred feet below, the river sparkled blue, with the steep, bush-covered hills above and beyond it. Three horses came and nuzzled my shoulder; what fun I'd have learning to ride. The men wandered into the sunlight and I was introduced to my mare Flicka. Riding lessons were to start now, and in earnest. My sweet understanding husband informed me that the road finished right here, the horses would be our transport for the next nine miles. New slacks, smart jersey, and undaunted, I was hoisted into the saddle. The fact that I crashed over the other side into the barbed wire fence didn't dislodge my bright, bride smile. The nine miles of winding track did and, in tears, aching in every joint, I arrived.

The next two years taught me many things, and I found my husband and myself in the solitude of the bush. I learnt to shoot a wild boar with a .303 and not bruise my shoulder. The lace cloths ended up in flames because the moths caught their wings alight in the candle flame and plunged to a fiery death. I could cook on a coal range, bake bread, boil a copper and I came to appreciate the things I now take for granted. I made many mistakes – packing the butter and flour next to the horse's flank, with a month's supply of butter running down the horse's legs. Scones and bread that bristled with horsehair reminded me for a long time of my stupidity, but we survived. The joys of the supply plane in the winter, with cigarettes after weeks of no tobacco. All the animals that tamed so easily: baby pigs, possums, goats, and turkey chicks.

When an older housewife tells me of the hardships she endured, I can truly say, 'I've been there, too.'

My Landlord Peter

Jackson Webb

Peter Thompson and I agreed over the telephone to meet at Tower Rock Farm about noon. He said if I liked the place, we could move right in.

If he'd expected us to come in Sunday clothes and a shiny new car instead of walking over the hill in overalls eating our lunch, he never showed it. Peter held out his hand and stepped from the shadow of the barn, where he'd been leaning with his arms folded and his slouch hat pulled down over his eyes.

'G'dai, Jackson! Well, here's a fine day for 't time of year!' And his brown dog wagged his tail, once, twice. It looked like they'd always been there.

He was about thirty, with grey-blue eyes and a short black beard. He wore a wool-lined army coat and Wellingtons plastered with red mud, shuffling along at ease, tapping his stick ahead of him as we went through the empty rooms of the old house and walked around outside. I liked the board floors and the rusty, grass-grown machinery out behind the shed – and the bathtub-troughs and the stacks of licheny planks in the courtyard. There was a bright, pure peace of age about the place. A hedgehog waddled surely down a drainpipe and off across the grass. A hen clucked. The only other sound was the brook flowing into the sluiceway under the millwheel.

We went out to the great monkey-puzzle tree in front, exchanged cigarettes and agreed on a modest rent. He didn't seem to notice my accent, or ask what kind of work I did. He was also very polite: he said nothing about the cat's tail hanging from Hepsibah's basket, or my three typewriters, or the swing I hung up for myself. No one had lived in the house for years: we both wanted the rooms dried out.

Every morning, Peter's splattered Land Rover rattles down the hill with its engine off and glides in under the low-roofed shed. If it's raining, and it usually is, he just sits there a while with his dog, looking straight ahead: thinking, maybe, or reading the paper, or simply working up to being out all day in the miserable weather. After a while, he stumbles past my window with a sack of feed on his back or a lamb under his arm, with his boots thudding by and the rain streaming off his hat, humming in a little boy's falsetto. At first, we didn't know where the sound was coming from – the wind? a singing mouse? a fly in a web? These days, we just think, 'Peter's here.'

Sometimes he comes in for a coffee and sits uncomfortably at the table for a minute,

1977, *Islands* 18

crumpling his hat in his hands, crossing his sock feet, preoccupied, obliged, too big for here. But most of the time, he's moving around the farmyard and up on the hill on his frosty jobs, checking his rat traps, counting stocks, bringing the sheep down and closing the gates, then driving away again home to Kohukohu in the red evening with the dog wagging his tail in back, fainter and fainter: a blurr of slow, similar days working here by himself with a kind of neutral regularity, thousands of such days long before we came here.

Every nicheful of twine and nails, every initialled, mossy fencepost and extra roof slate is here for a reason and is known to Peter. I borrow a block under a cart shaft to chop kindling on, and the next morning it's gone and another, better one is in its place. I knock a stone off a wall walking across the meadow to the Pawarangi road, and on the way back I notice Peter's put it back again. Hepsibah loses a mitten up by the cairn, and it appears back on the windowsill in the evening.

He never says much, just a nod of his brimmed hat from the hay loft or a wave from the group of leaning eucalyptus trees by the quarry. He's everywhere at once, bringing a long arch of sheep across the field, whistling for the dog, forking bales into the cart, pounding on the anvil in the lean-to, such a cold little sound, hardly there at all, going lost now and then in the silent marshgrass around us.

My best impression of Peter is still the first one: a man waiting in the rain. I've been here four months and I've never really got to know him. The moment has never been right somehow.

I take the rent money out to where he's propping up the mountain of bales or struggling with some other difficult object in the sleet, and he only says, 'Thank you, now. Just put it in my pocket.' Or he's standing like a school-teacher in front of his gathered sheep, counting with his stick, or he's jacking the fallen floor of the henhouse, too busy to talk. He never stops what he's doing, and he never needs help. So, every time, the weekly meeting on rent-day ends up just a brief, crisp transaction, and then we both go back to our different days. Anything else seems a bother to him. The situation is always wrong.

For example, Hepsibah carries a cup of tea and a biscuit around the corner of the barn exactly when he's having a temper tantrum: the cows are in the turnips and the dog just sits and rolls its eyes. 'Get on there, y' daft tyke! Nah, get round 'em! Get on, y' useless bugger!' Peter's livid – he sees Hepsibah there with her wee cup, but he still can't help himself. He turns purple and his beard sticks out straight, as he splutters and runs off in the hopeless mud. A little later, he passes my window in the downpour and sees the deceptively comfortable sight of me writing by the fire with my loafing cat asleep.

Our times and movements don't coincide. He deals in mutton and beef. We're vegetarians. His rasping tractor never takes a siesta. We're here together at the end of the road all day, but we only meet at the corners. It seems as if there is always a last little distance between Peter and us, like a peculiar, natural boundary that we've grown to appreciate and accept as normal.

Shaping Up

Neroli Cottam

'It's raw looking country,'
The agent says,
'Gouged out,
Scrub-covered
And brown as old nugget
Gone hard in the tin.'

You look at the
Promise of green
Where the water's been
You see how the light
Threads silver stitches
Along the ridges,
And you smell the wild thyme
That's a patchwork of purple.

'It's not easy country,'
The agent says,
'Much of it's been
Given back
To the rabbits and hawk.'

Against the glare in the gully
You see something like
The shape of a man
Perhaps an old timer
Still pecking for flecks
Of gold washed down.

'The ghosts,'
You say,
'Do they come with the land?'
And the agent just laughs
As he tips back his hat.
'You'd be better off,'
He says,
'With those good river flats.'

1996, *Under Mount Pisa: Central Otago Poems*

Quite a Lot of Bull

Elizabeth Underwood

When in 1988 my leg became too bad for me to continue with normal work, I decided to make a radical change in my life. At the time I was running the clerical side of an urban Probation Office. I had always wanted land of my own, a farm. Now I was determined to exchange the Mongrel mob for the cattle mob, the Black Power Gang for the black sheep flock. This was all well and good but what I knew about farm animals you could have fitted on a fingernail – and I chew mine. However, I successfully sold my small home in a commuter suburb of a big city and embarked on farm hunting. I was fortunate enough to have friends in a farming area and I stayed with them while searching for that one place that would be just what I was looking for.

I had thought that finding a farm would be simple. I had a large sum in cash and a clear idea of what I wanted. That only went to show I had no idea at all. Land agents appeared from all points of the compass to offer properties. I demanded 5 to 25 acres and in quick succession was shown farms that ranged from 2 acres of bare land up to 80 acres so vertical that a goat would have been hard put to it to maintain footing in wet weather. I wanted two to three bedrooms with a good range of outbuildings. I was offered the latter all right – everything from orchid houses to six-car garages.

I was on a limited and fixed income and had a certain sum to purchase. I had no desire to add a mortgage to my budget. Most of the agents appeared to be under the impression I was a close relative of Aristotle Onassis. Either that or I liked to be encumbered with crushing debts. Perhaps I looked like a masochist? I hastily rejected farms with huge mortgages, farms with medium mortgages and finally, farms whose owners were prepared to leave a bit in.

Personally I thought my requirements modest. Easy to understand. Simple even. An assortment of land agents continued to drag me away to see farms that were 'exactly what you want, madam'. I was shown farms that would have taken me a day to walk across. Farms that cost five times what I wanted to pay. And farms that either had no outbuildings at all, or an assortment bewildering in its range and complexity. Since my leg was badly damaged in an accident in 1977 I have had problems walking far. My right leg complains if I over-use it even now; because of the massive bone damage I am unable to run and am confined to a slowish walk even in emergencies. For that reason I had also stipulated a smallish farm with most of its land on the flat.

1993, *Farming Daze*

The final insult was when I was hauled out to inspect a farm of three times the land area I wanted, and twice the price I could afford. Just to make my day complete it was so steep it looked as if it could have been successfully used to make a Barry Crump advertisement. I turned in exasperation to the agent.

'Just how would I manage to get about on this?'

His reply was in casual tones. It was clear I was a typical female, always making difficulties. 'You get a farmbike, of course. A four wheeler'll laugh at a little slope like this!'

I gazed at the little slope. Any steeper and the land would have slid off itself. During the winter rains it probably did, judging by the scars in the hillside grass.

'And if the bike stops running when I'm on the other side of the place, I can always crawl home on hands and knees,' I said sarcastically. The agent sighed. People were so hard to please. I removed myself to the car and we returned to my friend's farm in silence.

After that I spent more time with other agents and even inspected a few places on private sale. At least with these they tended to be closer to my idea of the farm I wanted. It was the owners who were the trouble here; I hated to say no when it meant so much.

A time came when I'd been hunting for my dream farm for almost six months. I was rapidly becoming discouraged. Then in rapid succession I was shown two places that could be suitable. One was an old farmhouse that had begun life as four rooms. At a room per generation, it now had eight – all of them showing signs of the amateur carpenters who'd been responsible. The outbuildings were old and scruffy but there was everything I needed, from a three-suite hen house, to a big hay barn, pig sty and covered yards. I wasn't crazy about the house but it would take my four thousand books with the lounge shelved. There was an enclosed fire, two bedrooms, and a toilet you could have held square dances in. I think it had originally been a bedroom. Now a toilet sat there in solitary splendour.

The other farmlet was several acres less but the house was newer. It had been built all at the same time and the rooms were all of an appropriate size. It had far less character but at least the roof didn't leak. With the first farm went a single stand shearing plant and 60 ewes. I didn't know what went with the second. I could never find anyone at home when I rang to ask.

I'd seen over it briefly but the owners who had it on private sale had been out. I'd been shown over by a friend of theirs and seen nothing of the land.

At last I was able to get an answer on the phone. No, they weren't letting any stock go with it. Yes, I was welcome to come and look over the outbuildings. Just name the time and they'd be there. We agreed on a suitable time and promptly at two o'clock I wandered up the drive. There was no answer to my knock so I ambled around the house to try the back door. Still no reply. I sat on the step to wait.

After half an hour I was becoming restless. My farmer friend who had brought me here was engrossed in her knitting. I was unable to resist the temptation to explore. People who made appointments should keep them. I rose and drifted around the barn. I studied it, then passed on to look over several pig sties. Cow bails, yards – and what was that intriguing little building over in the middle of that paddock?

I found the gate and strolled through to look. As I wandered idly over the grass I noticed a large cow towards the trees on the right. I glanced again – a steer, not a cow. It also glanced in my direction and began to drift my way. That didn't bother me. I'd had animals most of my life and was aware that cattle tended to be curious creatures. As a small child I had often made friends with the steers grazed on One Tree Hill park just up the road from my home in Auckland. I continued toward the shed and discovered it to be a shelter for goats or calves. Hummm, useful. I hadn't decided about goats yet.

The steer arrived and stretched out an enquiring nose. I scratched him gently under the chin. My horses had always loved that. My new friend proved to be no exception and angled his horns so I could scratch around them too. Across the paddock my friend was waving. I waved back; it looked as if the owners had arrived and I'd better get back. The steer followed me nudging indignantly. Surely I wasn't deserting him just when we'd become pals? I was. He trod on my heels and I halted to reprove him with a gentle slap across one muscled shoulder.

He tossed his head but allowed me room to walk again. My friend's arm signals grew more urgent. I couldn't make out what she was bothered about. We weren't trespassing, the owners would understand. I paused at the gate and gave my large friend a parting scratch. As I opened the gate I was seized by the arm, catapulted through, and the gate slammed behind me.

'What's all the excitement?'

My friend surveyed me with a jaundiced eye. 'That's a bloody bull, you idiot.'

I stared back at the steer. For the first time my gaze slid further back. I gulped.

We left quietly. The owners never appeared and a week later I signed the documents for the first farm. I am now the proud owner of a housecow, geese, hens, a pig, and sheep. However I do not own a bull!

The Rise and Fall of H.G.-S. and A.M.C.
W.H. Guthrie-Smith

It was upon the 4th of September 1882 that the new owners of Tutira took delivery of their sheep station. They were wild with anticipations of sport, of riding, of
the mastery of animals, of life in the wilds. At least, by one of them, every hour of that
golden day can still be vividly recalled. He remembers wakening at dawn and rushing
out to forecast the day. It was a perfect Hawke's Bay spring morning, and be it said, no
weather in the world can beat a fine September in Napier. The sky was cloudless, the
faintest crisp suspicion of frost mingled with the salt tang of the beach. Behind the
town rose the magnificent snow-clad ranges, Ruahine and Kaweka, in front heaved the
Pacific's vast expanse.

What magic there is in possession! What pleasure the sight of the hacks! They were
not quite like any other horses in the world; they were our own, they belonged to us, an
earnest of that glorious sheep station which was to provide after a few seasons easy
enlargement of our minds and fortunes, endless rivers, moors, and forests in Scotland.

We rode through the picturesque town – our horses' hoofs sounding loud on the
quiet streets – where half the inhabitants were still asleep. We passed through Port
Ahuriri, crossing the newly built wooden bridge which linked the northern and southern portions of the province. We followed the beach road along the western spit; peopled
then only by a few fisher-folk, some of them living in homes built of biscuit and kerosene tins in lieu of iron sheeting. We passed the Petane Hotel, then run by the redoubtable
William Villers. We forded the Esk River, and, riding through the *kaianga* of Petane,
scanned with deep interest the reed-thatched *whares* of the owners of Tutira. O Ananias,
Azarias, and Misael! that morning our happiness overflowed the world. We even loved
our landlords – after all, they had been heathens until recently; they had never read
Henry George; they knew no better. We rode along the shallow sandy turf of the
Whirinaki Flats and over the Beach Hill to the County Boundary Peak. We were then
in the county of Wairoa, one of whose divisions was the Mohaka riding, within which
lay Tutira; it was another step towards our new possession. Farther on we reached the
Tangoio Bluff, and turning inland at right angles passed the homestead and wool-shed
of the Tangoio run. Tangoio and Tutira marched with one another.

We followed several miles inland, but parallel to the sea, the switchback track, the
old coastal pack-trail, so lost to common-sense as to think its deplorable grades good

---

1926, *Tutira*

going. We struck the First Fence, and saw for the first time the Tutira station mail-box. To ordinary eyes it might have seemed, as indeed it was, a kerosene case nailed to the top of a strainer-post. To us it was much more; that box, simple and unpretentious to the outward eye, had been the receptacle of communications about Tutira wool, about Tutira stock, about Tutira interests of a dozen sorts. We viewed it with a kind of reverence.

We turned sharp inland and followed up and down over the hill-tops, the trail faintly marked by the station pack-team. Three miles further on we struck Dolbel's Boundary Gate, and saw in the distance the Delectable Mountains of our pilgrimage – the ranges of Tutira. Shortly afterwards we looked down upon the Waikoau tumbling along amongst its boulders. We led our horses over the 'shoot', the almost perpendicular drop, down which the pack-team used in muddy weather to slide with stiff legs and unlifted hoofs. We zigzagged down the steep trail of Dolbel's Face, disturbing mobs of wild cattle, each of them raising pleasant anticipations of future huntings. With the delight of Scott crossing his Tweed at Abbotsford, we splashed across the unsung ford of the Waikoau. We trod Tutira soil. We viewed for the first time our own sheep. They were merino ewes – skin and bone, scrags, their wool peeling off – anxious to escape yet balked by the river, the kind of stock always in the very worst of condition. Such was our fatuous folly, that we believed against the evidence of our senses that they were not so very, very, very wretched, that not every single solitary bone in their lank frames was visible.

We climbed from the river-bed to the Reserve – long afterwards rechristened Racecourse Flat – and rode very quietly through the lambing ewes. We could hardly bear to tear ourselves away. If the sight of the scrags at the Waikoau ford had thrilled us with pride of possession, our hearts exulted at the sight of these lambs – lambs that apparently came from nowhere, but were even now swelling the numbers of our newly purchased flock – as if thrown in gratis, a gift from a beneficent heaven to H. G.-S. and A. M. C.

We rode along the shelf of the flat until suddenly, in an instant, the lake lay at our feet. The feelings of one of the new owners were those of Marmion's squire at sight of Edinburgh. Had the grass-fed pony permitted the feat, its rider, like Eustace, would have 'made a demi volte in air' at joy of the prospect. Before his eyes lay the whole length of the lake, picturesque in its wooded promontories and bays. Along its steeps grew brakes of native woodland brightened at this season with the deep yellow blossoms of the kowhai. The silky leaves of the weeping willows were in their tenderest green, the peach-groves sheets of pink. The south-westerly breeze that blew stirred the flax blades, making them glitter like glass; west of the lake the land was dark in shadow, the eastern hill-tops were bright in sun. I have looked at this lovely sheet of water a million times since then, but have rarely seen it more fair.

Animals

Farming in this country just wouldn't be the same without them – and not just from an economic viewpoint either. New Zealand agriculture revolves around livestock farming: millions of little to large, four-legged factories that convert plant material into meat, fibre, milk and methane. It is an industry, as we stubbornly insist, that capitalises on the most efficient grassland farming system in the world.

Despite New Zealand's temperate suitability for livestock farming, running sheep, beef or dairy cattle, thoroughbreds, deer and goats has its challenges. These animals are susceptible to a wide range of disorders, some of the body, others of the mind. Often the two conditions go together, which makes the task of gathering and treating them even more daunting. Just the same, life among farm animals is not a continual tussle, though in the previous book, in the section entitled 'Battling the Beasts', I was probably guilty of giving the impression that stock handling was a long-running war of wills, hooves and horns. Yet many of those stories and poems were sheer slapstick, and very funny: contributors of the ilk of Peter Hammond, Ross McMillan and Frank Anthony made sure of that.

No one has been better able to encapsulate the unfolding of one fiendish dilemma leading to another, and yet another, than sailor turned Taranaki dairy farmer Frank Anthony. His pen was the first to create deadpan and perfectly timed treatments of man versus beast episodes that always resulted in the former coming last. 'My New Heifer', which appears in this collection, is but one of several battles of will. By contrast, other stories describe less injurious occasions or commemorate old friends and loyal workmates. Many's the creature who has become a 'best friend' – a classification that is not the preserve of dogs alone. Lambs and calves are the traditional companions of country children, along with ponies whose range of personality traits is the stuff of family legend. Elderly farm hacks and packhorses are also regular members of mutual admiration societies, along with the horses and ponies that became this country's first school buses. On the Elworthy family property, Craigmore, in South Canterbury, every child on the station was issued with a tough little Timor pony. At the other end of the equine scale, Nora Sanderson recalls her father selling a very large Clydesdale – ex-Auckland Tramway Board – as school transport for six children, all of them on its back! 'Those kids treated that huge creature like one of the family. They even piled in under its wide tummy to keep out of the rain and it never raised a foot to dislodge them.'

Other regular animal companions included pigs, goats and deer. But membership has been extended to any member of the animal kingdom, including a few wild ring-ins – although why anyone would want to keep a possum for a pet, let alone a stoat, weasel or hedgehog, I don't know. All the parties concerned seem very happy with the relationship until someone gets bitten, severely scratched or 'top-dressed' once too often.

To many people, the most memorable creatures are those who were their close friends when they were young. They are recalled here, along with those who will always find a place in adult memory: animals with a great capacity for work. A bond of respect is formed between those who, day after day, develop a practical relationship that's built on trust. As Timothy Gambrill says in his book, *Flock House, Reminiscences 1948*, 'Whereas one *uses* a tractor, one *works with* horses.' The same can be said of farm bikes and four-wheelers compared with the now rarely seen station hack. Sheep dogs still fit into the indispensable category. So too, in their own way, did the house cow or dairy goat who always came when called, never put a hoof in the bucket it had just filled and let anyone milk her, anywhere. Although this section celebrates animals, tales involving them are to be found throughout the book; rare is the rural incident or occasion that doesn't involve one of 'God's creatures' or something they've left in their wake.

The old way of learning to ride

Rod Campbell

We learned to ride on quiet horses that had been ridden all day, every day, for many years. Some had spent almost all their lives in harness or packing big loads over the hills. Some were as quiet and gentle as it was possible to be – totally different from horses that were only ridden for a few hours a week.

As babies we were often carried on the front or back of someone on a horse; we almost learnt to ride and walk at the same time. Many children just loved their horses and could find all sorts of ways to get on a horse's back when there was nobody there to lift them on. The method used most often was to get the horse near a fence or gate, then climb on from the gate. But many horses would let you spend hours climbing up onto a gate, then just move away enough so you couldn't get on their back. When there were two children it was much easier. You could get the horse behind the gate and open it wide and have it between the gate and the fence. That way he couldn't move sideways until you were on his back.

Where there is a will there is a way, and children always found *some* way of catching their horse to be ridden. One child I knew used to take the bridle out into the paddock and spread it out in front of the horse where it was eating grass. Then he would just wait until the horse moved forwards and put its foot into the bridle. He would then gather up the bridle over his shoulder and lead the horse, by its front leg, home to his mother. She would then put the bridle on and lift him onto the horse's back. He would stay there for many hours, just being with the horse while it fed its way around the paddock.

Other children used to take a few pieces of carrot to where the horse was feeding and put them in front of it. While he had his head down, one child would climb onto his neck, then, when he lifted his head, crawl along his neck onto his back. Then they would put down more pieces of carrot and the next boy would get onto the horse's neck, crawling along its back in the same way. Many times, though, they would slip off while trying to turn around to face the right way!

Sometimes they would put a bridle on while his head was down, so they could try and steer him the way *they* wanted to go. Other times they were content to just sit on his back while the horse wandered along feeding.

There was one thing we learnt: it was a long way down to the ground from some of those big horses. Especially if they walked too fast downhill and you slipped off and

1994, *At One With Nature*

landed with another child or two on top of you! But after many years of riding bareback like this, by the time these children had grown up they had perfect balance, with horse and rider moving as one.

Accident Prone

Nora Sanderson

I was always a great admirer of my brothers' horsemanship, probably because I was too scared to learn to ride. To me my brothers were daring heroes. They seemed to deliberately court danger and take it almost as an insult if their horses refused to buck, bite, or try in some more subtle manner to unseat their riders and, if possible, break their necks.

Father, in what I can only think of as an absent-minded moment, bought the boys a copy of *Bar-20*, Clarence E. Mulford's Wild West novel. There must surely have been a sale of Western rough-and-tough novels in Hokianga at the time. Hopalong Cassidy's influence was felt strongly all over the district – almost overnight becoming one great wide-spreading rodeo.

My brothers were the toughest riders of them all. Even when still at primary school the dangerous delights of buck-jumping had begun to pall. They looked around for fresh fields to conquer and came up with the idea that it might be fun to try and ride Father's beef bullocks running wild out the back of the farm. These were huge, mad-headed beasts, uncontrollable and highly dangerous. The boys finally managed to run one of them into a rope trap – a snare was, I think, the correct term – and from the overhanging branches of a tree lowered the most daring of their buck-riders onto the beast's heaving back. With the wild-eyed animal fairly cornered, the other boys oblig-ingly passed a rope under its tummy and tied the rider's feet together. Nothing could dislodge him now, short of the rope breaking.

Great satisfaction was expressed by all the humans present, though I must except myself. I took no part in the proceedings and had forfeited the right to even comment – I was up a tree some distance away, terrified and bawling loudly as usual.

The riding arrangements went very well indeed. It was only after several successful buck-jumping rounds of the paddock that the bullock found the perfect comeback: it decided to roll on its rider. The result, several cracked ribs and Heaven only knows what other injuries. The poor lad must have been in agony but no one told the grown-ups how he got hurt. After all, Hopalong Cassidy would have made little of such minor injuries …

Shortly after this I caught my brothers making preparations to visit an old apple orchard at the back of the farm. I hated the boys to go anywhere without me, but in

1999, *One of the Family*

that blistering Northland heat I hesitated to follow along behind their horses, on foot, over the red-hot scoria dust. They kindly offered to take me up behind the saddle, but I was, perhaps unfairly, a bit cynical about this arrangement. I knew I would certainly die of terror if they started their horses bucking, even ever so playfully.

'Try riding Schneider,' they suggested – an elderly retired racehorse Father had bought for a song. My probing glance caught no hint of sniggering smiles on their faces. Perhaps I could really trust the old horse to treat me gently? So on board Schneider's obligingly immobile old back I was duly hoisted, and we set out for our destination. This was rather fun. I began to wonder why I had never found the courage to do this sort of thing before. Fancy being scared of old Schneider!

But now the scoria land was behind us, the smooth heavily grassed river flats rolling out beneath our horses' trotting hooves. No rocks on which a nitwit of eight years could bash her ginger head if she and the horse parted company rather suddenly.

'Want me to teach Schneider to amble?' The question was put enthusiastically to me. 'All good horses amble. You know, something like a broken cantering motion, DER-rum-ter-rum-ter-rum-tum-tum. White horses prancing with Wirth's circus, remember?' It sounded attractive and would certainly be easier than the way I was being jogged about like a sack of potatoes when Schneider broke into a trot. I thought, yes, I'd give ambling a go.

'What you have to do is hold the horse's head in with a tight rein and belt him with your riding switch. It won't hurt him, he's got a hide like a rhinoceros.' They were paying me flattering attention, the three of them; I guess being the centre of interest must have gone to my head. All right, if they wanted me to make Schneider amble that's exactly what I would do. With any luck I'd come out of this not looking such a cowardly idiot. They were all watching me, the reins slack on the necks of their own horses. This was my big moment. I held the reins tight and switched my trusty steed in the ribs.

The next thing I remember is coming slowly back to consciousness. I was lying on the ground. Blood had had time to dry round my mouth and nose. My tongue felt as though it had been put through a mincing machine, my head pounded and I felt desperately sick. I could see two or three of everything within my sight. I remember wishing the ground would keep still, instead of rocking like a crazy hammock. Schneider was nowhere to be seen but I vaguely realised I still held his bridle in my clenched fist. I must have pulled it off over his head as I took a somersault.

One of the boys was saying in a scared tone, 'We didn't know he'd buck so hard, he usually just pig-roots.' Another of my fond brothers was feverishly trying to force between my lips a handful of squashed, ripe blackberries. He was deadly pale, his expression suggesting that he fully expected me to die of malnutrition before I could recover my scattered wits.

Some time later I made one last trembling attempt to master the gentle art of horse riding. They say a horse knows when its rider is nervous. Be that as it may, my mount began to pig-root and act the fool, putting its foot through the stirrup where my own foot should have been. My brothers watched proceedings with hilarity. 'He sure knows how to use a stirrup. If he's getting into the saddle, you'd better get off.' It was an old gag but fitted the occasion. I slid to the ground and that was that; I'd remain a live coward rather than a dead heroine. After all there must be thousands of people in the world who can't look an honest horse in the face.

Harsh Mistress: A legacy of winter …

Amanda Jackson

There's a dark side to spring that nobody ever writes poetry about. A Jekyll and Hyde side.

On one side stands birth; new life, beauty and the fulfilment of hope after the darkness of winter. In the shadows, the long fingers of winter linger, turning the hope of spring to a brutal and heartrending season.

So much can go wrong. Ask any farmer, or any ewe, or any hard-working pair of birds of the risks and tragedy that lurk below the surface of brighter days and welcome sunshine.

And so it was with us.

A vicious drought had hammered the stock, through a long and late summer. A group of horse trekkers had grazed their horses on our paddocks, and we had been eaten out of any surplus pasture, sorely needed when food became scarce.

Stock faced the winter in less than good condition, and winter gives no favours. Early snow froze their thin bones. Grass, which had died off in the summer, was unable to make a showing through those gaspingly cold early weeks. Winter offered little comfort, and less fodder.

Tough decisions. The stuff of nightmares for a farmer. We sent away a lot of our stock. Sheep and cattle. We didn't even keep the obligatory pigs because we just couldn't make the sty dry or habitable. Most of the chickens died.

As the first signs of spring melted the blanket of snow and lifted our spirits, the fogs drifted away to reveal the aftermath.

Among the casualties were our horses. The young gelding had fared reasonably well but the bay mare, and our lovely old white mare, Misty, looked miserable and thin, even covered.

Their age was against them. The years wear away their front teeth to expose a gap which cannot close over short bites of grass and they had lost a lot of condition.

Misty looked worst. Nobody knew how old she really was. We guessed about 28. Her coat, when the cover came off, was staring and rough, her flanks sunken.

Her belly was hugely round, every rib showing. She stood stock still, head low, hooves planted squarely, breathing heavily and decidedly uninterested in everything around her.

December 2000, *Growing Today*

She was a sorry sight, and I felt guilty that I had dragged her through such an awful winter. Another tough decision. It was with heavy heart we left her, the paddock gate closing with the awful clunk of finality.

The children would take it hardest. Their relationship with the farm animals had always been a happy one; of puppies, pet lambs, calving, egg collecting. Children hope for a miracle, against all logic.

My husband decided to make a final decision early the next morning. I could hear him, moving furtively in the darkness, cursing softly as he searched for enough clothes to keep out the biting chill.

I lay there until I heard the door close, sick with guilt, tears pricking. I decided to join him. It was an awful job and he could do with some support.

Trudging along the track that morning, memories flooded in of long treks with Misty, all the kids on her back, the waterfall day, pet days, pony rides. Her two foals long since gone.

I could see a lonely shadow ahead of me, head bent, bag slung over his shoulder, no doubt thinking similar thoughts. She had been a lovely pony. All the kids had learnt to ride on her.

As we reached the paddock the sun was just rising, casting an apricot glow over the hills behind the house, lighting the tops of the fence posts. The birds sang everywhere, yet all was breathlessly still.

I joined the figure leaning on the gate. We stayed that way for a long time without moving, unwilling to break the spell of a new day. Dawn touched every sparkling blade of dew drenched grass as a gentle white head turned and fixed us with soft, trusting eyes.

At her feet, curled in leggy repose, lay a tiny brown foal.

Rajah

Jim Morris

He was 17.2 at the wither,
A touch of feather, but still,
Plenty of sting in the rough stuff,
Ton of guts on the hill.

His father a Clydesdale entire,
His mother a big barrelled mare,
You could bet when the going was toughest,
Old Rajah would always be there.

Nothing pretty or polished about him,
A big Roman nose and large feet;
But for nature and honest endeavour,
This horse could never be beat.

He was great with the kids on the station,
Safe as a church with them all,
Couldn't be faulted for riding,
Except for the distance to fall!

When the river was roaring about you,
And the water the pommel would lap;
He'd forge ahead gamely as ever,
And never get into a flap.

When the water was swirling and dirty
And the boulders were rolling below,
And other horses were baulking,
He would always give it a go.

The water pulling your upstream leg
Trying to drag you under;
He'd strike out with the current and swim,
And never was known to blunder.

Riding out to the heads of the rivers,
Over boulders and shingle banks too;
He would pick his way carefully but surely,
With barely the clink of a shoe.

Packing posts up a hill for a fenceline
You could really pack on the gear;
He could handle as much as two others,
And still never be in the rear.

Four bundles of standards for sideloads,
Two coils of wire for the top;
I've seen him pack this for an hour,
With never a sign of a stop.

As soon as the breast-plate tightened,
He'd lower his head with a grunt;
Dig his toes in and stride ever upward,
Making sure that he kept to the front.

Coming down loaded with a porker,
He'd sit on the breeching and slide;
And something has gone from this station
The day that old battler died.

1997, *Different Worlds*

83

Uncle Wally's Pacer

Barry Crump

Tallfern was a fair-dinkum thoroughbred pacer, the dirtiest-tempered, ugliest ratbag of a horse you ever saw in your life. More white in his eyes than a Maori with a green eel on his hook. Uncle Wally bought him off a Chinaman for two cows and thirty quid, and poured more oats, chaff, hay, good grass, time and bot-bombs into his miserable hide than all the cows were getting between them. We made a track to train him on and every morning I had to get the milking started while Tallfern got his workout. Wally used to say how we was going to play merry hell with his horse at the races and Aunt Sarah said the only playing he'd ever do was 'Remembrance' on its ribs with a guitar pick.

When the trotting season started at Epsom, Uncle Wally bought a brand-new sulky and patched up all the harness. Then he had to have a trailer and horseshoes and entry fees and more bot-bombs. Aunt Sarah and I listened on the wireless to the first race Tallfern was in but he was only mentioned once. Somewhere near the start of the race the announcer said: 'And six lengths further back to Tallfern!' I think they had to wait for him to get off the track before they could start the next race. The bit had come out of his mouth and Uncle Wally couldn't pull him up when the race ended.

When he came home Uncle Wally said how he'd had a bit of bad luck, but he couldn't possibly lose the big race the next Saturday. Aunt Sarah said he'd better not or we'd lose our account at the store.

We lost our account at the store. It got so we'd have boiled mangels and mutton for tea every night so there would be oats and bot-bombs and entry fees and things. Uncle Wally still swore he'd just been unlucky last week and he couldn't lose next Saturday, but Aunt Sarah and I didn't even listen on the radio any more.

Then came the great day. Tallfern won a race by half the length of the straight. The first we heard of it was when Uncle Wally came home early – in an ambulance.

An ambulance?

Yeah. Bruised and burnt all over. He was in bed for two weeks.

What happened?

Well Uncle Wally used to feel the cold a bit so he wore his old leather coat under his racing mocker. When the race was due to start he knocked out his pipe on the sulky shaft and stuffed it in the pocket of his jacket. It wasn't out properly and when they

1974, *Horses and Horsemen*

started racing the wind fanned the sparks until Uncle Wally's coat suddenly burst into flames. He was amongst a bunch of other horses at the time and they shied off in all directions. That put most of them out of the race. By the time they came into the straight there were horses and drivers and broken sulkies scattered all round the track. Tallfern suddenly saw what was going on and he galloped past the post like Johnny Globe. Uncle Wally was blazing like a forge and let go one of the reins to try and beat the fire out – and they shot through the rails into the crowd. Four people got knocked around and the horse broke its leg. Had to be destroyed. They put Uncle Wally out and brought him home all done up in bandages and instructions.

The racing clubs suspended him for a year for being careless, and Aunt Sarah and I had to do the milking till he recovered. It was worth it, though, because we knew there'd be no more racehorses and bot-bombs.

O'Reilly's Pig

Glynellen Slater

During the Great Depression, Dad left the city for a country school, and we were lucky enough to rent an old house with a little land. Mum bought a few day-old chickens and eventually we had our own eggs, while Dad converted the backyard wilderness into a magnificent garden in which he grew just about everything which was known in those days. There was a small paddock with half a dozen fruit trees in it, some dead and some dying, which we called the orchard. What little fruit it produced was so full of codlin moth it couldn't be eaten, and the only spray available was soapy water out of the copper after the weekly wash. Mum traded eggs with the grocer and Dad helped out with hay-making and wherever an extra hand was needed. It wasn't long before we had our very own house cow, and then a hand separator for cream which was hand-churned into butter. We did very well.

Down the back road Jack O'Reilly kept pigs, but since everyone was always too busy to visit and the little O'Reillys were much smaller than us, we didn't see much of them. Dad used to help out now and then, and every time Mrs O'Reilly went off to have a new baby Dad would go over to feed the pigs, and often the little O'Reillys as well, while Jack was away in town visiting Mrs O'Reilly.

In return Jack O'Reilly would select one of his finest piglets for us to raise, and he and Dad would inspect and admire it every so often until judged just right for bacon, when Jack would kill it and we'd have half each to home cure. It usually lasted almost a year, even with all the relatives coming from the city at holiday times for a bacon and eggs and cream breakfast, a real luxury for town dwellers.

Pig was always put in the orchard, where it rooted happily for codlin moth grubs and grew huge, and gradually the orchard began to bear again.

I think it must have been the last pig which I remember best, because it was the friendliest, most talkative and most intelligent one we had. Pigs like company, and this one used to run squealing to the end of the orchard nearest the back door every time anyone came in or out. Mum's job was to check the fence line every day and to hammer in loose pegs and mend holes in the wire. Pig loved this exercise and would sometimes show Mum a peg which needed attention and watch with great interest while she hammered it back in. Pig grew bigger, the pegs grew heavier, and the hammer was replaced by a great heavy wooden mallet kept by the back door.

1987, *Province: New Nelson Writing*

One day several pegs in a row had been loosened and Pig was still working away. Mum took the mallet and went out to effect repairs. She shooed Pig back and swung the mallet round her head. Mum's brothers were bushmen and well she knew how to swing an axe. Down came the mallet, but at that precise moment, Pig chose to reach forward and sniff the peg. Mum never missed and she didn't this time either. Pig rolled over without a grunt and lay still. Mum, horrified at what she'd done, dropped the mallet and rushed inside. No close neighbours, no phone, no transport and a sleeping toddler. There was nothing to do but wait it out until Dad came home. But every time she glanced out the kitchen window there was the body lying still and silent.

It was too much. She couldn't avoid seeing it, so she spent the rest of the day at the front of the house. When Dad came home, a distraught Mum rushed out crying, 'I've killed the pig!' Dad dropped his bike and ran down the passage and out the back door. Mum heard him roar. Then she realised that he was roaring at someone or something and ran out herself.

Broken pumpkins, half chomped cabbages and onions, uprooted caulis, parsnips, potatoes and carrots were strewn everywhere. The strawberry bed had been uprooted, the raspberries flattened.

In the corner nearest the orchard stood one bloated pig, perfectly still, with closed eyes and a bloody snout. He was too full to walk. Mum and Dad had to push him through the gate back into the orchard. As I remember, I think he was the last pig we got from Jack O'Reilly.

Sausages for Tea

Heather Browning

W e'd been living here for about two years when my friend from town, Vivienne, came to stay. She hadn't been to the Sounds before, so I warned her to bring her gumboots. Fortunately she also brought her sense of humour or it could have been a disastrous visit.

I'd cooked roast lamb the first night of her stay and, just as we started eating, Hilary, my daughter, asked me, 'This isn't Trip Trop, is it? Cos I'm not eating it if it's Trip Trop!'

'Trip Trop?' asked Viv.

'Mmm,' I said, looking guilty, 'Hilary's pet lamb.'

Of course it was Hilary's pet lamb. It had met with an accident and rather than waste all that meat we'd butchered it and shoved the poor thing in the freezer. Great! Now Vivienne was looking green and Hilary was refusing to eat.

The second night we had roast chicken – home-grown!

The thing that Vivienne remembers to this day is Hilary announcing loudly during tea, 'Gosh, Peter had a big breast bone, didn't he?'

'Peter?' Viv asked, fork poised in the air.

'Mmm,' I said bravely, taking another mouthful, 'the rooster.'

'Oh God! Does everything you eat have a name?'

The third night we had sausages, bought from the shop, unknown and unnamed. Well, except for the ones we put on Vivienne's plate.

We christened them Simon and Cecil Sausage.

1999, *Sleeping Dolphins*

Cats

Pat White

When the old cat finally
fell to bits and chucked it in;
kidneys, appetite, the lot
we planted a smoke bush
where we buried him

given time, we got a grey kitten
she opened me up, made space
where cats had never been
when we walked down to pick her off the
road
a mess of guts and smashed bone, we had
to wait while another car ran over her
going over a ton, no trouble
bastard never even swerved;
she'll get an olive tree
if this drought ever ends

a few weeks back, we got a couple of little
scrubbers
one tabby, one black and white … thought
we'd increase the odds a bit

1999, *Drought and other intimacies*

My New Heifer

Frank S. Anthony

A fellow sold me a heifer one year. He said she was a well-bred little thing, and all she wanted was gentle handling, and she would probably be the best cow in my herd. He said if I cared to take her, he would pop her in at my gate straight away, as he had her out on the road.

I was short that spring, so I snapped the offer, and went out on to the road to help turn her in. Right from the start that heifer looked scary to me, and before we got her on to my farm she had jumped three fences, and led us a dance over about four miles of country.

The owner said it was only to be expected, because he had mustered her up with the dogs that morning, and of course she was excited and unsettled. I think now that the reason I got a cheap heifer that morning was because he had made up his mind that he could never get her as far as the saleyards, but he never mentioned anything like that to me. He suggested that if I kept her about the sheds for a day or two, and hand-fed her on hay, she would calm down and follow me about like a dog. I tried that, the same afternoon. I noticed that as soon as I got anywhere within a hundred yards of her, she would commence to circle round and eye weak spots in the fence, so I used a little tact, and finally got her penned up in the stockyard. Then I went to the hay-shed and got a big armful of hay. I threw it over the rails of the yard, and gave my new purchase such a fright that she got her head stuck between two rails of the fence, and nearly broke her neck. By the time she had cleared herself I was over the rails, and advancing on her with the hay in my arms again.

The man made a bit of a mistake in his calculations, or else I misunderstood him, because she certainly followed me round – but not like a dog. Unless he meant a mad dog, and I don't think that's what he said. I had to hurry myself a little in order to get over the fence before she got me, and then I sat on the top rail for a few minutes, and watched her tear that heap of hay into single straws and trample on each one separately. That set me thinking, and I decided to leave her to it for a while and try her again when she was hungry.

The next time I tried to feed her, I lowered the hay over the rails on a long pole, but my dog went into the yard to inspect an old bone there, and spoilt things. He didn't stop there very long, and the heifer knocked off a horn showing him the way out, and

1977, *Me and Gus*

both of them got excited about it. I tied the dog up for my next attempt, and tried her with a few swedes instead of the hay. Every time I threw a swede over, she jumped at a fresh part of the fence. Then an old cove from close handy happened to drop in, and said, 'What's the use of doing that? Can't you see the heifer's frightened of you? Take her quietly, man, take her quietly.'

He said it was a queer sort of heifer would beat him, and he'd show me how to work things.

He took a short stick in one hand and a wisp of hay in the other, and climbed down into the yard. Then he said, 'Watch me,' and advanced on the heifer.

I must say that for an old man he was worth watching.

As I told him, it was as pretty an exhibition of aerial acrobatics as I have seen for a long time.

I think my performance was a trifle better, because I had two horns to side-step, while I have an idea that the absence of a horn saved that old chap from a very unpleasant experience. When he was firmly planted on the top rail of the yard he started to say some things about it. Why hadn't I told him she was like that? I was the sort of person that would let a man go to certain death sooner than say a word in warning.

Then when I saw a man mangled to death he supposed I'd laugh. Well, he'd come over to give me a hand, but in future I could do my own dirty work.

He called in at my house as he passed back, and borrowed my saddle and bridle so I have an idea he really came over for them, but whichever it was, he never stopped to help me any more. I sat on the rail and admired the latest acquisition to my herd for a while, and then opened the gate and let her out with the other cows.

I was feeding out hay at the time, and every day I used to cart a load out and fork it about the paddock. While I was busy doing this my old cows used to gather round and get in front of the horse, and chase each other for tasty tit-bits, and kick up a deuce of a row.

My new heifer would occupy the time in trotting up and down the furthest fence, waiting for me to go away. When I was well clear of the paddock she would circle round the feeding herd, in ever diminishing circles, and by the time they had eaten up all the hay she would arrive about the outer edge of the feeding area, and start looking hungry. There wasn't much grass anywhere at that time, and I began to feel anxious because she was going down in condition.

Then one morning I went out and found her trotting about with a calf nearly as active as herself. This was where the real business began, because somehow or other I had to inveigle that heifer into the cowshed, milk her, and capture the calf. I wasn't in love with the idea at all, but it had to be done. I refused to be enticed more than a chain away from the fence, when I sallied forth to bring her home, but I needn't have worried myself.

As soon as she set eyes on me she went off like a shot, and left me to capture the calf without any interference. The calf took after its parent, and went off like a packet of crackers as soon as I clapped my hands on it. I had it jammed in a corner, and when it found there was no escape it turned round and charged, like an old hand at the game. I carried it home and tied it in the cow-yard, in the hope that if I planted myself out of sight the heifer would eventually pluck up enough resolution to pay it a visit. Nothing happened that day, so in the evening I was reduced to the necessity of trying to drive the heifer home. Something had to be done, because I couldn't leave her all night without milking her.

I mustered all my cows, drove them down to the heifer, collected her, and then headed them for the shed.

Three times she broke away, and I patiently worked the cows back and got her again, and then finally, by the aid of a loud 'Whoop!' and much noise, I got her through the gate and closed it on her. Although she was such a blood-thirsty creature, she didn't seem to have much heart when it came to fighting her own species, and while I was preparing things my cows filled in time horning her round the yard.

I only had five cows in at the time, so I decided to milk them first, in case they got upset when I started to break in the heifer. I thought I might as well run the whole lot into the shed at once, and while I was busy with the cows the heifer could have a look round and get used to things. The first thing she inspected in my shed was a gap under the door, about six inches wide. She got down on her knees and tried to crawl through it, and when I hauled her back by the tail she doubled like an eel, and I escaped sudden death by half an inch. I let her out into the yard again so that I could milk the cows in peace, and then I nipped over to a neighbour, and asked him to come and help me. Sam Turner isn't the kind of man I would choose to help on a job like that, as a rule, but he lived close by, and it was a case of go for the nearest.

Sam has a squeaky voice, and is inclined to be excitable. He has great ideas about everything. Sam can sit by his fire of an evening, and explain how to break in the wildest outlaw, horse or heifer, that ever lived. One great theory of his is to fix the animal to be subdued with a steely eye, and mesmerize it. When we got over to my place he had worked out a plan of battle, and as we entered the shed, he was telling me not to be afraid to call on him again in the morning, if I had further trouble. Sam didn't anticipate I would, after he had settled her. but he said he could always spare a few minutes to help a friend. We got a rope, and made a running noose on it, for a start. I got up in front of a bail with one end and Sam fixed his steely eye on the heifer, which was backed into a corner of the shed, lowering at us, with only the whites of its eyes showing.

'When I slip the noose over her horns, you pull her up into the bail,' said Sam, and advanced slowly. I hadn't much faith in Sam's idea myself, but I didn't like to hurt his feelings by telling him so. thought he might be right, and anyway he couldn't do much harm trying it. When I went over to get Sam's help, I was under the impression I told him the heifer was wild. I thought he understood that was why I wanted his help. But after I had woodened the heifer with a sledge-hammer, and dragged Sam out on to the grass by his heels, he said, 'No!' He said he wouldn't have dreamed of coming over if he'd known she was like that. He wanted to know what he'd ever done to me to warrant my putting such a dirty one across him, and when I wanted to help him to his feet he said I was to keep my murdering paws off him. I listened for a while, and then went away to get the embrocation bottle, but I needn't have troubled. When I got back with it Sam had disappeared, and was half way back home. I followed his track back by listening to the groans and curses, as he crossed fences and creeks, but I did not know till later that he had done the whole distance on his hands and knees. After Sam had gone I began to ponder.

I went into the shed, and had a good look all round. There was a beam going right across the roof, about eight feet from the ground, so I climbed on to that, and tried lassooing the heifer from above. After several misses I managed to get the noose round her neck, and then I climbed quietly down with the end in my hand, and ran it through the front of one bail and back down through another. Then I stood in the one bail and hauled her up by the neck. It was a good job she was small, or I should never have handled her, but finally, by taking advantage of every time she rushed forward, I had her safely bailed up and her head tied in as well. But the fun had only started. When I went to leg-rope her I found that she could balance herself on one leg and kick with the other three all at once.

After I had both her hind legs tied, she fell down in such an attitude that it was a case of let her go again, or choke her.

Then I did it all over again – with the same result. During quiet moments – when I was trying to undo a knot that had jammed – before the rope broke her leg, or strangled her, my mind dwelt lingeringly on the man who had sold her to me.

I hoped that I would meet him again, so that I could express my gratitude in a fitting manner.

Every time the well-bred little thing let out a bellow, or went through a spasm of shuddery flinches, I saw that man's face, and heard his voice in my ear, advising me to hand-feed her, and I would have her following me round like a dog. Before I could milk her I had to put two ropes across underneath her to prevent her falling down. Then I got about a cupful of milk, and comforted myself with the reflection that she would probably give more in the morning. I went to the factory next morning before I attempted to milk her, and then, after going through exactly the same procedure, I got another cup of milk. I did this for a week, and neither she nor I got used to it, so finally I turned the calf on to her and shut her away in my back paddock.

Then I waded in and did all the work I had neglected when I was subduing her, and went out the back to see how she was getting on just in time to save the calf's life. That well-bred little thing wasn't producing enough milk to nourish her own calf, and the poor little beggar was simply fading away. I had to bring it home and bucket-feed it again, and then I hunted round and tried to find someone I could give that heifer to.

Several people accepted her, but none of them ever got her past the middle paddock of my farm, so in the end I went back there with a gun.

* * *

That was the year something went wrong with the hide market, and when I took the skin to town it fetched one and sixpence.

* * *

The only sort of heifer I buy now is the sort you can go up to and pet in the paddock.

94

Texas Longhorns

John Dawson

Basil McGurr was typical of many part-time West Coast farmers. In fact in the '70s about half the farmed land was run by part-timers, so there were plenty of them. Basil did a bit of most things, but mainly not very much, as supervising his ill-defined holdings and wandering stock took most of his time. He basically had the 'run' of most of the roadside between Kumara and the Taramakau Settlement, plus a few scattered clearings in the cut-over bush. Although he was a stranger to superphosphate and fences, he was an expert musterer and a master at extracting sheep and cattle from both the gorse-covered tailings and the bush where they grazed. This was achieved with the aid of a canny old heading dog and a rusty bicycle. Indeed, Basil was a distinctive sight, as were his stock.

His sheep were unique. From Perendale stock, they were mostly long-tailed, of assorted sex and age, with one distinguishing characteristic – what little wool they grew was confined to their hindquarters. This was because the gorse continually pulled the wool off the front half – hence their name, 'Kumara Half-wools'. They were probably the most inbred, motley, malnourished flock in the South Island, but they were also very hardy and unbelievably cunning. Basil knew every one of the 300 or so and woe betide anyone who pinched one for the table or even innocently ran one over.

His cattle were equally variable and about 70 of them were scattered in small mobs over a distance of 70 kilometres. They were of Shorthorn ancestry, lived deep in the bush and were completely wild. Despite the harsh conditions, the mature cattle were huge. Indeed their size, appearance and lack of respect for humans had scared the hell out of several possum trappers and deer stalkers.

Clinton Lonergan was a Texan who was staying at the Mitchell's Hotel on the southern side of Lake Brunner. He was a rancher and oilman who these days spent four months of the year fly-fishing around the world, and was at Lake Brunner to fish the tributaries of the Grey and Taramakau Rivers. Unfortunately, he was typical of many Texans, large, loud and very wealthy. He was also not very well advised. It was September when he arrived too early for fly-fishing but not too late for the heavy spring rains the Coast is known for. In short, his fishing trip had been a disaster of flooded streams, washed-out tracks and high winds.

1998, *Whitebait and Wetlands: Tales of the West Coast*

After six days at Mitchell's he was utterly fishless and presented a lonely and miserable sight as he sought solace in the bar. By this stage the locals had had enough of his company as he regaled them about the deficiencies of the place, and how everything was bigger and better in Texas. But Coasters are good people and patient listeners – especially when the visitor buys the drinks.

And so it was that Clinton Lonergan was drinking with three well-known locals – namely Pat Fitzgerald, Martin Shaffrey and the one-and-only Basil McGurr. Pat Fitzgerald was a local farmer, while Martin Shaffrey was helicopter pilot whose reputation was made on deer recovery work from his base in Jacksons. His skill and daring were legendary. Clinton Lonergan had just told them that the fishing was better in Texas and if they saw how big the cattle grew, 'Why you would be just plumb green with envy!'

'How big?' asked Basil McGurr.

'Well my three-year-old steers just hung up at a carcase weight of one thousand pounds average,' bragged the Texan.

'That's pretty good,' muttered the humble Basil, 'but I own bigger cattle than that. Some of mine weigh three-ton liveweight and stand six foot high at the withers.'

'Why you people must think that us Texans are just plain dumb to believe that,' spluttered the indignant Clinton Lonergan. 'I'll bet that is not true.'

'If you bet us enough we will prove it's true,' said Basil.

'Why, I am willing to put my fishing gear on it.'

'Done,' said Basil, extending his hand. 'As long as you throw in your Stetson hat.'

They shook hands and agreed to the terms, with Lonergan suddenly aware that the entire bar had congregated around them and were taking a great deal of interest in proceedings. Still, as he told his wife, he had nothing to worry about. 'No chance of any cattle growing that big outside Texas.' Although he wished he hadn't bet his fishing gear, as it was not only obscenely expensive, it was state of the art and his pride and joy. Good thing there was no chance of losing it he mused, reassuring himself.

For Basil and his two mates there was no time to lose. To win this bet he would have to muster and present the Slatey Creek mob, and he had only three days to do it. They were 12 in number, hadn't seen humans for two years, of legendary size (and age) and notorious for their disposition. Unable to be mustered for TB testing, they were under sentence of death and had successfully evaded the two Forest Service cullers who had spent a week hunting for them in June. Three years ago the mob had terrified a Canterbury couple. Desperately hungry, in the middle of a severe winter, they had emerged from the bush between Mitchell's and Inchbonnie, blocking the road. They then surrounded the couple's vehicle, rendering it completely immobile for two hours while they slobbered all over the windows, licked the paint and gave it the odd playful 'nudge'. This incident was mostly responsible for their fearsome reputation.

As it happened, Basil knew exactly where they were. Martin Shaffrey had seen them as he flew over a clearing two days ago. They were some four miles off the road, east of Greenstone, and they looked hungry. A plan was hatched.

By noon next day Martin Shaffrey had dropped off four bales of a Rotomanu cow cockie's best hay, out of a deer recovery net slung under the chopper. By mid afternoon the bales had been devoured, including the twine. The next two days were not as straightforward, and a lot more risky. While Martin Shaffrey dropped off strategically placed piles of hay, Niko and Pat Fitzgerald formed a trail through thick bush, old tailings and swamps to the Mitchell's road to Kumara, about five miles past the pub. Miraculously, the Slatey Creek mobs obliged and were tossing their hay around the roadside when Clinton Lonergan and his wife turned the corner heading for Kumara and South Westland.

While three days of hay feeding and full bellies had quietened the mob to the point where the distant sight of Basil and Pat on horseback didn't upset them, the Lonergan Range Rover certainly did. As it skidded to a stop, most of the mob crashed into the bush. Not so, the five protectors of the small, feral herd who glowered and snorted their anger at the noisy invader of their peace.

Clinton Lonergan coldly surveyed the scene, utterly disbelieving what he saw. They were without doubt the biggest, meanest cattle he had ever seen, even by Texas standards. Of the five that had him bailed up, two were roan Shorthorn bulls, a nine- and an eight-year-old. There was nothing between them – each was immense, at least three-ton liveweight, and very angry. With them were two huge cows, one completely white and the other brindle, whose three-month calf peered nervously from the bush.

The largest of the five was a blue roan steer aged about 12 years. He stood 18 inches higher than the others and would have been half a ton heavier than any of them. He was enormous. A sight probably only seen in the bullock teams used for logging in the last century. The huge blue steer was not as aggressive as the others were, and more curious. Like his herd mates, his horns were large and fearsome. By the time he had flicked off the indicator light and scraped a panel or two, it was time for Basil to intervene.

Slowly Basil, Pat Fitzgerald and their six dogs approached the scene as the cattle sniffed and stamped their unease. From thirty yards away Basil showed Clinton Lonergan a large grass seed sack, 'This is to put your fishing gear in.' Clinton Lonergan was at a loss. He was outfoxed and humiliated. But for all his noise and pride he was an honourable man and painstakingly he transferred his beloved fishing gear into the sack as the cattle gingerly backed away from the vehicle. As he engaged first gear, Basil shouted, 'What about the hat?' With a stoic smile Clinton Lonergan passed up his Stetson to Basil.

As he eased down the road to Kumara, he reflected on his stay at Mitchell's Hotel. Wet to the skin most days, bogged twice, no trout and he had lost his priceless fishing gear to a local who now wears his Stetson. Still, the size of them West Coast cattle; wait till I tell the boys back home …

Bulls' Horns

Nelson Cooper

One quiet afternoon I sneaked off down Gisborne's Ormond Road with my typical drover's mob of bulls, cull cows and odd cattle. There were quite a lot of them and they were well behaved, so well behaved that I was walking along behind them, leading my horse, when one of them, a bull, decided he wanted to go somewhere and peeled off towards Stout Street. On the corner, where he chose to do this, there was an old pork butcher shop with an extensive verandah built out over the footpath. Dropping the reins, I headed him off by taking a short cut under the verandah. The bull was not an aggressive type and returned to the mob. I went back and picked up the reins of my little horse, who was so good that he would stand while the traffic drove all around him. We walked along past another few corners until we came to one on our left, and it was here that my friend the bull took it into his head to have another go. He peeled off to his left and away he went along McLean Street and then turned left again into Clifford Street, by this time I had mounted the horse and rode after him and headed him off. A few strokes over the head with the supple-jack and we turned back.

When we got to the first corner, he hopped on to the footpath and we didn't have far to go before we were going to be back to Ormond Road. But on our right was a tall, clipped, evergreen hedge all the way to the corner. It suddenly occurred to me that if there was somebody walking along just around the corner, a woman with a pram perhaps, there was a danger of their getting tramped into the carpet. So I stoked and had the bull going so fast that he couldn't turn the corner. He would have to go straight ahead on to Ormond Road, which he did, all according to plan. But now, coming down the road, and slowing down as he approached the back of the mob, was one lone motorist in a Rugby car. He looked to his left and saw a large dark bull approaching at considerable speed, so he did what anyone else would have done under similar circumstances, he stopped. Had he not stopped just where he did he would have been quite all right. Just another two metres forward or backwards would have been OK. Just there, certainly not, because the bull was coming at such speed that he couldn't possibly deviate from his line of travel, which was straight ahead. Ferdinand the bull, being suddenly confronted with this barrier to his progress, let out an ear-splitting BLAW as his horns penetrated the centre of the front passenger's door, lifting the car to about a 45-degree angle, but not quite tipping on its side. Now there was still about a half-ton

1999, *Memories of a Stockman*

of fired up, very fresh bull beef to be accommodated somewhere, and this fitted perfectly, below the running board on that side of the car.

At that time there were a pair of tram lines embedded in hard tar seal along Ormond Road and the car was travelling on this prior to stopping to give way to the bull. With his horns stuck in the door and the rest of his body jammed under the running board, the bull was not able to get a grip with his feet. But then, somehow or other, he managed to kick himself outwards and upwards and on to his feet. With considerable force he freed his head out of the door, tearing a big sheet of metal out as he did so. The glass from above the door had come showering down on the top of his head and neck, and he stood there gathering his wits and shaking his head. Both horns were liberally coated with green paint. He blew his nose, backed off and waddled down the slope towards the mob, very obviously disorientated, counting stars and trying to work out what had been happening these last few minutes.

It was time to interview the driver, who appeared to be suffering from shock. His teeth were chattering, he was pale and appeared to be short of breath. He told me his name was Mr Boag. I recalled being at school with a boy by the surname Boag and this helped set the scene for negotiations. His breathing improved and his teeth stopped chattering as I assured him there were no more bulls to come. They were all there in front of us now. Was his car insured?

'Yes.'

'Which Company?'

'South British.'

'Ah, good. Well, you take the car down to them, they have the Public Risk cover on these cattle and will no doubt be pleased to know that nobody has been killed.'

… Another mishap occurred [different day and mob] when one Arthur Whiting, who had a farm at Manutuke, met the mob on the short, straight stretch of tar seal as we approached the Waipaoa bridge. He had an Oldsmobile or Hupmobile or similar type of car: canvas hood, side curtains, wooden spoked high wheels and slow-revving motor which could eventually reach a considerable turn of speed, given time to build up.

Now in the mob was a tall, skinny young jersey cow with short, turned-in horns, and as Arthur drove through the cattle, she decided to turn back towards Manutuke. She cantered along in front of him, he put his foot down, and the race was on. I naturally expected him to overtake the cow in short order, but she had immediately accelerated, whereas he had to build up revs. Eventually he started to overtake her and would have – no trouble at all – had she not decided to cross the road obliquely in front of him at top speed. Her feet skidded from under her on the tar seal and she fell. The left-hand front wheel of Arthur's automobile mounted her face, rose up and over the uppermost of her two short, turned-in horns and dropped down on to the road again.

99

The cow got up, shook her head and Arthur proceeded on his way, with a decided shimmy on his left-hand front wheel. As there was no further danger to either horse or dogs, I gathered her up and away we went. We rattled our way across the old Waipaoa bridge and along toward the Saleyards Corner.

Bart and the Cows

Ormond Burton

The world is not, of course, inhabited only by men and women, cats and dogs. In fact, the greater part of the population of New Zealand is made up of cows, with a fair percentage of bulls, pigs, and sheep. In our part of the world, it was cows with a fair sprinkling of bulls. Any time from five in the morning until eight and again from four till seven in the evening the milking-machines filled the air with their pleasant chug-chugging. Our neighbour, who owned Old Don [a dog] (or was owned by him, according to the point of view), also sang to his cows. They liked it, too. Some day, a lover of cows will write a book about them. I never formed any passion for them myself, but, after all, they are human like the rest of us, and to those who love them have a fascination all of their own. In the main, they are extremely tractable beasts and very docile, but there are, of course, points on which they feel strongly, like other feminine creatures – calves and so forth.

An angry cow is not a pleasant person to meet. Fortunately, it is rarely that their staid domesticity is disturbed. Despite their placidity, they strongly resemble other women in their highly-developed bump of curiosity. There is, moreover, among the members of a herd a certain clannishness which develops into something like militant trade unionism on the question of dogs. Their own dog is accepted. They may or may not like him, but he being a proper part of the scheme of things, they will allow him to muster them and take them to the shed. (This, like other things that female creatures apparently allow themselves to be dragooned into, is because they really wish by mustering time to be milked.) But they will have no dealings with another dog. I remember one day Bart bounced into a neighbour's paddock full of high spirits, conceit, and arrogance. He would show the world how a herd should be brought in.

'Get up, you fat beasts! Get up!' said he, giving plenty of voice. 'Get up! Move along!'

Thirty heads came round curiously and suspiciously. Thirty buxom wenches turned with their heads toward him. Thirty heads went low and a wordless message passed from one to another.

'Get up!' shouted Bart. 'Move on, fat ones!' There wasn't quite so much conviction in his barking, though, for the heads were all the wrong way. Of a sudden they started to move forward slowly, but purposefully. Bart made a dash at one old beldame, but she still came on and her wide-open eye was nasty. The pace quickened, and the thirty

---

1944, *Bart, the Story of a Dog*

broke from a slow walk into a lumbering gallop. I should imagine Bart's feelings were somewhat akin to those of an infantryman armed with a rifle caught by himself in the great open spaces with a *Panzer* division hurtling down upon him. There was nothing for it but an ignominious flight through the nearest fence. It was one of the few times I saw him turn his back upon a foe.

It was not long after this that he and I were paying an evening call upon the parents of one of my pupils. Their herd had been turned out into a front paddock, through which ran the pathway up to the house. Dark shapes were lying about us in every direction, but as we went in they rose and started to converge about us. I picked what the worry was and told Bart to hop it and make himself scarce, but the idiot, instead of getting back on to the road, which he could have done quite easily, turned in behind me and started to walk demurely at my heels.

'Go on, you old idiot. Get back! Can't you see these brutes mustering round us for a rush?'

'Dear master! I will be good and chase no one. I will not nip the heels or swing on the tail of one of these dear old ladies.'

'No, you silly ass! But they will be trampling on us in a minute.'

'Master, I have every confidence in you! I know you will protect me from these unpleasant females.'

I wasn't thinking at all of protecting him. I was thinking of myself and what a miserable widow Helen would make. Bart could save himself by streaking out into the darkness. I heard a nasty sound a bit to the side of me. One of the cows was a bull. At that moment I would have given a lot to have been dumped down into no man's land again, with the flares going up and a machine-gun sending nasty vicious bursts overhead. The phalanx was forming, ten yards to the rear, and every second I expected the rush. Fortunately, at that moment the front door opened, a stream of light showed forth, and the voice of my host was heard. The cows checked for a moment and by that time I was at the garden gate.

Sheep

Fiona Farrell

Last week they stood about the paddock
solid as a chesterfield suite. They
moved slowly, their black feet concealed
beneath the fleece. They took seriously
this business of eat and sleep, teaching
their lambs to chew slowly, to conduct
themselves as sheep. On Saturday the
truck came, rattled up the road, and the
lambs were taken. Oh, heavy load! They
cried, the mothers. How they grieved,
calling all night to the dark hills.
Where are you, my sweet-scented darling?
Where are you, whom I licked one slick
green day from bloody ground? The valley
echoed with the sound of lamentation.
But today they have forgotten. They have
been shorn and stripped in an instant
they leap free, creatures new-born.
There is no hill too steep, no creek
they cannot cross. Light enough to leap
fences, and a whole lifetime before it
starts again: the loving and the loss.

1997, *Sport* 19

Drama at the Yard

John Gordon

A one-act play for three lambs, four gates (one opened) and a narrator.

Scene 1: A sheep dog trial ground. Beside a two-metre square pen, a frustrated man (or woman) and a panting, heading dog are trying to turn three elusive sheep towards, then into the yard.

NARRATOR: Dog trial sheep are usually referred to as she, because at most trials female stock are used: lambs, hoggets, two-tooths and even mixed-age ewes. There are rare exceptions where entire males are used, though only as ram lambs, and the bolshie little buggers have a lot more fun than the competitors, especially at the yard! Ewe lambs of five to eight months of age are a very regular challenge. Small and innocent looking they may be, but looks, as always, are deceiving. They're too naive and have no real personality or confidence of their own and, too often, all three will lack the boldness necessary to become a leader. Having one lamb with an independent streak gives a competitor a chance of coaxing it in the right direction, so that the other two can be encouraged to trot along behind it. Alas, a regular scene at the yard has three fidgety adolescents going nowhere in slow circles; playing their traditional roles in an ongoing drama of indecision.

LAMB ONE: What do we do now?

LAMB TWO: I don't know.

LAMB THREE: One of us is supposed to be a leader.

LAMB ONE: What's a leader?

LAMB TWO: I don't know.

LAMB THREE: One of us does something and the others follow.

LAMB ONE: How do you know?

LAMB TWO: I don't.

LAMB THREE: My mother told me. (pauses, then adds with pride) She won lots of dog trials.

LAMB ONE: How?

LAMB THREE: By just standing here.

1998, *Three Sheep and a Dog*

LAMB TWO: Don't we move at all?

LAMB THREE: You can, but only in little circles and (inclines head towards yard) you're not supposed to let them push you towards that.

LAMB TWO: Shouldn't we go in there at all?

LAMB THREE: Not if you can help it!

LAMB ONE: And if we stay here, what happens then?

LAMB THREE: Eventually they just get sick of it.

LAMB TWO: That's good. Then what?

LAMB THREE: We'll be sent back to our paddock.

LAMB ONE: How will we know when that is?

LAMB THREE: A man comes out of that hut and yells out 'time' or something and these ones (nods towards triallist and dog) have to go away and take us with them,

LAMB TWO: And what do we do then?

LAMB THREE: Everything they want us to do.

LAMB ONE: But you said we weren't to help them.

LAMB THREE: Only when they wanted to get us in there (refers to yard). Once that man has called out, it's all over and we'll have won.

LAMB TWO: And then we're to be good?

LAMB THREE: That's what my mother said. It really annoys them when we're well behaved and it doesn't matter!

Baa, baa, baa

Millicent Bennett

His few sheep
produced
not one lamb –
they were barren
without exception;
but did one of them
guess
how they'd
shattered his dreams?
Not they –
they just had
no conception.

1969, *New Zealand Farmer*

Au Revoir

Joy Cowley

They limped out of the sunset, the man's back bent under the old army haversack, the dog's nose drooping in the dust of the country road. When they reached the verandah of the pub, the man eased the straps from his shoulders and sat down on a wooden bench near the door, the dog at his feet.

'Sorry,' he said, loosening its collar, 'sorry, Dog, but you see how it is. Don't you?'

The dog grinned and thumped the dust from his tail against the bare boards.

'I wouldn't be doing it, only – well, you understand.'

As the door of the bar swung out, the dog sat alert, ears straight, whimpering softly.

'No,' said the man. 'Not yet. Not that one.'

They waited, and when the door opened for the fourth time, the man stood, hitched at his belt, and called to the stranger:

'Hey, mister! Want to buy a cattledog? Cheap?' The stranger turned away. 'He's a beaut worker. You can have him for five quid.'

'What's the matter with your dog, Hori?' said the stranger.

'Nothing, honest. It's just that I don't need him now I've chucked in droving. Don't want a dog in the city.' He looked down at his dust-coated boots, then added, 'Matter of fact, I'm stony broke. I need the cash real bad.'

The stranger walked up to the dog and pushed him with his feet.

'Looks all right. But what guarantee have I he'll work?'

'Oh, he works right enough. Like I said, he's a beaut. Want to see him?'

'Yes, I do,' said the stranger, looking at the dog, who stared back with upturned eyes. 'Tell you what. I've got some bullocks in a run-off not a quarter of a mile away. We'll take him down there and see how he makes out. If he's as good as you say, I'll buy him. Could do with another dog.'

The stranger opened the boot of his car, and the dog leapt in beside the man's haversack.

'What do you call him?' asked the stranger, as he swung the car into the roadway.

'Just Dog,' said the man.

The car pulled in beside a gate at the other end of the town. In a small paddock the cattle stood motionless, black humps pinned to the grass by long, dark shadows. When released from the boot, the dog sniffed at the still air and circled the car twice before he came back to the man.

1967, *Return to Open Country*

'The gate's open at the other end,' the stranger said, leaning against the fence. 'Get him to take them into the next paddock.'

The man ruffled the wiry coat. 'Go on, Dog,' he pointed. 'Way back there, way back.'

The dog, like an arrow, twanged the fence wire and shot across the grass, ears twitching for the man's whistle. The signals came loud and clear, the bullocks bellowed and shifted nervously, but with short, sharp barks the dog snaked the herd into a tidy bunch and drove them cleanly through the far gap. Then he sat by the gate, waiting.

The stranger scratched his chin. 'But will he work for me like that?'

'He will if you whistle him right,' said the man. 'Why don't you try? Get him to bring them back.'

At the stranger's shrill call, the dog stood uncertain. Then, when the orders were repeated, he moved swiftly behind the mob and herded them back through the gateway.

'Here boy,' called the stranger, but it was to the man that the dog returned. He sat beside his master's boots, panting.

'He works well enough when you're here,' the stranger said, 'but when you've gone it might be a different matter.'

'Not if I tell him he's yours. This dog's real bright.' And the man bent down with his mouth close to the dog's ear. 'This is your new boss, understand, Dog? Go to him now. You're his for keeps. Go on.'

The dog's eyes turned towards the man, and he whimpered. But the man shook his head firmly, pointed, and the dog moved over to the stranger.

'He's all yours,' said the man. 'You try to make him come back.'

The stranger tried, but the dog merely sidled closer to his legs.

'Like I said,' the man shrugged. 'The dog's got clues.'

The stranger felt in his back pocket for his wallet, leafed through the notes for a fiver and crumpled it into the man's hand.

'Will you write me a receipt?' he asked.

'Me? Write?' The man looked surprised. 'Mister, I never been to school.'

'Okay then, forget it,' said the stranger. 'Do you want a lift back to town?'

The man shook his head. 'No, I'll walk. You take him straight home and treat him well. What time does the pub close?'

'When the last one's finished,' said the stranger. 'And don't worry about this chap. I'll look after him.'

The man folded the note into his pocket and hoisted the haversack over one shoulder.

'Goodbye, Dog,' he said softly and stepped on to the road.

'So long,' the stranger waved. 'Be seeing you.'

The man turned his back and smiled. 'Like hell you will,' he said under his breath.

No moon shone that evening. The small fire in the clearing made an island of orange light in the dark ocean of scrub.

The man unpacked his haversack slowly and methodically, unwrapped the steak, put it in the billy with tomatoes and a slab of butter, fastened the lid, and set it on the coals. Then he put out the chipped cup with NZR stamped on it, and two tin plates. A couple of sacks and a blanket were spread beside the fire, a pair of boots kicked off near them.

The man padded on bare feet to the edge of the island, and stood beneath a tree rolling a cigarette. He did not wait long. A rustle of dried twigs, an eager whine, and the dog dragged his belly across the clearing.

'You're late,' said the man, glancing at the wet muzzle that rested on his foot. There was another enquiring whimper, but the man did not speak again until the cigarette butt had been thrown into the fire. Then he slapped his thigh twice. The dog leapt at him with a bark and tried to lick the hands that fastened a thin strip of leather about his neck.

'Cost me a fortune in collars, you do,' the man grunted, but there was no resentment in his voice. 'Come on, tea's ready.'

The dog laughed and laughed, his tail sweeping the dried leaves around them. The man laughed too and his teeth were as strong and white as the dog's.

Uncle Trev and the Howling Dog Service

Jack Lasenby

I woke and heard a dog howling across the farms out the back of Waharoa and, somewhere further off, so far away I could hardly hear it, another dog howled back.

'They're barking at the moon,' my mother said next morning, but Uncle Trev had a different story when he dropped in for a cup of tea on his way home from the Wednesday stock sale at Matatmata.

'They're not barking at the moon,' he said. 'Don't go telling your mother now, but they're trained howling dogs. Mine. I trained them myself years ago.' I looked at Uncle Trev and he looked back at me. 'Years ago,' he repeated, 'I got sick of paying the post office for toll calls. It took ages to get through, then half the time you didn't get the person you wanted, and when you did, you couldn't hear them for noise on the line.

'I don't suppose you're old enough to remember,' he said, 'but people had much smaller ears before the telephone. They've only grown into these big flaps on the sides of our heads since we started squashing them with the telephone receiver.' I heard Mum give a sniff from the bench where she was making a cup of tea. 'Have a look in the album at the old family photographs, if you don't believe me,' said Uncle Trev. 'You can't even see ears on your grandmother.

'Besides,' he said, 'that old Mrs Eaves on the telephone exchange at the post office, she was always listening in. I could hear her breathing whenever I was talking to somebody. Sometimes she'd even join in the conversation.

'I was lying awake one night, thinking about it,' Uncle Trev went on, 'and the dogs were barking across all the farms between my place and Waharoa, and I thought, "Those dogs are talking to each other!"'

He stared at me. 'That's when I got my idea!' he said.

I stared back at him. Mum put a cup of tea and a plate with a few slices of cake on the table. 'Isn't it time you were in bed?' she told me.

Uncle Trev waited until she'd gone back to the bench. 'A howling dog service,' he said, 'that was my idea! I remembered how we used dogs to carry messages in the trenches in the Great War, and how my mate Squeaker Tuner always said we should teach the dogs to talk.

'Well, it took me a few years, but I got hold of some expensive huntaway bitches and bred pups from them for their voices. They had to be able to bark high and clear so the

1991, *Uncle Trev*

messages would carry, and they had to be able to remember a long message, that was the other thing. I started selling my dogs cheap,' said Uncle Trev, 'and they were good working dogs too, so in no time I had them planted on farms from one end of the country to the other.

'From Waharoa on a clear night, a good howling dog can make himself heard in Matamata. From Matamata they howl the message up the Hinuera Valley, round through Cambridge to Hamilton, and up to Auckland. The reply comes back through Morrinsville and Walton to Waharoa before the first dog's finished rattling his chain. Of course,' he said, 'if the wind's from the north, they howl the message round the other way.

'You listen,' said Uncle Trev, 'and you'll hear them howling off messages in all directions, specially on a clear night. Auckland, Wellington, Christchurch, Dunedin – our howling dogs cover New Zealand.'

'What about Cook Strait?' I asked.

No trouble!' said Uncle Trev, 'sound travels good-oh across water. I'm even thinking of putting a dog on top of Mount Cook to howl messages to Australia.'

'It's long past your bedtime,' Mum said to me. 'As for you,' she said to Uncle Trev, 'if you've finished your tea, isn't it time you were getting home to your farm? You've got cows to milk in the morning.'

When he called in next week, I asked him how the dog was doing on top of Mount Cook.

'You wouldn't believe the trouble I'm having,' said Uncle Trev. 'It's so cold in the snow, the first dog I put up there got chilblains and wouldn't bark, so I'm crossing my best huntaway with a beardie collie to get a longer-coated dog. It's going to take a year or two to get a good pup though, and even then it's still got to be trained.'

'How much do you charge for your howling dog service?' I asked him next time he called in.

'It's cheaper than toll calls,' said Uncle Trev. 'You see, the dogs earn their tucker working in the daytime, and it costs me nothing to get them howling messages. There's nothing a dog likes more than to have a good old howl at night, specially if there's a moon.

'Actually I've had a bit of trouble with the post office. They were really scared when they found my howling dog service had taken most of their business. They sent their Post-Master General in his uniform with red stripes down the trousers and a shiny brass helmet. I asked him if he was a fireman, but he got off his horse and begged me with tears in his eyes to stop the howling dog service. He said the post office was going broke.'

Mum was banging some pots around on the bench. I didn't want her to hear Uncle Trev's story or she'd send him home. 'What happened?' I asked.

111

'I felt a bit sorry for him,' said Uncle Trev, 'so I said I'd close down my howling dog service if the post office cut the cost of its toll calls in half. The Post-Master General couldn't thank me enough. He wanted to give me a free telephone, but I told him I didn't want big lugs instead of ears. I said I'd go on using the howling dog service for myself and a few friends. I couldn't stop the dogs talking to each other, of course. They still howl dog messages all over New Zealand.

'The Post-Master General thanked me and put on his shiny brass helmet and rode back to Wellington.'

'Are you going to sit there talking nonsense all night?' said my mother. 'Isn't it time you were getting home to the farm?' she asked Uncle Trev. 'As for you,' she said to me, 'you're supposed to be ill in bed, not sitting up listening to a lot of silly stories.'

I said goodnight and heard Uncle Trev's old lorry rattle away. It was warm under the blankets. I lifted the blind. Outside it was frosty, and there was a moon. Somewhere down Ward Street, a dog howled. I listened, and out towards Uncle Trev's farm under the hills at the back of Waharoa, another dog replied.

The Commentators

This section represents some 70 years of magazine and newspaper columns written by people who lived on farms and were able to reach beyond the front gate and express their thoughts, hopes and fears to others. For many decades this material was usually advisory. As well as proposing the adoption of new management techniques, the writer-farmer – usually male – would remind readers that certain seasonal tasks needed to be done, then describe how best to do them. During the Second World War some changes were made, beginning with the advent of 'J.J.' in the *New Zealand Free Lance*. She was a landgirl who wrote to encourage her colleagues and, I suppose, create support for our farm-based war effort.

Towards the war's end a nameless correspondent began to appear in the same magazine, whom I think must have been the first of the opinionated farm-based columnists. His approach is best described by an extract from his first entry: 'Only those who live in the country are qualified to write about country-life'.

From the mid-1940s to the early 1960s, country life was very much the theme of the *Listener* column, 'Shepherd's Diary', written by the magazine's first editor, Oliver Duff, who retired to a small farm not far from Christchurch. From there he penned reflections on day-to-day happenings that were an always thoughtful mixture of the comfortable and the questioning. From at least the 1920s onwards the *Dairy Exporter* had a succession of farmer columnists who were always 'how to' rather than 'how dare they!' In fact it wasn't until the mid-1960s that a full-time farmer used a pen to cut and thrust his way through the attitudes and complacent traditions that abounded in agriculture. He was Roland Clarke who, as 'Nor'wester', wrote a *New Zealand Farmer* column, 'The Month Down South', for over 20 years. Clarke, an Ulsterman, came to this country after management experience in the linen flax industry and brought to the farming scene a fresh set of eyes, directly stated views and a keen sense of humour. He described what was happening on his property and why, but never presumed to give advice – though he was never shy about giving his opinion on matters beyond the farm gate that threatened his livelihood. Now in his 80s, Roland Clarke still contributes material to at least one rural journal.

One of the most important contributions to this collection is an extract from June Slee's *Bloody Friday*. This book recorded the actions of a group of Southland farmers who, in August 1978, protested against the fact that, in the midst of falling prices, a drought and trade uncertainty, they could not get their stock killed at the local freezing works. Their protest proved that whipped cream and raspberry jam had disappeared from the rural scone for good, putting an end to the cosy image many urbanites had of farming folk as harmless grumblers. The Southern demonstration was the first time that a large group of New Zealand farmers had made such a public and arresting stand against outside pressures. They not only showed their contempt for the actions of the Freezing Workers' Union, but also took a heavy swipe at the industry as a whole, the government and the restrained and behind-closed-doors approach of their own representative group, Federated Farmers.

This was a watershed day and its written record is an important one, especially to me. *Bloody Friday* commemorates the time when a very representative group of my generation, and in my home province, drew a line, stood on it and stared the rest of the country straight in the eye.

The Farmer's Wife

Anne Earncliff Brown

1932

To-day I helped stake up our 'tall' table peas, and also planted my own carefully hybridised sweet pea seeds. It may be because of this that I have read with special interest of Mendel and Mendelism in recent issues of the *North Canterbury Gazette*. Long ago, when young ladies wore their hair in 'rolls' and their legs in black (silk for Sunday) stockings, I remember listening to my uncle discoursing lengthily on Mendel. At that period, also, it was fashionable for youth to show deference to its elders. Therefore I strove to appear interested in the results of the monk's experiments with peas. If a sombre leg swung a trifle impatiently, or an enterprising finger, intrigued by novelty, sought a hair-pinned roll, who shall blame me? Outwardly polite, I listened eagerly for the releasing 12 o'clock gong. It is not surprising that the green peas for dinner interested me vastly more than the contemplation of their possible ancestry. The appetites of youth are keen.

Yet now, minus the rolls, and much of the appetite, I share my uncle's enthusiasm for the Moravian monk. How much we farmer folks owe to that first geneticist! To-day with the aid of research and breeding stations, farmers can obtain accurate data of wheats, etc., can procure pedigreed seed producing increased yield or the desired quality. Our cattle are no longer bred haphazard. Definite aims with regard to butter-fat or beef influence our selection of breeding stock. The characteristics of sheep are carefully studied, with due regard to market requirements. Wool and mutton breeds today are not blindly sought after. Our pigs are built to carry the correct proportion of fat and lean.

Yet how many of us have heard of Mendel? The application of the laws of heredity, first propounded by the son of a peasant, in a distant Augustinian monastery, has become the everyday practice of progressive farmers all the world over. It is fitting that New Zealanders, an agricultural people, should learn something of the great debt which they owe to this earliest of research scholars.

And yet, the study of heredity is a little disturbing. Many a mother, in blissful ignorance of the Mendelian laws, comfortably attributes her child's virtues to herself, the faults of the father being plainly stamped on his erring offspring. A pleasant and harmless habit, not at all convincing to the paternal one, since from the time of Adam man

1932, 1933, *North Canterbury Gazette*

has naturally 'blamed the woman.' Alas! Modern theology, or evolution, now threatens that ancient stronghold – the Garden of Eden.

This recalls to me that ours is no garden paradise, wherein weeds are unknown. Since the rain, which falls on good and bad seeds alike, I have a settled conviction that weeds are the Ishmaels of the plant world. Without doubt they enjoy a superior vitality to legitimate vegetation. With every man's hoe against them they thrive exceedingly. Natural selection – the survival of the fittest – has chosen fat-hen for its own.

Autumn 1933

Across the orchard, the smoke from a chain of bonfires eddied and swirled round the figure of Bunty. She stood, eyes aglow, waiting like a priestess with her sacrificial offering – four lovely 'Arran Banner' potatoes. Only when the mounting blaze from the dried orchard prunings had died to a glowing ember would she fling, with expert aim, her treasures into the soft white flakes that blanket the slow burning heart-wood of a fallen cherry plum. Nearby, fresh cut clippings from Lawsoniana and Macrocarpa hedges smouldered pungently, their green ferny beauty crisping but slowly to the urgent flames below. A waft as of bitter almonds betrayed the presence of Laurel amongst the dry, crackling thorns of gooseberry and rasps. Carelessly, her thoughts on the feast to come, Bunty scattered the leaves of a last year's pocket calendar amongst the high-piled smoke-shrouded green … August … September … October … I watched them flare, blacken and vanish – my year of busy days – burnt offerings on the green altars of this island land I love.

Rounding Up Recalcitrant Cattle:
Female Drovers Have Exciting Moments

'J.J.'

It is not so long ago since hiring the services of a drover was a small matter of giving a few directions, but lately it has become much more complicated. Most of the regular drovers are in camp. This year many motorists have met girls on the road with stock, their dogs varying from a well-trained team to a fox-terrier 'doing his bit' for the war effort. Whenever possible, communal methods are used and any one mob may have stock from up to six owners.

My first experience in droving cattle was not lacking in excitement, though there were two of us girls on the job. As if sensing their destination, which happened to be the freezing works, the cattle were determined to give us as much trouble as possible. It took us over an hour to get them out of the paddock. Once we were started we realised that we were a dog short. As his soldier-boss was home on leave, he evidently felt that he no longer owed me allegiance. So we had no alternative to getting along as well as we could without him.

When we reached the main road our herd divided in two. Half of the cattle decided on a hike to a town some 60 miles distant; the rest made a wild bid for home again. While I pursued those that were making for home I wondered what drovers did in cases like this. It was just as my mount reached full speed that a lad who had been an interested spectator rushed to the middle of the road and flung his oilskin into the air. It turned the cattle all right, and I just managed to stop myself when I reached the proximity of the horse's ears, as she had just slid the last yard. From then on the cattle took the wrong turning at every opportunity and broke back several times. To add to our enjoyment, there was another large mob not far behind us, and when we reached the railway crossing the weekly train came along. My companion had a chilly moment when she was galloping uphill while heading a steer and met a car off-side on a bend.

Many motorists seem to look on drovers and their stock as trespassers on any road. Indeed, I used to feel that way myself. Yet after I changed places I found myself regarding motorists with much more venom than I had hitherto directed at drovers. One soon gets to know the different types of motorists and to wonder at the fate which decrees that a beginner-driver always meets one's mob on a uphill grade. When one is droving sheep the first few cars which come along get the most consideration as for a short distance a smile and a wave are ample reward for clearing the road. As the cars

23 September 1942, *New Zealand Free Lance*

begin to line up one feels deserving of more appreciation and lets each make its own way. If the motorist is bad-tempered and inconsiderate one can always send an extra dog ahead – but not in order to aid the motorist.

On arriving at the works one afternoon with a mob the shepherd told me it was quite their red-letter day, as I was the third girl to arrive with stock that day. Next season there will be many more girls on the road. So here's wishing good droving to the land-girls!

Age-Old Right of Farmers

For the *New Zealand Free Lance*

Missing Something

So many writers extol the pleasures of country life that we who live in the country have begun to feel that we must be missing something. At the end of each winter this feeling is very strong.

After months of cold weather the grass has disappeared from our paddocks, and on the face of every hungry sheep and bullock we can see an accusing look. It is too cold to drink the beer, which in summer gives us an excuse to meet our neighbours at the pub; tennis courts and bowling greens are closed until the sun's warmth returns. Worst of all, the lambing season is about to begin. Though a landgirl with a couple of pet lambs may make a nice picture, to the sheepfarmer or shepherd the lambing season is forbidding. To an outsider it may seem absurd to get worked up about the death of a few sheep, which in any case would sooner or later be killed for mutton, but to a countryman the untimely death of any animal comes as a shock. After months of worry about the condition of every sheep on the place, the farmer can recognise many of them on sight, and the death of one of the best ewes in a flock is like the passing of an old friend.

Apart from such inevitable losses there is the regrettable fact that the worst weather seems always to be reserved for the lambing-season. In New Zealand there is no more pathetic object than a newly-born lamb which, having lost its mother, stands on shivering legs in the south-west storm so typical of lambing weather. Nor does it make any difference should the lambing be early or late.

Hardened by years of exposure to our westerly gales, the shepherd's face shows few signs of his sympathy for distressed stock. In spite of his many coverings of oilskin and leather, he knows what the sou'wester feels like, and a young lamb has a very naked look. In sunshine we view the care of lambing flocks as a worth-while job whose unpleasantness is alleviated by the sight of the youngsters frisking in unusual warmth, but in cold rain it is just a job which has to be done. At such times our most cheerful thought is that the lambing will come to an end; our one interest is the weather-forecast, which all too often promises worse weather next day.

Countrymen all over New Zealand welcomed the return of radio weather-forecasts [after the war]. Among thousands I listened with bated breath: 'Wind changing to sou'west, reaching gale force in exposed places, temperatures very cold, snow on the high country.'

---

25 July 1945, *New Zealand Free Lance*

After a glance through the window at the starlit sky, I telephoned a neighbour.

'Did you hear that forecast Bill?'

'Yes. It looks like we'd be better without it, after all. Anyway the bloke should have taken a look at the sky before he started talking like that.'

Whoever made that first radio-forecast missed a royal chance of widespread popularity among country-folk. We got all he promised us and more but, right or wrong, he should have prophesied fine warm weather for the whole of New Zealand. Thousands of farmers could then have gone cheerfully to bed, and when next day proved that the meteorological office had been wrong, we would all have had something about which to laugh. The man responsible for these weather-forecasts should remember that it is better to be pleasant than to be right. His guess at the next day's weather is not usually any better than ours, anyway, and he might as well err on the bright side.

Only those who live in the country are qualified to write about country-life. Not for twice my present wages would I sell my dogs and stifle in some office-job, but I claim the farmers' age-old right to grumble. With so many towns-folk taking a bright, though fleeting, view of the distant countryside, that right is in danger of being forgotten.

A Shepherd's Calendar: 1953

'Sundowner' (Oliver Duff)

January 17

There are easier jobs at my age than dagging sheep in the open in a hot sun; and sweeter jobs. But there are not many farm jobs which it gives me more satisfaction to see done or even to do. Sheep have to be very filthy to be offensive to me, and if I could keep my hands clean when I am tidying them up they would not offend me at all. In other words sheep that are reasonably healthy never offend my nose. I do not feel oppressed in a wool-shed in the hottest weather, I can eat in sheepyards, and I find pleasure in the scented air sheep leave behind them for an hour or two after they have been driven along a road. I have sometimes wished that the New Testament miracle had happened in a sheepfold and not in a cattle-pen.

March 12

She was still in her thirties, young enough to be sorry for herself, and foolish enough to keep on saying so.

'I came too late to this country,' she said, 'and to this narrow life.'

'I call it a full life, full and satisfying.'

'I know you do,' she answered angrily. 'That's why I have been waiting for you. I think you are a humbug. I don't believe what you write about cows and sheep. What is there interesting in sheep? They all look the same, smell the same, behave in the same stupid way. Tell me what you see attractive in them?'

'I will if you tell me first what you found attractive in Birmingham.'

'I'm not going to be put off. Face up to these sheep I see all day and hear all night. Tell me what you see in them. Have they looks, or brains, or character, or nice ways?'

'You must let me praise them in my own way. I have never said that they have what you mean by looks, or probably mean by brains. But did you ever hear in Birmingham that beauty begins in your own eyes?'

'We're not in Birmingham. I wish we were. We're in Central Otago with its rocks, and rabbits and silly bleating half-breds. Tell me why you call sheep-farming a good life?'

'Let me take the short way. Sheep can't fly like eagles, or sing like thrushes, or dance like Bojangles Robinson. They can't paint pictures or play Beethoven. Neither can dogs or horses or monkeys or all but two or three of the people of Birmingham.'

1953, *New Zealand Listener*

'You're dodging. You know that sheep can't be praised. They're dull, like most of the men who own them. As for their women, you either don't know how they live, or you know and won't tell. But I know. For eight years I have done nothing but cook and wash up, bake scones and serve morning tea, listen to dull talk about fats and stores, or put up with being ignored.'

'That must have been terrible.'

'It *has* been terrible. It has been insufferable. And you add to the injury by calling it a good life.'

March 13

I did dodge and hedge with that farmer's wife, first because I could not think of the answers she demanded offhand, and second because it was fascinating to hear such heresy in such a place. But I find it difficult to answer her yet, I don't think she *can* be answered with the definiteness of one-and-one and two-and-two; with simple yeas and simple nays. Even to me, tied to them with more strings than I can count, sheep are not in themselves fascinating, or beautiful, or intelligent, or especially likeable. They hold me because they are associated with so many other things that hold me – the memories and experiences of childhood, the most satisfying experiences of maturity, the material things without which we could not live. The spiritual experiences without which we would not wish to live. The whole animal-angel combination we call human life and find richest and fullest when we get as close to the earth as sheep always are, and feel as little strangeness.

May 17

Two pups which saved their lives by getting born an hour after their three brothers and two sisters had been buried are making new assaults on my weakness. They are now nearly a month old and their method for three or four days has been to sit up when I approach the kennel and cock their heads sideways to look at me. But today they went further. They sat up, stretched, yawned, staggered round the kennel with their tails up, then looked at me for a moment and barked. I felt my resistance melting away and began pulling myself together to go. But suddenly one threw himself clumsily on the other and started chewing his ear. This, I knew, meant 'Let us be cunning. Let us be bold. Let us catch the old boy by the heart-strings and hang on until something gives. Another turn or two and we'll have him.' So they bit, and rolled, and growled, and yelped till there was nothing left inside me but water.

How far could I let it go? Was I farming or fooling; making the animals pay for themselves and a little more; or establishing an animal refuge? Before I could find an answer the pups rolled over and were sound asleep, one with his hind leg in the air. I hurried indoors to advertise them for sale, but instead of writing the advertisement made this note.

The Cold Shoulder

'Whim Wham' (Allen Curnow)

'I am satisfied that the proper processing of this meat – the article not to be called 'mutton' – would provide good eating and sell on any market in the world.'
– Mr J.D. Ormond, chairman of the New Zealand Meat Producers' Board, to a conference of the Waikato Federated Farmers.

Don't talk about Mutton, you Jokers,
Nor even of Lamb and Green Peas.
That tender Fore-quarter may make your Mouths water –
It isn't the Same overseas.

Don't think you can collar the Markets
With any old Slogan or Ruse:
And whatever you do with that stringy old Ewe,
Don't call it Colonial Goose.

Don't stow the old Carcase on Shipboard
And wait for the Cheques to roll in.
It's that muttony Look that repels the good Cook –
She'd far rather open a Tin.

Let's call it, say, Pate de Mouton,
With a View of Mt. Cook on the Label:
Or Filet Merino, with Olives and Vino –
A dish for an Epicure's Table.

But Mutton – don't MENTION it, even.
It's vulgar, not delicate – see?
If you're really awake, call it High Country Steak
And what succulent steak it will be!

Call it Corriedale Cuts, or plain Crossbred;
Don't carve it or serve it with Shame,
That old frozen Shoulder, grown colder and colder –
The Appetite's all in the Name.

1959, *The Best of Whim Wham*

High Country Diary

'Tussock Jumper' (Sean Pennycook)

27 January

Putting the wethers out on their summer country gives us probably the longest and most energetic day of our year. After a three o'clock breakfast, we begin to muster the holding paddock by starlight, each man taking a spur and hunting straight up it. The sheep are fresh and climb well, encouraged by plenty of yelling and barking; it will be broad daylight before any dog work will be required.

Gradually the mob builds up under the snow fence at about 3500ft, ready to be pushed through the netting gate. It is a ticklish job forcing the leaders out, with wild-eyed individuals on the perimeter of the mob trying to break back down the hill as pressure is applied, but once the first fifty are through we can relax and let the rest trickle after them.

In scorching sunshine now, we toil up the hill face in a long sidle. Steering the sheep as near as possible to the ideal route, without fatiguing them by taking excessive 'twists' with the dogs, and maintaining as fast a pace as the heat of the day and the length of the trek will permit. At 11.30 we gain the ridgetop at a saddle of well over 5000ft altitude, where the dogs gratefully scrunch at snow lying in drifts on the leeward side of boulders and spurs. This far side of the range is a wilderness of great bluff-bound ridges inter-sected by deep, well grassed and watered valleys. It is down one of these that our track now runs. After a precipitous scramble down the shale and scree of the cirque, we are on the open valley floor with the sheep keeping a good swinging pace, without need of urging.

Two pleasant hours bring us to the mustering hut. From here the mob is split up and hunted out in various directions so that the sheep will distribute themselves over the 20,000 odd acres of summer country. First man back to the hut is responsible for a brew up; then, about 4.30, it's 'Head for home and the Devil take the hindmost!' On the way back up the valley, the long gradual slope is just steep enough to keep breaths whistling and leg muscles at full stretch. The final thousand-foot pull from the valley head up to the saddle is a mankiller at this stage of the day.

With only the briefest of glances at the breathtaking view – the panorama of serried ranges and the patchwork of paddocks and toy buildings almost a mile below – we plunge down the front face, all weariness forgotten in the exhilaration of running down-

1966, *New Zealand Farmer*

hill. Three-quarters of an hour lands us panting and lathered with sweat in the station yard, where soon we are supping ambrosia, cold bottled beer; truly the nectar of the gods, when drunk at the end of such a day. It is long after 7 o'clock, and more than 16 hours of work have been accomplished since breakfast.

26 May

Our wethers, as I described in an earlier article, spend the summer on the far side of a 5000 to 7000ft range and are, therefore, our first concern in the fall muster. An early snow on this country would not necessarily be fatal, but it would increase the difficulties of the muster a thousandfold. So a sigh of relief goes up each year when the mob finally heads back over the top to the homestead side of the range.

To muster this area requires three long and strenuous days; with two nights spent in one of the roughest of the many rough mustering huts, with which I am acquainted. Situated in the depths of a narrow sunless valley, inaccessible even by packhorse, it is inhabited for 360 plus days only by possums, rats and earwigs; but each fall its 15ft by 12ft must serve as 'home' to seven weary men. The frame is of roughly split slabs from the stunted local mountain beech (or 'birch' as it is usually mistakenly called). The roof is of reasonably sound iron, but the walls, originally clad with tar-paper, are virtually wide open to the elements. Every year we tack, tie or prop the tatters back into as weatherproof a wall as possible, but like the Bark Hut in the song, 'You can leave the old door open, or you can leave it shut,' there's no fear of suffocation.

The fireplace of unmortared stones is a champion smoke producer, but the chief glory and star feature of this palatial residence is its bed! Half the floor space is covered by this edifice of beech poles and snow tussocks, and in the evening, the hut's scant complement of damp and noisome blankets (inadequate for individual bed-rolls) is spread out and all hands crawl in together. Like sardines I was going to say, but no tin of sardines was ever as tightly packed as this. With all seven 'on board', no one has room to lie on the flat of his back, and one can change position only with the permission of the other six. Very hilarious, in retrospect, but at the time, conducive to neither good temper nor sleep! ...

For the first two days the weather treats us kindly; gradually the wethers are gathered from their maze of gullies and basins, and hunted out at each day's end into a confined gully, still to be mustered on the third and final day. Overnight showers 'icing sugar' the tops with a skiff of snow, but a dawn of broken cloud promises an ideally cool day for the long uphill grind. While five of the gang muster the big mob up the final gully, the other two push on by a different route to take up strategic positions.

The gully pinches in to a horseshoe of bluffs through which the track spirals up; a snack of sandwiches is the order of the day as the interminable mob clambers up in Indian file. Out through a narrow saddle at the gully's head, 6500ft up, the gang is reunited and, with high spirits, urges the sheep over the springy carpet grass of a series of high-rolling, hanging basins till, at last, about mid-afternoon, the long-anticipated moment arrives. Beneath our feet the ground suddenly drops sharply away, giving an uninterrupted view down to the tiny homestead buildings far below.

After the jagged, topsy-turvy, stood-on-end environment in which we have lived for the past three days, the spacious level of the valley floor looks wonderfully restful: the rich green of the paddocks soothing after the austere yellows and greys of this world of tussock and rock. The back of the fall muster has been broken; it's down-hill work from here on!

Sheepmen and their Dogs

Peter Newton

Deals in Dogs

Anyone who has knocked around mustering camps will have memories of dog deals. On wet days when held up in camp someone was bound to try and quit some half-pie 'Sunday dog'. The most common deal was a swap; all hands would know that each of the dealers was trying to put one across his mate. But what the dealers didn't know, was just how poor the other bloke's dog was; only the owner of the dog knew that. I've been stung myself a few times. On the other hand there has been the odd occasion when I have got the best of the deal.

My introduction to the art of dog dealing came when I was quite young, and on that particular occasion we both missed. I swapped one of those old His Master's Voice phonographs with the great big horn (you needed a spring cart to carry it around) for a huntaway bitch. The phonograph broke down about a week later and the bitch worried, so honours were about even. The next deal I made was a straight out purchase and, this time, the other party was a real artist.

I was just a boy at the time, a sort of rouseabout shepherd on a little place up the Waimakariri. However, feeling that it was time I was doing a bit better for myself I'd got a beat mustering up the Ashburton Gorge, and the next thing was to get some dogs; all I had was a young huntaway and another dog it would be a bit hard to describe. First, I needed a heading dog and, as anyone knows, they've always been hard to get. However, I'd got to know one of the local musterers, Bill, pretty well. I didn't really know what his dogs were like but I'd been greatly impressed with his whistle; he used his fingers and you could hear him 10 miles away. I also knew that he had a heading dog called Help, one of old Joe Allan's breed; and the cowboy on the next place told me that if you had one of Joe Allan's breed in your team you couldn't go wrong. So I went down to see old Bill. Would he sell Help, I asked?

He looked at me in amazement. Sell Help! Good gracious, boy – not Help! He just wouldn't know how he would get on without Help – the dog was a whole team in himself, No, no, not Help. Why, only yesterday old Jimmy-what's-his-name had recalled a run Help had done on a break of lambs, when they were tailing out in the valley last week. Just as they were yarding the mob, about 50 of the little devils broke and man, did they go! Anyway, old Bill started Help, and you should have seen that dog –

14 September 1967, *New Zealand Farmer*

it was an education to watch him work those lambs. All hands reckoned he'd never have a show, but do you know that dog got every single lamb. I gathered that if old Bill had been a betting man he would have made a pot full. No, he just couldn't part with Help.

As I said, I was only a boy at the time and easily knocked back; Help wasn't for sale, so I turned to go. But mind you, old Bill said, that would be just the dog for a young fellow – it would be hard to get one that would suit a boy better. And anyway, he reckoned, a man never wants to get married to any dog. Feeling that it would just about break old Bill's heart to part with that dog I hesitated to ask again and just stood there looking hopeful.

Shaking his head sadly, old Bill stood looking at Help. I stood looking at him too, and we just seemed to be getting nowhere. Finally old Bill broke the silence; he did have another heading dog that only needed work, and as long as he had old Help that dog wouldn't get it. He'd be good too, if he got a chance. But do you know, he never thought the day would come when he would sell old Help.

Half an hour later I led the dog away – minus a fairly substantial was of notes. I've seen better heading dogs, but I reckon that lesson in the art of selling dogs was worth that wad of notes anyhow.

Toprail Talk

H.N. Munro

A pet aversion of mine is the visitor who gushes after watching the horses at work or play – 'Aren't they just like HUMANS?' My recollections of the theory of evolution are distinctly hazy, but surely primitive eohippus appeared on the scene before primitive homo sapiens?

Anyhow, I prefer to believe that humans, in their rare better moments, act just like horses. In both cases there is a vast amount to be learnt from horses by anyone who has the time to lean on the toprail, merge as much as possible with the surroundings, and quietly observe their goings-on. Follow me through Pandy's gate to the stableyard, and I'll show you what I mean. Mind that latch – I haven't got round to fixing it since Pandy and I crossed swords about it last week.

Pandy is the kid's pony and his sagacity is nothing short of diabolical. You could say he's the conscientious-student type, I suppose; he spends hours studying a problem from every angle, particularly problems to do with evading capture or avoiding work. You can almost see the thoughts going round in his head as he nuts out the riddle of a new gate latch. Wire hooks, sliding bolts or loops over the post are child's play to him – he beat those years ago. I put this length of heavy chain on his gate about a fortnight ago, and I'd hear him worrying away at it during the night, trying to lift it off the hook with his teeth. Three nights it took him to solve that one. Then he put his muzzle under the chain, gave a sharp upward flip and, Bob's your uncle, off to spend the night chasing the yearlings round and round their paddock.

Each evening I'd visit him, last thing, with some new dodge to fix his gate; head down munching his hay, he never appeared to notice me, and that alone was highly suspicious. You can bet your bottom dollar his wise eyes didn't miss a move I made, and his very indifference shouted louder than words, 'Do your darndest, I'll find a way out!' I tied the chain with twine – he found the bow and pulled the correct end. I knotted it firmly, planning to cut it in the morning; there was no need, he'd already cut it with his teeth and taken his departure. I bent the hook away at an acute angle – he bent it back, heaven knows how!

Wait until I just pick up these feed-buckets. The housekeeper always leaves them lying round untidily. She's that bay mare over there, asleep in the sun, now her morning duties are done. For some reason or other, ever since she was a baby, she's insisted on

25 September 1979, *New Zealand Farmer*

cleaning out the last stray scraps in the buckets when I finish feeding-up. It's not that she's hungry – if I increased her breakfast ration she'd leave it – but she has this compulsion to lick each bucket clean. If I don't open the gate and let her into the yard to do her chores, she frets up and down the fence and works herself into a real state.

Now that big brown horse is a real character. We call him Bub, and a real baby he is, in every way. Scold him and he almost weeps; pet him and he basks in your approval. If he gets the slightest scratch from a fence, he's lame for a week – always in front of you, and often in the wrong leg.

Look at Miss Prunes and Prisms in the grass yard there, very conscious of the bright green canvas of her new cover. Beneath its skirt her long slim legs remind you of a black-stockinged flapper of the 'twenties', and her little round feet are placed demurely close together, as if in obedience to her mother's dictum that that is how a lady should always stand. Butter wouldn't melt in her mouth, you'd say, and the way she comes up to make friends with a stranger is nothing short of charming – just as long as she thinks there might be something in it for her. But a voracious appetite rules that willowy body and dainty head and she'll bite, kick or trample anything that comes between her and her feed-bowl.

Most stables have a clown, and ours is that big brown horse with the white stockings behind. He's the kind of practical joker who creeps up behind you when you're not even aware that he's in the vicinity, then snorts like a dragon for the pleasure of seeing you jump out of your skin. When you turn to pick yourself up and turn to curse him, the sardonic grin on his face convinces you that 'horse laugh' is no idle expression. He's also a kleptomaniac, and we always search the straw in his box first, when brushes, straps and other oddments go missing.

I could go on indefinitely like this but what I've said is, after all, only another version of the cliché, 'Horses are all different.' It should be obvious that the more you study them, and the more familiar you are with their individual characteristics, when not directly under man's influence, the greater understanding you will have of each one's needs and capabilities. But a word of warning, we must not be guilty of anthropomorphism – lovely word! It means, in this instance, the tendency to attribute to our animals the manners, thoughts and behaviour we would like them to exhibit, as if they were humans.

The Month Down South

'Nor'wester' (Roland Clarke)

4 November 1965

… The school is a mile away, but it was a favourable wind and my old dog had decided which way he thought the sheep should go. I disagreed and let fly at him, and the primers heard the lot! It made me think. Gone are the days when swearing was an art. I feel the Elizabethans could have eased their feelings and told the dog just what they thought, in front of the Luton Girls' Choir.

I feel their tirade would have gone something like this: 'You misbegotten cross between a poodle and a pekinese. You wall-eyed excuse for a dog. Get in behind you revolting, smelly, short-legged, lousy, mother's mistake! You blind, stupid, horrible caricature of a dog.

'If you don't stand still I'll sell you to the Japanese for mutton.

'You re——volting creature!'

13 January 1966

It's been an extraordinary November with snow lying on at least two mornings. As a result we have plenty of soil moisture, but there has been no flush of feed and the lambs are not as far forward as at this time last year. I intend weaning next week …

We had a lot of fun ridging the swedes last month. Last year, 30 acres wintered the flock; this year I'm putting in 60 acres, of which 30 will be for sale. If I'm lucky, I'll graze some 1500 sheep at a bob a week each. These paddocks are on my new block, which needs building up. Besides, one man can normally look after all my sheep in winter, so these grazers will mop up idle labour – that's me.

Sixty acres is a longsome job for a 2-row ridger, so my neighbour and I fixed up a very natty multiple-hitch, to tow his ridger and mine in tandem. This worked a treat and saved days of work, but we did have a terrible run with super. It's not a word of a lie, but in my two paddocks we had five major smashes caused by foreign bodies in the manure. We found: 12 only, worn, ⅜in bolts, a 12in strip of rubber tyre, a length of lace, numerous rocks the size of walnuts and one bird's nest, all in the super!

You can imagine, but never surpass the expletives and ill wishes we directed towards the fertilizer works. I was hopping mad and rang up the manager. Next morning his minion arrived and pocketed some of the bolts we had found. Unfortunately, we found

---

1965-70, *New Zealand Farmer*

no further bolts while he was there, though we did get a 2in x 1in piece of wood …. He was sympathetic and tells me that within the past few weeks his firm has started an engineer in charge of their dispatch department. They have fitted new screens, rather like the ones on a header, and have placed powerful magnets over each conveyer belt. They have been astounded at what comes out …

Of course, all this is the Farmer's Fault. There are several well-known ways of stopping such monstrous inefficiencies. The Russian method is the most certain. They would shoot the manager and start again. Then there is the puppy dog method: rub their noses in it … Ring up the head-man personally with every complaint and send all the bolts and rubbish from your super to his home address, till he realizes you mean business. Another approach is the Spiv: if you can't stop a racket, join it. I'm sure there's an opening here for some bright fellow to contract for the supply of old bolts for fertilizers. They cannot have all come from the works or their machinery would have fallen to bits years ago.

Long, long ago, when even Mr Nordmeyer had hair on his head, I served my time as a linen yarn spinner. Even in those days we had magnets over the machines to pick out nails and bolts. The fertilizer works are not to be congratulated on finally installing these aids but castigated for allowing this unbelievable state of affairs to continue so long.

13 July 1967

'We've got your pig here,' said the railway clerk. Pig indeed! It was my new Drysdale ram, which had just come down from Massey. A Drysdale's a Romney, only not quite. He looks a bit like Paddy M'Ginty's goat; covered in hair from his John O'Groats to his Land's End. He's got horns that wouldn't disgrace a Dorset Horn and, to a Romney man, he looks dreadful. Drysdales stem from one very hairy Romney ram that was presented to Massey some 30 years ago. He has a dominant wool gene, and two doses will fix the wool type on his progeny.

I said I'd try one just for fun, and he's running with 100-odd ewes just over the fence from my neighbour's Romney stud! Once I got accustomed to him I began to quite like him. He's very free moving, maybe rather light in the bone, and produces a very coarse wool – about 28's – which will replace the 500,000lb of Scottish Blackface, which we import every year. I picked out my coarsest ewes, the end result of years of breeding producers of high-grade 46's. They're in a paddock of their own and I'm going to winter them separately, to avoid a 'orrible botch at lambing.

What do I hope to gain? Well, to start with, it gives the neighbours something to criticize. Then I could end up by being first in on a new breed of sheep, producing wool with a guaranteed premium over straight Romney. The first cross commands a premium of 2 cents over similar Romney wool, the second cross, 5 cents. …

… Why oh why does wool cost so much, when we get paid so little? I went into

Ballantyne's in Christchurch last week to buy some underclothes. Cotton singlets were 95c each, wool singlets from the same manufacturer were $3.80!

12 October 1967

… I rang up Mr Lance McCaskill at Lincoln College recently, about grass grub; his immediate reaction was *Silent Spring*. It bears thinking about.

The best insectivore of all is the starling. Mr Ted Mackenzie of Baccleugh remembers when the sky was darkened with great flocks of starlings, and the telephone lines sagged under their weight. How few we see nowadays. I remember when I first put on DDT here, and had a good kill of insects, I noticed quite a number of dead magpies around the farm – a most unusual sight. I presume that the quick-acting dry mix had provided a regular feast of grubs on the surface and the birds had made pigs of themselves. Once farmers start spreading the new oil-washed DDT super, there will be a massive kill of succulent insects, and a further diminution in the numbers of our birds.

Each year our local Federated Farmers executive arranges a bird-poisoning week; I hate it! They dish out poisoned wheat to kill the grain eaters. Sparrows are enemy No.1. … In 1907, a Mr Shury of Ashburton observed in a department of agriculture booklet, that a pair of sparrows had been seen to feed their young 36 times an hour, in a 14-hour spring and summer day. He calculated that they feed their young with 3400 worms and caterpillars in one week. Mine is a plea for all birds, not just for sparrows, which are like booze, good in the right quantities. It is a suggestion that we may be our own worst enemies. That we have deserved and brought on our own heads the plague of insects; that we should have put the money we spent on sprays and insecticides into trees and bird shelters; and, that we should pay the birds for their work each year, with a fair measure of grain.

10 October 1968

No forward-looking, provident young farmer should marry between the ages of 22 and 44. It's a new development, a deplorable child of this increasingly intricate, technological age. Take the case of Don Dunderhead down the road; married last year at 22, his son is now a year old. That's fine; Don can grow up with his son, if he hasn't grown up already.

All will be lovely for 16 years, then Don will be faced with the prospect of young Dunderhead leaving school and coming home to work on the farm. The young one will take maybe 6 years to know as much as Dad and will then be looking sideways at the old man, wondering when he'll hand over and go to town – leaving the young fellow to marry and repeat the pattern. …

Let's be honest, farming in the old sense is child's play, mentally, as easy as marrying young. Think of the jobs we do: would it take a week to teach a man to drive a tractor?

Could an intelligent young fellow not make a success of a lambing beat after a season's training? How long would it take to teach a man to put up a fence, mow a meadow, draft sheep? The more I think about it, the more our job seems to consist of a collection of easy-to-learn jobs. Farming has been so easy in the past that any of us could get by. How many farmers went broke through inefficiency between 1955 and 1965? The efficient managers made a mint of money.

Now the position has changed and some of us will go broke. In fact we are in the same position as any factory in town; we're going to have to learn to *manage*. I spent years under a ruthless, hard-driving boss in Ireland whose hobby was management. He nearly sent me cuckoo and, in fact, I came out here! But some of his teaching rubbed off on me.

I define management as the art of making forthcoming events conform to my wishes. I want to make money out of sheep, so I try the Drysdale and mark my twins. I want my super for drilling on October 20, so I order it in July. … I hasten to add that I'd like not to do silly things, like turning on the water heater for my new couple, without any water in it. I'd like to be good at paper work and advance from my present deep-litter system of filing, and get rebates for prompt payment. I think that my son, if he farms, will have to manage well in every sphere. From the catalogue of errors above, you'll agree that he won't learn perfection from me. …

Let's plan out a sensible course for young Dunderhead. Naturally, Dad will keep him at school as long as possible. Ideally he will then go to university … then let him go out into the cruel, hard world, let him find a job in some efficient organisation, and let him work there for five or 10 years. … By now Dad will be finding the wheat sacks a bit heavy and wondering how he can reconcile the extra work involved in expanding production with his increasing baldness, obesity and shortage of breath. He'll be thinking he'd like a hand. Young Dunderhead will come in, assess what is sound and good of his father's practices, find out what is new, and spur the farm on to greater production. In a couple of years he'll have mastered all the small technicalities, like lambing a ewe, and he'll be a leader in his industry.

9 October 1969

… My dogs aren't much cop. I like them and they'll bring in any mob I want, but they're just not lambing dogs. Normally I lamb without them and today I heard of a novel solution to the ewe-catching problem.

It appears that this joker, not far from Pleasant Point, goes lambing with a shovel. Not to bury dead lambs or even to use for hitting old ewes on the snout. No sir, it replaces a dog. When he wants to catch a ewe, he approaches her quietly, till he's in range and she turns to flee. At this very moment he throws his shovel over her head and the old girl breaks hard and lets him catch her.

9 April 1970

Dear Nor'wester

I'm 45 and farm 400 acres. I spent the best years of my life breaking it in and now carry 1600 sheep. All my profits have been ploughed back into the farm and I still live in an old, two-bedroom, wooden house.

We have a good rainfall, but it's not cropping country. Year by year I see less money coming my way and the only possible move is to increase stock faster and faster. Every extra lamb will mean more work by me – drenching, dagging and crutching.

I'm fed up. I can see nothing ahead but more and more work, as I grow older, with less opportunity to relax. Should I sell out now or keep plugging away?

Sincerely

Jim Smith (Sen.)

Dear Jim

Sell now.

Sincerely

Nor'wester

I cannot remember such a widespread feeling of frustration among my friends. We are told we are the most efficient farmers in the world. So we are, in our line of business. But how many of us will get a living and reduce our indebtedness this year (assuming an average mortgage)? Darned few I suspect.

We are in the middle of one of the most widespread and severe droughts on record; this on top of ever-slumping prices and surging costs. But what has been done to deliberately sabotage us? *Interest rates.* I now pay 8 per cent to my firm on current account. Presumably their rate has been forced up by the Reserve Bank.

I will have to pay quite a lot extra each year for grass grub control, now that DDT is banned – to please the Americans, who lead the world in pollution. I will have to pay more to the freezing workers to kill my lambs. Make no mistake, I'll have to pay, and if ever my ire was roused it was when the freezing workers resumed normal slaughtering to 'help the drought-stricken farmers', and went slow again a few days later …

I believe that this drought could be the best thing possible for farming if it emphasizes to the Government, and the country at large, just how quickly they are killing the golden goose. It could possibly make people wake up this year, rather than after another, two or three, normal years.

The EEC

Anon.

Tune: 'Age of Aquarius'

Now De Gaulle is in obscurity, the Poms will soon align with Bonn,
They'll join the big community, our export market's gone,
This is the downing of the age of the EEC, the age of the EEC,
The EEC, the EEC,
Surpluses of dairy produce, meat and lamb will be of no use,
Freezing works will all be shut down,
No more lambs or sheep get put down,
No more artificial breeding, no more shearing, killing, bleeding,
The EEC, the EEC.

c.1960s, *How You Doing*

The View From Our Hill

Bob Linton

Presenting the farmers' case

Farmers are angry. Protest meetings are being convened up and down the country, prompted by three factors: low prices and rising costs (the 26 per cent drop in farmers' purchasing power in the last three years is always quoted), the drought, and industrial unrest, particularly in the freezing industry. There's no doubt that we have a case, it's how we present it that disturbs me.

At these protest meetings there's always someone who calls for direct action. I've never found out just what these people have in mind, and I've tried to think of ways in which we could force Government's hand. But any that I've thought of would embarrass us more than they'd embarrass the Government.

If the employees of one of our major manufacturers have a grievance with management, they can threaten certain things that cause inconvenience or loss of income to the other party in the dispute. In our case it's impossible to directly inconvenience those who are in a position to make changes. The common causes of action suggested, involve withholding produce intended for local consumption or demonstrations similar to those held in France and England, where farmers have blocked streets with cattle and tractors. We would be injuring an innocent third party in an effort to get action from Government. We've got no quarrel with the housewife, whom we deprive of milk or meat or with the city commuter, when we block the streets. We would lose more by alienating public sympathy, than we'd gain by pressuring Government.

So what can we do? Our strong card is that the nation needs our export income. The Agricultural Committee's report to the National Development Conference calls for a 2.6 per cent annual compound increase in livestock from 67/68 to 78/79, for which we'll need $140,000 *annual* capital expenditure on our farms. There is also a fair bit of superficial evidence that, in spite of rapid progress between 1962 and 1967, we are now falling behind. Breeding ewe numbers are static, and there is evidence that farm capital expenditure is well down.

One survey shows that, in the past 12 months, the average dairy farmer's position has worsened by over $1000. This means that dairy farmers are borrowing, not for improvements to increase carrying capacity, but for day to day living and maintenance …. I don't know how serious the situation is, as it's always difficult to tell. Farmers are

14 May 1970, *New Zealand Farmer*

very volatile and tend to over-react. Two years ago farmer confidence slumped in the Waikato and replacement heifers dropped $30 in three weeks, but at the following October's clearing sales, prices reached record levels.

At the moment I'm sending surplus replacement dairy heifers to the works because they're worth more there than if I sold them for milking. But this, by itself, doesn't mean very much. We need more information on the farmer's economic position, and we need it urgently. In the meantime, we need leaders who are prepared to do their homework and marshal the information we've already got, to present it to Government. Colin Gordge of Waikato Federated Farmers' is to be commended in this respect.

It's Cabinet as a whole, and Treasury, we've got to convince. They'll be far more impressed by information showing how far we're going to lag behind NDC targets, than by threats of direct action. They need to be reminded that the main source of capital investment on farms is ploughed-back revenue. If profit isn't there, not only is there nothing to re-invest, farmers lose confidence. We get our tails down, we refuse to borrow, and we make no progress.

Follow Fellow

M. Weatherall

Sheep
    following
        each
            other
                down
                    the
                        hill
                                rhetorically
                        with
                  placards
                would
            make
        splendid
      protest
marchers

14 May 1970, *New Zealand Farmer*

Bloody Friday

An Account of the Southland Farmers' Protest, 9 June 1978

June Slee

Background

In a climate of fear and mistrust, a small group of farmers organised a protest at what was likely to be the most disruptive killing season in the history of the New Zealand freezing industry. The season had begun late, and had been constantly interrupted by industrial stoppages, load-out bans and strikes. The four freezing works in Southland had been involved in at least 80 disputes or industrial stoppages in the first five months of 1978.

Unable to tolerate the situation any longer the farmers went into action, choosing the busiest time of the week in the busiest place in Southland – Friday afternoon in Invercargill's Dee Street – to stage their demonstration. Their aim was to draw public attention to the seriousness of the situation, and the impossibility of their plight. While the freezing companies, the union, Federated Farmers and the various mediators all argued and got nowhere, sheep were dying on Southland farms at the rate of more than one thousand a day. Old ewes, which ought to have been slaughtered as far back as November, were still waiting for space at the end of May. It was estimated that there were still one million ewes and lambs waiting to be killed in the Southland province. …

On a bleak Tuesday afternoon on 6 June, Syd Slee shifted cattle which were being grazed at his neighbour's back to his own bare property. While he was there he decided to ride around the old ewes on his hill block. What he saw distressed him. There was very little feed left and several ewes were dead. The live ones were hobbling among the tussocks looking in vain for something to eat. Syd estimated that most of them had a life expectancy of two or three weeks. Twice he came upon collapsed ewes, too weak to walk any more, lying with their eyes pecked out by seagulls. It had become his habit now to carry a knife so that he could put these poor things out of their misery. Looking at his old ewes so pitifully thin, and feeling tremendous compassion for the pain that those who had been attacked by the seagulls had been through, Syd experienced a feeling of complete and utter frustration …

On that very day there was no kill at Makarewa or Ocean Beach, and at the Alliance works the men had worked for just half a day. At Mataura they had just gone back to work after a week of stoppages, in which not one head of stock was processed.

1979, Bloody Friday

Syd decided it was time for some positive action, it was past the time for talking. A group of farmers should each select about ten of their thinnest sheep and take them to Invercargill and dump them in the main street and leave them there. He believed that this would surely bring the country's attention to the fact that the farmers had had enough. This was his original plan, which he later modified, because he was convinced that it would be more responsible (although less dramatic) to drive the sheep through the streets, then slaughter them, rather than just letting them loose … Being on horseback, Syd had more time to scheme, and by the time he neared home he had made up his mind that he was definitely going to take action. And he had a fair idea how that action was going to be carried out.

He was just about to go in his road gate when he saw his neighbour, Peter Gow, coming along the road. He stopped him and outlined his plans. Peter looked stunned at first. 'You can't be serious,' he grinned, thinking that Syd was just joking. Russell Fallowfield, Peter's head shepherd, was with him. An ex-freezing worker, he too took it lightly.

'You've got to be joking,'

'No, no, I'm deadly serious. Something has to be done, it's gone on for long enough like this.' It slowly sank in to the two men that Syd was in earnest.

'Well I'll be right behind you if it does get off the ground,' Peter promised him. 'It's just what we need really …'

The protest was aimed at the delays at getting stock killed, and Syd wanted each farmer to choose ten to fifteen of his thinnest old ewes and put them on a utility or trailer and take them down to the Lorneville saleyards, on Friday, arriving before 1.30 p.m. From there they would drive in convoy to the centre of the city and let the sheep out. They would then drive them to an empty section nearby and slaughter them.

One farmer on almost every country exchange was contacted and asked to mobilise support. There was no advertising; it was organised solely by word of mouth. Syd attributes a good deal of the success of the protest to this personal contact from one farmer to the next. On Wednesday morning Syd Slee went to Invercargill with his younger brother, Roger, who was very closely involved in the whole issue. There was a great deal of organising to be done. Southland Butchers' By-Products were approached and asked if they would accept a then unknown number of carcasses for rendering down on Friday afternoon. The general manager, Mr T.J. Cooke, agreed to this and to keep quiet about it. They went out to the Lorneville Saleyards to ask the caretaker for permission to use the yards for the meeting to be held before the demonstration.

The final difficulty lay in arranging transport of the carcasses out to the abattoirs at West Plains. In the end, the two men realised that no carrying company would take this on for fear of retaliation, so the obvious thing was to do it themselves. On their way back to Blackmount that evening they discussed who should be spokesman for the group. Roger suggested Owen Buckingham and that night phoned him at his Te Anau farm. Roger went straight to the point.

'What do you think of farmers having a protest about the freezing industry and taking a ute-load of old ewes into town and cutting their throats?'

Owen's reply was instant. 'Bloody oath, I'll be the first down there.'

'I like your style, Buck, you're our spokesman.'

'Hang on,' argued Owen, 'there are plenty who would be better.'

'You're the spokesman until you find someone better,' and Roger went on phoning other farmers.

Protest

Friday morning and the hectic preparations were over. All that remained now was to see how many farmers would turn up. Syd was apprehensive about this aspect, but estimated there would probably be about 100, if the assurances given over the phone were kept. …

Owen Buckingham felt extremely apprehensive as he drove down alone, because he saw no one else bound for Lorneville. As he passed farms he would peer into the backyards looking in vain for farmers getting ready to go, but there was no sign of activity. As he neared Lorneville he saw one other utility on the road.

'At least I'm not going to be the only one,' he thought. The hundred miles from Te Anau to Lorneville is a long way when you are feeling uneasy. Owen was early, though. Had he been half-an-hour later, he would have felt as many others did. Participants said later that the sight of so many trucks laden with old ewes bound for Lorneville with a common purpose, inspired them and they lost any diffidence they might have had …

One thing that puzzled Syd Slee on the day was the apparent change of mind by the caretaker at Lorneville, Mr B.A. McKenzie. 'You can't use the other yard, not after what was in the papers this morning.' Syd thought the man had been over-ruled, as there was very little in the papers that morning, and certainly nothing that the caretaker hadn't already been told. A short time after, Syd was approached by Federated Farmers' leader, Gordon Pullar, and police sergeant, Derek Beveridge.

'Where are these sheep going to be killed?' was Sergeant Beveridge's first question and indeed, his main concern. 'Are you aware that you can't kill them in a public place?'

'They're not going to be killed in a public place,' Syd assured him.

'Where are they going to killed then?'

'I'm sorry I can't tell you that, but it's not a public place. It's private land.'

'That's okay then. I wonder can I meet the group organising this before you go?'

The committee for the day was: Gavin Evans (Hedghope), Stuart Allen (Castlerock), Owen Buckingham (Te Anau), Chris Glynn (Orawia), George Buckingham (Waikawa Valley), Alex Miller (Tuatapere) and Syd Slee. It was only at this stage that Owen learned that he was definitely spokesman for the group, and he wrote a few quick notes for his address to the crowd.

The assembly at Lorneville was probably the most critical part of the demonstration. It was here that the organisers had to make it clear that they were running the day, and that what they said, went. This sounds authoritarian, and it was, because the organisers had an immensely difficult job to do. They had to act as moderates, steering a way between the demands of the radicals and the counter-demands of those who wanted them to water down their proposed action. Some farmers wanted to drive onto the main street, cut their sheep's throats and then leave, having spilled blood everywhere. They had to be told that this was not on … then there were the doves – mainly represented by Federated Farmers officials – who asked the organisers to tone down their protest. At the most they wanted just a token few slaughtered. The committee was adamant. Syd Slee told them, 'This is our show. You can run yours next week.'

Owen made it clear when he addressed the crowd that letting sheep go was illegal. 'You have two options. You can drive down Dee Street and the ones who want to can let their sheep go. If you don't want to break the law, you can keep them on the back of your trucks. These are the only options. If you don't like what we are going to do, you can pull out now.' No one pulled out. He continued. 'After we drive them down the street, we are taking them to an empty section where we shall cut their throats.'

'Whose throats?' someone yelled from the crowd, drawing some laughter. The crowd was raring to go. The group from Te Anau was worried that the organisers would back down and let Federated Farmers talk them out of their plans to slaughter stock. John Heany, a farmer from that district, threatened Owen. 'Don't you dare bring all us farmers here and then go and back down on us or you'll never get us to join in anything else.'

Owen left the crowd with the warning, 'No one is to carry knives and there is to be no cutting throats in the street. You are to treat your stock as gently as you would at home.' Someone yelled from the crowd, 'Well, I don't know about what you do, but I treat mine gently.' Owen responded quickly, 'I want you to handle your stock carefully. Put any that are too weak to walk back on the trucks. Remember, the eyes of the whole country will be on you today.' He finished his instructions, 'Okay we've got a job to do, let's go.' A cheer rose from the large crowd, and many of the men were quite moved by this feeling of new-found unity. At 1.30 p.m, precisely, they drove out of the sale yards and headed towards Invercargill … They drove the 7 or 8km to the city in single file and at Tapper's corner, about 1km from the Trooper's Memorial, they began to travel three abreast.

Owen, travelling in one of the front vehicles, recalls that the police had no idea they were going to let the stock out. He followed the police escort car until the memorial, then stopped and had the gates on the back of his ute opened before the police realised that he was no longer following. He was releasing the second ewe when he felt a tap on his shoulder.

'I'm going to have to arrest you.'

'Arrest me then,' said Owen, neatly putting the old ewe through the policeman's legs. No arrest was made though, probably because the police were as bewildered as the old ewes that surrounded them.

Roger Slee was in one of the front vehicles, his truck carrying the slogan, 'we've had a guts full'. He unloaded his sheep before Inspector Harris approached him and put his hand on his shoulder, 'You're under arrest.'

'What for?'

'For inciting a riot. Do you want me to arrest you?'

'If it's going to make our protest heard then I'm prepared to be arrested.' At this critical point in their dialogue Roger noticed that the old ewes he had released were heading off down towards the Crescent, the bulwark of Southland's stock and station firms. Yelling 'I've got to get those ewes,' Roger disentangled himself from the inspector and ran after his stock. Seeing that his words had little effect on Roger, Inspector Harris spoke to the rest of the crowd from a public address system. He was very serious.

'Please keep the sheep in the trucks or you will be liable for arrest. I want you to round up the sheep you have already let go.' Again, his request was ignored.

One of the oldest demonstrators, war veteran Allan Jones of Hedgehope, was unloading his ewes when stopped by a policeman. 'You can't do that.'

'Can't I?' Allan pointed to all the other farmers, 'What about them?' The policeman saw the futility of it all and left.

Five minutes later, a block beyond this scene, twenty more trucks were unloaded. Further on, Mr Cockroft, the chief traffic officer in Invercargill, refused to allow the remaining trucks to go past Yarrow Street. So, at this intersection, they were unloaded. Dee Street, often boasted as one of the widest streets in New Zealand, was now overflowing, and the flowers in the centre-plot were rushed by starving old ewes. This indicated as well as anything could just how hungry they were. But the pitifully thin appearance of the sheep would have been enough. All around them the protesters heard the crowds say, 'We didn't know things were as bad as this.' It spurred the men on. 'The poor old sheep.'

'Good on you, boys, you ought to have done this long ago.'

Some of the sheep went down towards the railway station. Some went towards the *Times* office. Some collapsed, too weak to walk, and had to be carried back to the trucks. Outside the Grand Hotel a group of freezing workers hurled abuse at the protesters. Syd began yelling back at them, as Owen walked over. 'You're wasting your time with those blokes, Syd, you won't win that one!' Meanwhile, Barney Barrett, a tall Maori farmer from Tuatapere, an ex-freezing worker, walked slowly past them, amid a mob of sheep, with a slow grin on his face, wearing white gumboots and all …

The demonstration lasted for one hour and by then the 300 protesters had rounded up their ewes and had driven them to an empty section near the Borstal Bridge. A trench had been dug around the perimeter of the section to allow the blood to flow away. Hurricane netting gates enclosed it. The crowd that gathered to watch the slaughter was fairly silent. The killing had just begun when, again, a request was made to slaughter just a few. Syd Slee was adamant; the slaughtering must continue until all the sheep were killed. He pointed out to the crowd that these sheep would have died of malnutrition in a few weeks anyway.

The first load of 39 carcasses was taken to Southland Butchers' By-Products at West Plains at 3 p.m. The slaughtering continued. Expert butchers, mainly ex-freezing workers, cut the sheep's throats and piled the bodies up neatly, while other farmers loaded them onto trucks. The police maintained a close survey of the whole proceedings, and at one stage a group of freezing workers was asked to disperse, in case an open brawl between them and the farmers erupted … Towards the end of the kill, the protesters were surprised to see the 'Black Maria' police van draw up. Three policemen jumped out, ran round the back and opened the doors. Chris Glynn muttered to a companion, 'This is it. We're all going to be arrested.' He was immensely relieved when three old ewes that had missed the muster hobbled out.

Later that night, the farmers who had taken part felt a sense of achievement; they had finally done something. Everywhere the general reaction was that the farmers could not be blamed. In a unprecedented way they had revolted and shown that they were sick and tired of being the object of union irresponsibility, of freezing company weakness and greed, of their own federation's continual ineffectual bargaining, and of the government's ineptitude in industrial relations.

Most knew, in the words of one of the older demonstrators, Bill Foster of Hedgehope, that 'it would be a hard act to follow'. And they fervently hoped that there would be no need for a following act. But the realists among them knew there could be no instant panacea for the troubles of the freezing industry and they guessed, and rightly so, that this was just the beginning. As Syd Slee drove back to Blackmount that night, he thought about what George Buckingham had said to him when the kill was over; Syd had remarked that it had been a good day. 'Yes, it's been a good day, Syd.' George was thoughtful, then continued in his slow fashion, 'It's been a good day, but I think this type of thing is a onecr for all that.'

Syd laughed to himself. George was right, it certainly was a oncer.

The Land

John Kneebone

Call yourself a peasant

Despite tight credit and gloomy meat and wool prospects, some fertiliser is being spread, fences renewed and houses painted. Store stock prices are bit shaky and feed is not too plentiful. But compared to prospects in mid February, we have been pretty lucky. The autumn recovery and not too much eczema mean we are in reasonable shape to face the winter. The great exception has been the devastating drought in Canterbury. Individual farmers must be facing a pretty bleak winter with empty barns, silos and bank accounts.

Probably because of the political diversions, there has been little media coverage of Canterbury's plight. The region, it is assumed, can cope because it enjoys such a reputation of solid affluence. The impression a traveller gains when passing through is of substantial 'baronial manors', trimmed hedgerows and permanence. Canterbury cockies tend to be tidy fellows and keep their farms pretty ship-shape. While they are no strangers to dry summers, they have no more fat in their system than the rest of us, so spare them a thought.

Hearing daily news bulletins, we easily forget the power of the media to condition our thinking. Our news is honest, for with New Zealand being little more than an extended village, fabrication is easily checked out. What we are less confident about, however, are the criteria used to decide what events are given prominence and turned into news. This is an issue that can never be resolved to everyone's satisfaction. We will always question just who chooses to give priority to issues … As something of an insomniac, I frequently tune in to all-night radio. The news items selected for the wee small hours are quite different and rarely make the daytime broadcasts or newspapers. Very curious?

SMP's [supplementary minimum prices], very much in the news, have raised again the topic of diversification. I become very nervous on this topic because of the misconceptions of the urban community, and its difficulty in critically evaluating the feasibility and practicality of suggested new options. Farmers, historically, have been criticised for tardiness in adopting new ideas and methods. The opposite is, in fact, true. Kiwi farmers have a history of rushing prematurely into new practices long before they are properly evaluated. Millions of dollars are lost annually by farmers experimenting with new

June 1982, *NZ Journal of Agriculture*

plants and animals, and new treatments and techniques that would make a witch doctor look like a Fellow of the Royal Society.

In the field of new ventures, New Zealand farmers have no peers; you name it, we have tried it. Animals of every shape, colour and origin can be found in this country. The Government was bulldozed into building the only maximum security, animal quarantine station in the Southern Hemisphere. It is now little more than a monument to our impulsiveness. The Government's glass houses in Auckland are bulging at the seams with imported plants passing through quarantine. New Zealand has pioneered developments in artificial breeding and ovum transplants for animals, and plant breeding and tissue culture are in top gear, so we are not exactly dragging the chain in seeking improvements.

For the size of our country, our Government research is surpassed nowhere in the world. Official activity, while impressive, is only the tip of the iceberg. The great bulk of experimentation and innovation goes on behind the farm gate, and most of it is kept pretty quiet. Bank managers develop ulcers, stock firm managers, heart ailments and mortgagors, nervous twitches, whenever they get wind of customers dabbling in non-traditional activities. The odd few entrepreneurs make a few dollars in short-lived bonanzas, with publicity and euphoria exaggerating profits. New enthusiasts follow; their financial losses are massive and legendary.

The most suitable land use very rapidly sorts itself out. The only viable alternatives to sheep or cattle are dairying, deer, horticulture and forestry. Dairying has definite requirements for rainfall and proximity to processing plants. Deer farming for export is yet to be proven, as is horticulture. Forestry, under today's economy, must be large scale, with suitable land contour and nearness to export ports, so it is not a practical alternative for an individual farmer. If meat and wool returns remain depressed, there is little scope for diversification, and New Zealand will simply have to lower its rather lavish living standards. Easily said but less easily done …

Several people in recent times have chided me for referring to myself as a peasant; they felt it was demeaning. It may sound odd, but I do believe that it does no harm to strip away much of the pompous nonsense with which we surround ourselves. My sentiments were echoed by an old forestry friend in Auckland, as he surveyed the endless sea of houses and muttered, 'What the hell do all these people do – pay one another to take in each other's washing?' While I live close to Auckland, I rarely go there. But I've always marvelled at the activity, the affluence and the arrogance – all financed by farmers' exports.

Closer to home, I find myself being amused by the 'beautiful people' who fly in by helicopter, garbed in expensive suede, to experience the rural environment, tipple a few pink gins, and proceed to outbid each other for investment deer. Flushed with the experience and the imbibing, they waft their way back to their high-rise apartments;

refreshed by the bravado of their bidding, the rural ozone, and smug in their manipulation of the taxation system. By comparison, I am a rustic and rather slow – which is especially true when it comes to getting my house painted or desk tidied. Being a farmer, I am ruggedly independent, sound and reliable. Though not as snappily dressed as the 'suede brigade', I am house-trained, literate and usually vote National.

Peasants are historically resilient, independent, proud and persistent. Writers and academics are generally rather superior and condescending in their attitudes to the peasantry, but less so than to some other lower groups, such as miners and common labourers. For centuries, as I understand it, my ancestors wielded picks and shovels in the bowels of the earth. They were miners, a social ranking markedly inferior to the forthright and sturdy peasant – or so the many novelists who influenced my youthful readings implied.

Being only a second-generation tiller of the soil, I would doubt that I yet qualify as a full-blown peasant. Some people think that the boilermakers at Huntly are tough, banning from work any tradesman with less than six months union membership. But most older farming districts in New Zealand accept nothing less than four generations of continual membership. I am therefore simply giving notice that we, as former pick and shovellers, are applying for permanent membership of the impecunious, but ruggedly independent, rural self-employed.

Sustainability

Jim Morris

They mutter of erosion
In their offices of glass,
And say this block should be retired
Before another season's passed.

They speak of soil and water
And the values they hold grand,
Then go and build another suburb
On some market garden land!

1997, *Different Worlds*

People

Heather McCrostie Little

Drought is more than a physical battle

When we put back our clocks from daylight saving and turned into the long run towards winter, we might have expected more obvious signs of an approaching autumn. But no, the summer heat continued, and the severity of drought.

Each morning I watched my neighbour feed out. For an hour or so the listless waiting of the stock was broken, and long lines of sheep, heads down feeding, were strung across the bare, baked paddock. As pastures shrivelled, receded and disappeared, these bare paddocks grew nothing but dung. The pattern of the day no longer included grazing the long paddock; there was little left on the roadside that was edible. For my part, I spent the early morning and evening hours hauling hoses round the trees and shrubs, checking the water, calculating where I should hose next, and assessing the tank supply against the need. I was unwilling to predict if I was winning or losing the battle in my fight to save the trees. Each day another would show signs of distress. I was unable to settle to any jobs in the house as my internal clock ticked round to hose-moving time again. Concentrate as I might on reading or writing, my subconscious was alert to what was happening outside.

But drought is more than a physical battle against the depletion of the soil, plants, and animals. Drought holds you in a state of siege, at once emotional and physical. It can possess you, threatening your stewardship of the land and stock and challenging the very basis of your need to live in the country. Over it you have no control. Before it you are powerless.

During the lunch break at our last county council meeting, discussion centred on the drought. Usually 'drought talk' contains four factors: stock, feed, water, and finance. This time the men added another dimension – their own depression in the face of the consequences of the continuing heat. One councillor volunteered the fact that that morning, in raging despair, he had found himself shaking his fist at the glowing sun. Nobody laughed. We lapsed into silence, understanding full well the impotent rage that sparked his gesture.

During droughts I experience a reluctance to leave the property, which is often too compelling to be ignored. I close in on myself. If the land is to suffer and I can no longer offer my successful guardianship, I must remain and share the suffering. It is a strong

May 1982, *NZ Journal of Agriculture*

but deep-seated feeling difficult to articulate, beyond acknowledging that whatever spiritual force binds me to the land, demands that I remain.

In the 1960s we lived through the 5- (or was it 7-?) year drought – the phrase itself has such biblical overtones – and that was before the farmer/county water scheme. The summer droughts were so severe that feed or water could no longer be guaranteed or supplied. To survive, farmers shipped their stock out to kinder climates further south. So did we, once. The sheep, flock and stud, were mustered in and trucked away. It seemed to take days of noise, heat, dust, worry and exhaustion and, when the last transport and trailer had ground down the drive, an oppressive silence fell over the property. The farm died. Its pulse ceased.

Tractor work continued. Outbuildings were painted. Machinery was overhauled. But the lifeblood of the property had flowed away, and everyone moved as if in slow motion, heavy with depression. The farm felt like ship tied up in port – empty and in a state of suspension. City friends said 'How wonderful. Now you can go on holiday.' We smiled wanly, thinking of the long haul south each week to check our sheep. We scarcely admitted that there were fundamental reasons preventing us from going away at this time. Our deep need to maintain contact with our stock was one reason; to leave a farm of empty paddocks would be a form of desertion.

What we were experiencing was being endured by most of the community. It was unreal – a community of farms that weren't. It was agony grappling with something that refused to be grappled with as we and the land waited, waited for the rain and the return of the sheep. For waiting – suspension – is what drought becomes. The land, open and vulnerable, lies waiting for the rain. At midday, in the shimmering heat, the waiting takes a different form. Then the hills and valleys lie crouched as if waiting to explode into some all-consuming fireball. The tension between land and sun draws taut.

Weather continues through its patterns. Only rain is absent. Black clouds build up over the hills. At any other time they would denote rain, but their bloated fullness is like a false pregnancy with no rain being spawned. They fill the sky for a short time with their mockery – and evaporate. This year they didn't fool me. Nevertheless, I felt the tension within me build as they formed and massed behind the hills, and I wondered and waited. Waited for the sweet release of rain.

The long summer twilights offered their own relief and how glorious they were this year. It was indeed a glorious summer. If I was living near the sea and a swimmer or near enough to sail and fish. If I was young and living in a city, what a tremendous summer it was. One to recall in one's old age as a 'golden year'.

But I don't live near the sea, and I do live on the land. And I see the other side to the bright summer coin.

153

Make a poem of this
Pat White

a few ewes stand
by poplars

the trees are dying
leaves fall
are eaten by the ewes
there is no grass
just shade, and

sometimes a dead leaf
...
nine live akeake
along the back fence

over one hundred planted
by Andy and us
last winter ... in the wet
...
up there the nor'westers
blow, break seedhead grass
at ground level
flatweeds, thistles grow
...
each autumn the north
faces are grazed
sheep cattle fatten
flush on the growth

this year, not
a beast
...

the old neighbour said
'I've never seen those
dams dry'

well, he has now
months since

    ...

last night, rain
I dare you to dream

make a poem of this

1999, *Drought and other intimacies*

155

Gilbertson

Tim Gilbertson

Tourist venture earns more aggro than EBIT

Statistics indicate that, not before too long, the average dairy farmer will need to milk 12,000 cows to remain economically viable. This may well squeeze out the last remaining pastoral farmer, who will need to graze the entire North Island to produce an EBIT of 4 per cent.

EBIT is a new word for nett profit and stands for Earning Before Interest and Tax. It's the sort of word that is popular among people who write reports about the average dairy farmer. I like to try out these words every so often. It proves you have read the business section of the *Herald*. But, to be ruthlessly honest – apart from that – it is the most useless piece of information on the planet. Since our finance and banking industry is now controlled by a computer program in Gnome, Alaska, in the near future any farmer with an EBIT of less than 4 per cent of CNAV (Current Nett Asset Value) faces the prospect of being sold up. Or being refused seasonal finance or sent to a business re-education course run by Jim Anderton, under a beech tree on the South Island's West Coast.

This is a fate too horrible to contemplate, forewarned is fore armed. But there is hope for those of us whose EBITs do not – and probably never will – cut the mustard. This is because the business page, as well as educating the novice in the new terminology, also introduces one to the wonder of 'how to' books. This is a literary genre that tells you how to get rich.

I always assumed that wealth was inherited, married or came via a Lotto ticket. But no! Anyone can become immensely wealthy by buying tomes such as Ezekiel Jerome Hemplebaum III's *The Six Successful Habits of the World's Richest Entrepreneurs: Your Guide to Instant, Effortless Wealth*, and following the few simple rules contained therein.

Unfortunately, book phobia is still widespread amongst the rural sector. 'Book' is a word with negative connotations. 'The books' once meant dashing into the accountant's, throwing a fadge full of invoices on his desk and shouting at him down the phone weeks later when he said you had to pay tax.

Nowadays, the modern farmer spends more time on his cash flow than his cash crop and knows more about EBITs than EBVs (Estimated Breeding Values). That, and doing courses. A mate of mine did a course on techno-farming recently. For $2500 he learnt to subdivide an acre into four parts with an electric fence. I could have taught

22 May 2000, *Rural News*

him that for the price of a pint! The trouble is, they're reading the wrong sort of books. They should be reading Ezekiel Whatsit and looking at the big picture.

The days of wandering into the bank every autumn and adding another nought to the overdraft are well over. The information revolution has seen to that and in this global environment, the farm budget is a living document, and investment opportunities exist beyond the farm gate. This makes lying to bankers a lot harder, which is fine for them but not so hot for the rest of us. But as Hemplebaum says in *Punching the Envelope: Your Guide to Immense Riches in Three Seconds Flat Via Internet Investing*: 'Limiting your vision to the horizon is like ordering goat's milk soup from the menu of utopia. You can dream your future into reality.'

A nod is as good as a wink to a blind man, and to me this meant alternative on-farm investment, which means grapes, olives or tourists. You are still allowed to kick olive trees, grapevines and sheep, under extreme duress, but not tourists. However, the tourist dollar is the quickest return by miles, so I re-roofed the shearers' quarters, fixed the plumbing – more or less – threw in a pottery teapot and some colourful bedcovers from the op shop and put up the sign.

In they drove. I pocketed the $200 and congratulated myself on launching a new agribusiness venture. Twenty-four hours later, the fridge had blown up, the rats were launching forays from the woodshed, and the smoke from the blocked chimney had tainted the ratatouille. The historic wire wove beds, dating back to 1927, had caused numerous slipped discs, the wasp nest in the roof was upsetting mother, and the kids all got hayfever. They demanded their money back and left.

Looking on the bright side, projections that indicate rural tourism is one of the fastest growing segments of the economy, are obviously bunkum. Which indicates that projections about the 12,000-cow herd are probably bunkum as well. This gives me hope. If all else fails and I do have to sign the hacienda over to the banker and the mega-farmer conglomerate in a year or two, I can retire to my lovely, renovated shearers' quarters and sleep the sleep of the well rewarded on my comfortable, old wire wove bed.

Local farmers seek assistance
– *Wairarapa Times Age* headline

Pat White

seein' is believin'

the pendulum of politics
has swung that far
to the right
(you're on your own kid!)
maybe in the year 2000
It'll hit the wall of the universe
and shatter everything in sight

1999, *Drought and other intimacies*

At First Hand

T here's nothing like being there,' so the old saying goes, and gaining *real* experience. In some of the stories that follow the writer is an observer and, somehow, the main target or scapegoat as well. This not only gives complete authenticity but also meant several bruises, stains and strains at the time, both physical and mental. Undoubtedly there are drawbacks to being in the middle of the action, experiencing a new environment or the tedium of post-incident damage control, but, because you were there, the story can be told much more realistically and honestly – with judicious use of additional colour and drama.

The 'I've been there too' element was useful during my time as a television presenter and director. There is a notion in many rural minds that a person who appears on television is 'a townie' and therefore knows naught about the land itself and what happens on it, let alone understand country people and their ways. In that ever-awkward, ice-breaking conversation I quickly learnt to comment on or interpret something I'd noticed on the way up the drive or could see in an adjacent paddock. The initial response would usually be a slightly raised eyebrow and the query, 'Where'dja learn that?' The ice would not necessarily be broken – one shower doesn't break a drought – but the prospect of a thaw was on the agenda. On the other hand, there's nothing better for brief and harmless rural entertainment than a visitor who says or does the wrong thing and causes harm only to him- or herself.

This section, more than any other, celebrates the role of women on the land – their contribution to both the workforce and to overall stability, as the linchpin of both farm and family life. Theirs is a strength as old as New Zealand farming itself, and it is never more needed than when times are hard and resources slim, and getting slimmer by the day. No one I've read in this country has described that as simply, yet evocatively, as Amiria Stirling in telling her story to Anne Salmond.

> We had the cream cheque, and the kumaras and potatoes, and we felt we were
> on our feet. We could pay for the house and the children's clothes and
> everything; we felt we were doing very well.

To fit the description, 'At First Hand', all the prose found here should be non-fiction, and it is – except for the work of the highly prolific Mary Scott. Northland-born, Hawke's Bay-reared, Auckland University-educated and domiciled on northern King Country farms for over 40 years, Mary Scott penned descriptions of agricultural activities, characters and events that reflected real life experience. Her first five books were based on the character Barbara, who first appeared as the central figure in Scott's *New Zealand Herald* column. These chronicles were at least semi-autobiographical and, for many, Barbara was the first female character in local fiction who was readily identifiable as 'one of us', doing what New Zealanders did at that time. Mary Scott then turned to writing novels of light romance, all of them set in the countryside, providing the most accurate commentary on rural life in the 1950s and 1960s that can be found in any branch of local literature.

The Khaki Pit

Field Candy

Khaki pits are only about 30 inches deep. Otherwise they're not too different from the front-line trenches of the 1914-18 war. Usually three or four feet wide, they can range in length from little 18-footers to prodigious affairs that stretch away into the distance. I refer of course to the pits in herring bone cowsheds. Although no one has ever been killed in a khaki pit, they are nevertheless difficult and dangerous places in which to work. Every year countless cockies suffer painful injuries to the hands and fingers while milking the national dairy herd.

The casualty list is always higher in the spring. At that time we are busy training the new intake of heifers, many of whom are convinced their hind feet have been designed for pulverising human hands. If you have no other way of identifying a cow-cocky in August or September, just look at his blue and swollen hands. And don't be offended if he seems disinclined to shake hands with you.

Cows are not only devastating kickers; they are also filthy great vegetarians. In the spring they are extra filthy and extra great. At this time of the year the khaki pit is more khaki than usual. In the spring the grass is lush. When the grass is lush the cows are loose. And when the cows are loose we get a khaki pit. They run amuck. Pardonable really. With all those herbs and grasses being taken in at one end, it's only natural that there's a certain amount of spillage at the other; a body can only take so much! Some people have runny noses. Well, cows have runny behinds. Researchers estimate that a dairy cow discharges 10 tonnes of manure a year. I believe them. Removing the khaki overburden from walls and pipe-work and restoring the sparkle to plant and equipment twice daily is enough to convince anyone.

In the field, cows are only reasonably efficient bulk-manure spreaders. In the cowshed they are positively irresponsible. But a cocky can make life better or worse for himself, according to his temperament. Cows love a quiet, unhurried routine (such as most women milkers habitually provide) and always produce best when kindly treated. Rough, ill-tempered milkers will never get the best results from these highly sensitive animals. Fearful cows, with the aid of powerful sphincter muscles in their udders, can withhold their milk, a tactic that nearly always coincides with a lack of control over their bowels.

A classic if humbling example of what can happen when cows become agitated

1988, *Every Living Thing*

occurred a few seasons ago when we converted our old walk-through shed into a herring bone. When introduced to this scary new system in the spring, they temporarily lost control of themselves. That period of familiarisation proved disconcerting for us too. In the old shed we had been on top of our work, now our work was on top of us! Relays of bovine juggernauts, 16 at a time, loomed above us, their unsavoury behinds and waterworks all pointing in our direction. Down in that shallow fissure we were at the mercy of all those fouling pieces. Even the trenches of Ypres provided more security and protection. But in the khaki pit there was that dreadful overhang, full of menace and manure. It became imperative that we learn new survival techniques.

In some situations it's a help if you can read people's minds. In the khaki pit it's a help if you can read cow's behinds. It goes without saying that hindsight is worse than useless. We soon developed nifty sidesteps in moments of peril. Sudden coughs from above caused us to duck instinctively, though not always in time. Hot from the place of manufacture, the cough drop, as we called it, was very hard to take with equanimity. Certain individuals fancied themselves as make-up artists. Flourishing loaded tails, they would daub our faces with khaki moustaches or gangrenous-looking eye-shadow.

However, no incident can match the one that overtook me on a bitterly cold morning in the newly commissioned herring bone. My hands were numb, my sidestep was slow and stiff, my behind-reading was malfunctioning. I was washing a line of udders on one side of the pit. I'd just finished washing No.76, a smelly old affair at the best of times, and had moved to the next one in the row. I was working away, minding my own business, when I suddenly became aware of this warm sensation on top of my cranium. At first I wasn't too worried. It was pleasantly warm, about blood heat, and as I say it was a cold morning. But a moment later this khaki-coloured stuff began to trickle down over my eyebrows. I realised I was in the middle of a disaster area. Telling myself it was only partly digested grass, I groped my way to the dairy where I dunked my aggrieved head in a bucket of warm water.

I suppose you have to expect this sort of thing when you hobnob with the 'effluent' society while making your pile.

Ever since the day old 76 jettisoned her payload on my head, I've worn a potae in the khaki pit.

Milking before Dawn

Ruth Dallas

In the drifting rain the cows in the yard are as black
And wet and shiny as rocks in an ebbing tide;
But they smell of the soil, as leaves lying under trees
Smell of the soil, damp and steaming, warm.
The shed is an island of light and warmth, the night
Was water-cold and starless out in the paddock.

Crouched on the stool, hearing only the beat
The monotonous beat and hiss of the smooth machines,
The choking gasp of the cups and rattle of hooves,
How easy to fall asleep again, to think
Of the man in the city asleep; he does not feel
The night encircle him, the grasp of mud.

But now the hills in the east return, are soft
And grey with mist, the night recedes, and the rain.
The earth as it turns toward the sun is young
Again, renewed, its history wiped away
Like the tears of a child. Can the earth be young again
And not the heart? Let the man in the city sleep.

1953, *Country Road and Other Poems*

Life on the Farm

Amiria Stirling and Anne Salmond

We didn't stay long at Kapongaro, only about a year. We grew one crop of maize there, and then we shifted to Otaimina. We had a mixed farm at Otaimina, milking and sheep-farming and later on, cropping. All our other children were born there: Wahawaha, Mokikiwa, Lily, Tama, Marama and Te Kepa the last. And I had all my babies at home except Tama; he was a floating baby and he didn't seem to bother about coming away. The time was up and he should have been born, but he wasn't worried, he was still there.

Dr Scott was the doctor then, and he said, 'I think you'd better go to Opotiki Hospital, Mrs Stirling, because a lot of things can happen, you'd better have that baby there.'

When I told Dick he agreed, and he said, 'If you go to Opotiki, go to Motoi's place, she lives close to the hospital. Just stay there the night, and we'll book you into hospital for the next day.'

He arranged everything, and when I got to Opotiki, Motoi was waiting for me at the bus-stop. She took me home and she had a nice little place. She said to me, 'Never mind about going to the hospital – you stay here. If anything happens and I can't manage, it's all right, I'll just ring the doctor and he can come.'

That night the pains started.

'Look Motoi, I think I'd better go to the hospital ...'

'Don't worry, it's all right!'

She wouldn't ring the doctor. I kept asking her but she said, 'No, *don't* worry about it. Come on, you have the baby and I'll look after you.'

In the end she was the one that helped me to give birth all right. The funny thing was, when the baby was born we heard all the rockets go off, it was Guy Fawkes night. I heard the crackers and the next thing, *bang!* Tama was born.

At Otaimina we had the Maori Affairs house. Eruera went and had a talk to Apirana [Ngata] about it, and after a while Maori Affairs built us a place.

With all the children and paying the Maori Affairs, it got pretty hard on the cream cheque, so we used to go out and pick seaweed, leave it on the beach to dry and then send it up to the Internal Marketing in Auckland, and that brought us a bit of extra money for the family at home.

1976, *Amiria: the Life Story of a Maori Woman*

A few years later, Eruera heard that some other people on the coast were cropping kumaras and potatoes, so he thought he might try it. He said, 'Gee, I think Mum, I'll plough up a patch of paddock here and put in a few kumaras and potatoes.'

There were people in Te Araroa growing these and selling them to Lou Gow, the Chinaman who came round in a truck between Gisborne and Opotiki, buying for the market.

I said, 'Do you think they'll allow us to do that? Maori Affairs is the boss of this ground now they've built the house.'

'Oh, *blow* them. It's my own land! I think that I'll give it a go.'

It was a lot of work getting the ground ready for cropping. The puriri stumps were the worst, and once the trees were all out, the soil had to be ploughed.

One old chap called Marama Brown said to Eruera, 'Eru – the horse is no good for ploughing, that's the trouble. They drag too fast, and if the plough gets stuck, they keep pulling until it's all smashed up. The bullock is the best. You try and train a couple of bullocks. Although it takes months and months, once they're trained, they're the best; if the plough gets caught, the bullock will just stand, not like the horse.'

Eruera started training steers, and the old man helped him. He was right, too; the bullocks were very good. Then Eruera got the kumara plants from his mother. She had a patch of kumaras, what they called the whakaika kumara, down at Stirling Castle. After that season she showed me how to do it; you put the kumaras down in a big bed and bury them, and when the shoots start to come up, you pick them, bundle them up in kits and plant them in the ground.

That year, we did very well. The next year we thought we'd like a really big batch, tons of kumaras, because it's an extra cheque to come in.

Dick said, 'Oh blow the Maori Affairs, we'll plough Otaimina up,' and he did.

That's how we got on; we had the cream cheque, and the kumaras and potatoes, and we felt we were on our feet. We could pay for the house and the children's clothes and everything, we were doing very well. Then Eruera was in Auckland one time, and he went to see the people at Turners and Growers. They offered to buy all his kumaras and potatoes, and told him to contact them about prices, not to bother with Lou Gow. In the end Eruera thought he could handle the other people's crops as well. He waited until Lou Gow went past in his truck, then he went up to Te Araroa and Ruatoria and asked the people how much Lou Gow had offered them for their kumaras. He wrote to Auckland, and Turners and Growers told him to buy all those kumaras, they'll give a better price than Lou Gow's.

When Lou Gow came back the people told him, 'Oh no! Our kumaras have gone, Dick Stirling has bought them.'

'What?'

'Dick Stirling – he gave us more money.'

He got so wild he came to see Dick, and told him not to chip into his business, to leave his customers alone.

'Well, those people deserve a better price.'

'Look here, you mind your own business!'

'If they agree to sell their kumaras to you, that's all right; and if they agree to give them to me, I'll take them.'

They had a bit of trouble over that.

Every now and then when we saw Lou Gow go past, Dick would take the bus and find out what the price was.

'Oh well, I'll give you this …'

When Lou Gow came back to collect the kumaras, they'd say, 'No, Dick Stirling's got my lot.'

Lou Gow bumped his price up, and that's how he went broke. Dick wrote to Turners and Growers about this price, and they told him to leave it, the prices in Auckland had dropped. So Lou Gow went broke, and the Chinese people in Gisborne put him back in the market gardens.

We had geese and fowls and ducks at Otaimina too, to give us plenty of eggs. In those days you had to bake all the time, it wasn't like the town where the bread is ready for you and everything is at your finger-tips. I'd boil up a big pot of eggs for the children to take to school with their bread, and they used to take the bread down to the cowshed for a feed. There was a big patch of strawberries near the shed, and they'd eat strawberries and cream and bread for breakfast. For a while our cream kept coming back from the factory, Second Grade. Dick couldn't work it out until one day he emptied out the can and it had breadcrusts and bits of strawberry in the bottom, so we had to stop the strawberries then.

After that the first of the children who got up in the morning to get the cows would collect all the eggs. The next thing you'd hear them yelling, fighting in the paddock over these eggs. I'd open the window and call out to them, 'What's the matter?'

'Oh … so and so's got my eggs, I found the eggs and they took them off me!'

'You should be in bed! Come on back home.'

Another thing the children liked was keeping pets. I remember when the boys went pig-hunting one time, they shot a pig, and when they started skinning the carcass a little suckling pig came squeaking out of the bush. That was Porky. They caught it and brought it home, then they came inside and asked me for the baby's bottle.

'What do you want it for?'

'Oh, we've got a little orphant pig out there.'

'You mean to say you're going to give the baby's bottle to a pig?'

'Mum, come and have a look, it's a dear little fella.'

When I saw the pig, it was white, pure white, and grunting along as though it was starved. It had its mouth open, ready to grab onto anything.

'Well, you'll have to ride down to Waihau first and get the baby a new bottle.'

'We'll go soon, Mum, but this pig needs a drink now.'

I had to give them the bottle. That poor little pig sucked away, it was grateful to have a drink. The children looked after it like a mother looking after her baby; they always remembered to feed it and it grew into a great, fat animal. If strangers came to the gate, all the pig's hairs would stand up on end, and you could hear it growling away, telling them not to come in. It was so tame the children even used to ride it to school, and it would follow Eruera when he went riding off to Waihau on his horse. One time when the pig went up with the cows to the top of the hill, though, somebody shot it and took it home to eat.

We had two pet horses on the farm too, Des and Hokey Pokey. Des was George's pet, and whenever George went to catch him, Des would run and dodge as if he was playing football. George would say, 'Don't run away, Des – just stay there, won't you?'

But Des always backed off and as soon as he saw a gap, he'd slide out and run that way.

'Watch out, Des, I'll knock your blooming head off!'

The horse would duck back, and run off in another direction. So George picked up a stick. 'All right, you do that again and I'll have your head off.' And when Des tried to dodge, bang! on his head. After that he seemed to understand, he'd just stop there and let George catch him.

Hokey Pokey was another one. Once when one of the horses was ready to foal, the children came in one morning to have a look and found her dead in the hay, with the little foal sucking away – no milk. They brought it back to the house, and that was another bottle the baby lost. The kids made a bed with an old blanket under the cow-shed, and they fed the foal themselves. I didn't think it would live, it looked so weak; but when Dick told the children it would be kinder to shoot the animal, they all sat down and howled, so he let them keep it. In the end Hokey Pokey grew into quite a healthy pony, except that his back wasn't quite straight.

I said to George, 'You people shouldn't be riding that horse, it's only a pony. See, its back is getting crooked ... .'

'I can't stop the kids, Mum, they ride him when I'm not looking.'

Hokey Pokey seemed to understand everything. When Waha and George went to get the cows, he'd trot along behind them, and if anyone was late for school after milking, they could hop on Hokey Pokey and he'd take them to school. There was no need for a saddle and bridle, he knew which way to go, and then he'd come back home by himself.

Just before three o'clock in the afternoon, I'd hear Hokey Pokey at the gate, pushing at the latch. When I opened the gate, he'd trot off as fast as he could go to fetch the children from school. Sometimes Porky the pig would go too, running along behind him. The first children to come out would say, 'Hey! Here's Hokey Pokey! We'll get him to take us to Waihau!'

'What about us?'

'Oh, you can ride the pig!'

So they hopped on Hokey Pokey's back and rode off to Waihau, pulling his ears so he wouldn't go home. When he'd get back to Otaimina, the children would say, 'Yeah! Where have you been, Hokey Pokey? You're supposed to bring *us* back, not cart those other kids to Waihau.'

Their other pet was a sheep. Its mother died, so the children looked after it, and it grew very big. One day when some people came to ask Dick for meat for a hui, he didn't have any animals ready, and they said, 'Well, what about that big fat sheep?'

'No, that's the children's pet.'

'We've got to have meat for the marae you know, there's a lot of people there and there's no meat.'

So he said all right. They took the sheep to the marae and killed it. When the children came home they were looking for their pet sheep, and we had to tell them in the end. Then there was a big tangi at Otaimina.

They said, 'We're not going to milk your cows any more, Dad – you killed our sheep.'

'Well, what could I do – let those people starve?'

'Why don't they get their own meat? There's meat at the shop in Waihau.'

For a whole week none of them would eat meat, they were frightened it might be their sheep. That's how bad it was, life on the farm …

A Day in the Life of a Farmer
My education did not prepare me for my chosen career.

Becchi Watt

Up at 4.30 a.m. Pack your lunch (Marmite sandwiches again). Chase your horse round the paddock for 20 minutes. Trip over the pigfeed bucket and spill it over the stable floor – all in the dark.

Out the back by 6 a.m. Dogs going berserk, cutting ewes and lambs in all directions. Throat getting sore.

Eventually get ewes and lambs into the yards by 8 a.m. – you have to pick up the biggest lambs because you're the biggest woman. Finish that paddock by 11 a.m. Help pack up. You have to help lift the hurdles and fold the scrim because you're the one that wants to do a man's job, so the other women keep saying as they count the tails or untie the scrim.

Set up in the next paddock. Have an early lunch; discover the thermos is broken and you've forgotten the milk. Start mustering again, and repeat the whole performance.

If things go well you're on your way home by 4.30. Throat is really sore, and the dogs insist on smelling out possums.

Home by 5 p.m. but there's still the horse to hose down and cover and feed. The dogs and pigs to feed and the pups to exercise, the milk and mail to pick up, tomorrow's dog tucker to get out of the freezer.

Finally you stagger inside and there's the fire to light, tea to make, bath to have. At last you sit down to dinner, and some well-meaning idiot rings up to find out what you have been doing! So you miss *Hill Street Blues*. Then it's the dishes and you're so tired that you trot off to your unmade-for-three-days bed – to remember the washing's still on the line for the fifth night and you have no clean socks. Your car is two weeks overdue for a Warrant of Fitness and, oh god, you made nothing for lunch so it's Marmite sandwiches *again*!

1986, *Herstory*

Busy

Katie Pye

I was busy sawing manuka whilst plucking a dozen chooks
when a squealing from the possum-trap took me over for a look,
then the shearer arrived, before I got there, to see if I'd fleec-o the mob,
so we set to as the rain started falling on him, then I went to a fencing job.
Instead of a lunch-break I dug gardens
instead of shearing I planted trees
whilst sprouting seeds I checked over the bees
and for a rest I sprayed fence-line weeds.
I cleared a drain of dense blackberry whilst mulching the fruit trees and leeks
I hung out the washing for afternoon tea (I'd been hanging it out for a week)
I inspected the dam while drenching the lambs
and mended the gate between breaths
and while sharpening a scythe-blade, I thought, I'm glad I'm not paid
or I'd think I was being worked to death.
I milked the stove and lit the cow and fertilized the phone
I heard the dog ringing, answered a crescent
and groomed the mare with a bone.
There's pig-scraps and butter and cheese to be done
while for dinner I foot-rotted the goats.
I mowed the lawns, with my feet picking pears, then I found this note in my coat:
'There's the eggs to take to market and the truck and chainsaw to mend,
collect the ram and make the jam and a tonne of potting mix to blend.
Could you feed the neighbour's dogs and cats?
and put that bull with the lost heifer;
Weed the beet, dip sheep, make soap from excess fat
and four rows of beans to gather.'
(and shift that hill!)
For supper I just went up the wall
but I whitewashed over the stains,
wiped my brow whilst heading for bed and met myself getting up again
saying: 'Check the chooks and I'll milk the cow, and water the horse while I groom,
and if you finish making the 100 metre ladder,
we'll maybe have lunch on the moon.'

1985, *Words of Whether With Scattered Scowers*

The Dipping

Mary Scott

When we muster in the hill country it is a question of all hands on the job. Yet I was dubious when Paddy offered his help.

'You've no dog, and no one can do anything on these hills and amongst these stumps and logs without a dog.'

'Is ut a dog then?' asked Paddy with superb scorn. 'Shure, yer honour, I've a little old trick of me own'll beat yer dog anny day.'

So I left it at that, since, where Paddy is concerned, I already know my place.

The dew of early morning was heavy on the grass when my wife mounted her *Kaiporka* and whistled old Mac to her side. Now this latter is sheer affectation on Barbara's part. Mac, who is almost as old as she is and far wiser, has long since seen his last day's muster. Lame, half-blind, and wholly senile, he yet lends that touch of verisimilitude that Barbara affects. He follows her for the first twenty chains and then goes to sleep under a log, rejoining her with enthusiasm on her return.

My own dog Spring knows all about hill musters and deeply dislikes them. Given his own choice, he would dwell upon the plains and wind slowly o'er the lea each evening after the lowing herd, for Spring is a determinedly lazy dog. Still, every time I set forth with a pathetic hope that on this particular day he will see me through. The hope is seldom realised. Meantime, there remained the erratic assistance of Barbara and the mysterious enthusiasm of Paddy.

'Where's that Irishman?' I asked irritably as we set out.

'He went ahead an hour ago and said he'd meet us on the ridge, if he was lucky,' said Barbara casually.

We rode out silently in the first flush of early morning. The high hill air was very crisp, the golden March sky clear and cloudless. As we went down the steep path and up the other side, the murmur of the creek in its stony bed, the occasional bleat of a sleepy ewe, alone broke the perfect peace of early morning. At moments a bird stirred and cheeped gently in the bush near by, but the silence was that found only in the country in the dawn hours. It was a scene of rare and perfect peace.

And then without warning a fierce and hideous clamour burst out and shattered for ever the beauty of the hour. The horses started and stood still; Spring raised enquiring eyes in mute appeal to me. As for the sheep on the opposite hill, the effect was electric

1953, *Barbara on the Farm*

and instantaneous. One and all lifted frightened heads from their dozing or the cropping, turned like Gadarene swine and swept down the ridge.

'What on earth …' I began feebly – and then stood spell-bound. Over the crest of the hill an extraordinary figure appeared. Paddy, his lank red hair blowing in the wind, the sleeves of his torn shirt flapping like some devil's wings, stood clear-etched against the primrose sky. In one hand he held a lump of wood, in the other a kerosene tin.

His method was unconventional, but at least it expedited our muster. By ten o'clock we were on the homeward track, with only the big creek to cross. Spring had worked surprisingly well and I could hear his steady bark from the stream. In spite of it, however, the sheep remained unmoved; they straggled up the banks, wandered in aimless groups, even scattered back up the track.

In despair I rode up the hill after a particularly stubborn ewe, and through the open wineberry had a clear view of the stream. Deep in its sandy depths, completely immersed and revelling in his crystal bath, lay Spring. Only his head was raised above the water and his 'throaty clamour' was hard at it to establish a satisfactory alibi. Wrathfully I descended upon him, but at the moment the din of a thousand devils broke out above me, and Paddy appeared, face crimson, garments more tattered than ever, but with the air of a drummer who leads on to victory. The sheep scattered in dismay before him, and I heard his triumphant voice, 'Was it a dog, yer honour? Sure, it's my little bit av music that moves them, an' it not needin' a bath to its comfort.'

The kerosene tin was battered to the size of a jam tin, but the sheep were mustered.

It had been agreed between the three of us that 'herself' should take a holiday from dipping this year; imagine, then, my surprise when I heard her liquidly regretful voice over the telephone: 'I'm so sorry, Mrs Warburton-Jones, but I shall be out today. I'm helping my husband with the dipping. Yes, we backblocks women have to be Jacks-of-all-trades,' and with a conscious smirk the perfidious woman replaced the receiver.

Mrs Warburton-Jones might justly be described as the Backblocks Bane. She is rich and she is idle; she doesn't play good bridge and has grown bored with parties. Therefore she has decided to find a new and original 'line' – and the backblocks woman is that line. She wants to find out all about their lives and, if they are not careful, she rushes out in her high-powered car to visit them. 'And don't make any difference, my dear. We'll all just picnic together.' So far my wife has eluded her.

When she left the telephone she avoided my eye, remarking with an air of high integrity: 'Of course I wouldn't tell a lie. I always intended to come to the dipping.'

It was one of the many occasions upon which the wise husband makes no reply.

We do not own a sheep-dip. It is one of those Eldorados of which we dream when mortgages have ceased from troubling and cement is once more within the humble reach of the small farmer. Meantime we drive our sheep three miles over clay roads deep in dust to the hospitable dip of a neighbour. Today I went on with the mob while Paddy and Barbara elected to follow with the rams. I did not witness the start, but my wife told me later that, in order to persuade the fifteen rams out of the yard, she was at one time reduced to barking like a dog, while Paddy on a brand-new tin executed a solo that drove the cows into the bush, the cats onto the hay-stack, and the fowls into the vegetable garden, but left the rams unmoved in the yard.

'Horatio was the trouble,' she admitted reluctantly.

Horatio always is, for once, in his far-distant youth, he was a pet lamb and that youth has remained as a pleasant memory now dedicated to evil ends. On this occasion he held the gate in the approved manner of his namesake, butted Barbara, blocked the other rams, and turned a cynical and disillusioned eye upon Paddy's drum.

Meantime I awaited them, leaning upon the sheepyard rails and looking down upon the quiet panorama of hill and plain that lay below me. Shadows passed gently across the distant ranges and all the air was so filled with magic that, almost unaware, I too became poetical. My thought turned to Barbara, even now winding her way down through the green and silent bush behind her flock. Softly I murmured:

'She walks, the Lady of my Delight,

A Shepherdess of Sheep.'

And then Barbara came … .

A shepherdess of sheep she might be, but a delight? Emphatically, no. She wore a skirt whose brevity practically cancelled its existence, a ragged hat through which her hair poked unbeautifully, and a torn khaki shirt of my own. A merciful shroud of dust enveloped her, but even Paddy, watching my glance of amazement and slight revolt, murmured gently, 'Is it herself, indade, or a small little gossoon from the *kaianga* yonder?'

But worse was to follow. I took the crutch and pushed the sheep under, while Paddy and Barbara helped, or hindered, each other in the catching-pen. All went fairly well until it came to Horatio's turn. Being a hardy perennial, he knew the procedure only too well. Balefully he glared about him, then, slipping and sliding on the wet surface, he charged my wife. Paddy ran chivalrously but too hastily to her assistance. There was a collision, a skirmish, a wail – and three figures as one plunged headlong …

As I watched paralysed, the voice of Mrs Warburton-Jones fluted forth just behind me.

'Here I am after all, you see. I came to call upon your neighbour, and she told me that you were all down here. I did so want to meet your wife. How sporting of her to fling herself into all your work like this.'

I was speechless, dumbly pondering that choice of metaphor, and she swept on, 'But where *is* your wife?'

There was a stir in the horrid brown mixture at our feet. Three heads emerged, dripping and beaver-like. But it was Paddy who rose superbly to the occasion.

'Herself?' he remarked, with all the instinctive courtesy of his nation. 'Sure, herself is the second to the left …'

Love Poem to a Farmer

Karalyn Joyce

this rural man
gives me the same consideration as a newborn
kindness as he plants a sapling
he envelops my hand in his
hands that push woolly arses through gates
slashed by the cutting edge of versatility
his feet firmly planted
he knows where he's at

this rural man
hands me wide clean sheets of space
bellowing in the southerly
the only concrete in sight
might be the floor of the implement shed
and the only cars the odd stock truck spilling past
kicking up a tail of dust from the paper road
'Look, can you hear it?' he asks, 'can you hear the silence?'

this rural man
patience flows after him like a line of sheep
he feeds out few words
suits himself but keeps an eye on the weather
and the odd ram that gets a bit stroppy under pressure
packs sixteen hours into twelve
to do what has to be done

this rural man
there is a calmness about him like
the space between day and night
'No use getting worked up,' he says,
'it'll all work itself out in the end.'
There's times when I wrap his great hands around me
And lie against him. Not talking
Just listening to the grass grow.

2001, *New Zealand Listener*

The Hired Man

Brian Turner

He has a valid reason
for doing what he is doing
and the furrows
are straight enough
to pass all but the strictest
standard.
        The work
is not easy, nor overhard;
but work alone
will not satisfy
or thrill him forever.

What's real
is a hot sun, the throb
of the tractor, the choking
wind that fills the air
with dust
sometimes thick as porridge
and covers the earth like burlap.

He has no time
to admire the hills' profiles
or the ache and impeccable
sweep of sky.
        Work is his means
to an end. Should his tractor's
engine stop, work will stop,

and so will he.

1978, *Ladders of Rain*

Of Cooks

Philip Kenway

The Candidate

Say, did your old boss beam, man,
    The sourest guest look pleasant,
Called they a come-true dream, man,
    Your kumara and pheasant?

Can you from nothing fake, man,
    Victuals for half a troop?
And can you really make, man,
    Proper pukeko soup?

And can you cook wild pork, man,
    Well – a la kopa Maori?
And is it common talk, man,
    That all your spuds come floury?

And does the welkin ring, man,
    Yet louder still and louder,
When they your praises, sing, man,
    Anent your oyster chowder?

No? But your chance ain't dead, man.
    You can still come out top.
Oh, *can* you bake good bread, man,
    And, *can* you grill a chop?

In New Zealand where the material for good food is abundant, where there is excellent meat and butter, and a good climate and soil for vegetables, there is, alas, hardly a soul who can cook. Waking at seven in the morning in the country, in a wooden house where everything is audible, you will be aware of a loud sizzling. It is the great panful of

1947, *Quondam Quaker*

excellent mutton chops, frying in plenty of fat. In half an hour the noise ceases, and you know that those chops will have been put in the oven to harden, while the billy is boiled. At eight you breakfast off something that looks and tastes like rather greasy boot soles. Cooking chops is easier that way and as few English know good victuals from bad, I suppose it does not matter much, but if a French housewife offered such food to her men, I shudder to think what would happen.

The general standard of cooking being so low, it is not to be expected that the man who prepares the food on a station or in a camp will be an accomplished chef. He may be an old soldier, he may have been a sailorman, a drunken schoolmaster, a stoker, a tinker or a tailor. He may have been of almost any trade in the wide world, but he will never have been a cook. And as it is a rather thankless, irritating job, this serving everybody at all hours of the day and night, the 'Doctor' as he is called, unless of a naturally imperturbable temper, is apt to become soured and cranky to the last degree.

My good neighbour, Hood, came to the conclusion, from long experience, that all cooks were mad and, when short of one, even applied to an asylum. For, he said, I shall then get to know in what particular way he is likely to break out and shall be able, in that direction at least, to be on my guard.

One howling wet day, when no work could be done, and the shepherds were taking their time over breakfast, the crusty old cook, hot with indignation, shambled up to the owner's whare with a big slice of bread. 'D'yer see anything wrong with this, Mr 'Oood?' Mr 'Oood did not. 'Well, if you'll believe me, sir,' the old man said, gasping with insulted wrath, 'the men are *toasting* it, sir!' …

It's nearly always the bread. A good loaf will cover up a multitude of sins, but the baking of it, in camp, is none too easy. Not only have you, in the first place, to make your own yeast out of potatoes and hops, but the kneaded dough must be kept warm till it rises. In a draughty shack or tent this is not always a simple matter. Then there is the camp-oven, a circular cast-iron affair with three rudimentary legs and convex lid, also of cast-iron. When partly filled with dough, this is stood on a bed of incandescent wood cinders, and more shovelled on top of the lid. The renewal of these cinders above and below in exactly the right amounts, and for the correct time, needs, as I know to my sorrow, a lot of practice. One big loaf I was responsible for in the early days was too solid for even our ravenous appetites and was cast out. It withstood the weather and the attacks of wild animals for months, and was in the end, at least so I was told, carried off by the Maoris to use as a grindstone.

'Killing a Bit of Beef in the Morning'

For the *New Zealand Free Lance*

When the boss announces that 'We'll kill a bit of beef in the morning', back-country hands prepare for what they regard as some fun. Reduced from their former greatness, when 50 men sat down to every meal, most of our sheep stations now possess only the remains of a stockyard and slaughterhouse. When a bullock is killed things often go wrong, as on a recent occasion at which I assisted.

Having left an uneasy bullock, with a couple of quiet old dairy-cows, in the yard overnight, the rouseabout and I were pleasantly surprised to find them still there in the morning. With a wary eye on the bullock, we began trying to drive him into the narrow 'race' where the fell deed was to be done. Alongside an orthodox slaughter-house there is a narrow yard, or race, about three feet wide. When a beast is safely corralled in this the professional butcher stands on top, one foot on each rail, and takes a full swing at the animal's head with a hammer. Stunned, the beast collapses, and is then dragged through a trapdoor to have its throat cut. In the hands of an expert the hammer is a humane and safe instrument, especially if the yard is soundly constructed.

As the station-hand is seldom familiar with the knocking-hammer, he usually prefers to shoot the beast in the head, for which job either rifle or shotgun is satisfactory. Old Puru, the Maori rouseabout, and I had a shotgun, with a couple of cartridges which belonged to the boss, and we hoped to get a shot at that bullock before the boss arrived to make his inevitable suggestions about saving expense by using the hammer.

Every time we edged the bullock into the wide opening of the race, one of the dairy-cows got in front of him and plodded patiently into the killing-pen. Then we had to back her out and start all over again, trying not to excite the bullock to the point where he would charge us. At the critical moment, just as we whipped the rails into place behind the beast, which at last had made a mistake, the boss arrived.

'Good!' said he. 'Nice quiet beast, eh? Now, where's your hammer?'

'We couldn't find it, boss. We'll have to shoot him.'

'Man alive, there it is on the rails over there! No need to waste a cartridge. Just give me that hammer, if you young fellows don't fancy the job.'

Mildly we mentioned the rotten nature of the rails above the killing-pen, which was in imminent danger of collapse as the big bullock wriggled this way and that. But it was no good.

9 August 1944, *New Zealand Free Lance*

'I've killed hundreds of them. "One-hit Seddon", they used to call me in the old days, and I'm as good a man now as I ever was. Just stand well back.'

Up he went. Teetering on the rotten rails, he waited until the bullock's head was in the right position. Then he swung the hammer with all his undoubted strength. The added pressure was too much. As the hammer came down, both rails cracked at once, and the boss landed astride the bullock's back. Though the hammer landed in the right spot, the force had gone from the blow and it did no more than enrage the beast. Up he reared. Crack! went two more rails. With one great plunge the bullock was out in the main yard. With the boss still clinging to him like a rodeo-rider, he put down his head and charged the outer gate. In a shower of broken rails he shot out into the open paddock, while Puru and I, shouting in two languages, made an anxious rearguard.

For 200 yards, while the rodeo lasted, it was worth paying money to see, but then, as his mount gave a vigorous buck, the boss landed on the ground. While the bullock galloped one way the boss galloped another. Old Puru and I, with two other station-hands who, as station-hands do, had materialised suddenly to watch the fun, have not yet been able to decide which of the two was making the better pace.

With a rifle from the station we then stalked our 'bit of beef', finally getting close enough to shoot it in the head. At the cost of much labour we got the beef on to a sledge and dragged it back to the slaughter-house, where the rest of the job continued amid bursts of merriment. In the back-blocks such 'bits of fun' are all too rare.

Yes, to the Very End

'Augustus' (R.A. Copland)

The service-car pulled out of Gisborne just as the sun was pulling in. We were a cold and melancholy lot, packed in rows down the car as in theatre seats without arms. One or two faces, wanner than the rest, had grown familiar to me during innumerable excursions to railway refreshment rooms the day before. The pies, sandwiches and tea from Paekakariki to Wairoa were still compressed and uneasy behind those faces.

The driver looked neat and fresh and efficient. He made me feel old.

The back seat was hilariously occupied by four Maori youths, whose provisions for the journey were some crayfish and a guitar. Soon the emanations of both were floating along the low ceiling. A hundred and fifty miles were certainly no hardship to those lads, and at the finish it was the others who were staring gaunt, glazed and emaciated upon the land of the long white cloud.

We left the flat country pretty soon and the driver began the long wrestle with the gear-lever which, from then on, was seldom out of his hand. All the way he maintained the utmost speed which the weight of his cargo and the precipitousness of the terrain would allow him. He swept round curves, plunged down chasms, hurtled over one-way bridges and surged up slopes with uniform indifference, and only the sweat of the engine whose fumes drifted back and mingled with the crayfish and the *Ferry-boat Serenade* betrayed the ardours of our progress.

The road was monotonously hair-raising. Its builders had shown a perverse predilection for the cliff-and-abyss style, declining always to saunter along the bottom of valleys, and blasting a track into the near-vertical sides of the grimmest mountains they could find.

Nature had done her best to soften the prospect, and the menace of gravity was everywhere glossed over with glistening dark-green bush. One felt that when the bus did plunge over the edge at the next bend the descent would be noiseless and comfortable into the torrent hundreds of feet below.

The road was just wide enough for our bus, and every now and then we would roar past a sheep truck coming in the opposite direction. The driver would wave an airy hand.

Once a red and yellow notice board edged into the roadway and had the effrontery

---

1950, *New Zealand Listener*

to suggest that as a slip had occurred on the road ahead, a certain amount of caution might be exercised. The bus sneered past the notice, no paint apparently being removed from either. The slip had gnawed a semi-circle back into the road, but the bus had sufficient speed to clear it. From my window I glanced down for a second into eternity.

Then an old hand behind the driver noticed a bush away on the other side of the world which was all ablaze with scarlet. 'What's that Mac?' he asked the driver, and everyone looked sadly in the direction of his pointing arm, expecting a volcano or a dinosaur. The driver left off driving and studied the flaring patch. The bus changed its gears and swirled round a bend.

'Hanged if I know, George,' the driver admitted at last.

'Would it be rata?' the lady near me ventured to the paralysed passengers. We all took up the cue. The psychologists call it sublimation, I think. The pressure of terror becomes so great that you feign an interest in the trivial. We all became wildly speculative about the scarlet bush, and I rummaged through the remains of Nature Study, thankful that no one knew I was the new Rector of Wairenga-o-roaroa.

When we came to a Public Works camp the driver actually stopped the bus. A vast weight of accumulated speed piled up and oppressed us in the sudden and silent no-motion. Outside the camp a Maori stood with his hands in his pockets. He was big enough and preposterous enough to have built the road himself. He might have had a hand in landing Maui's fish. Just to look at him made the tale a shade less fabulous.

The driver asked him about the coloured bush. He suggested rata, and we all smiled knowingly and shook our heads at him. He wasn't in the least abashed. He thrust his trousers forward from the pockets, shrugged his shoulders and beamed at us.

'Aw, the hell,' he roared, 'how would I know – I don't belong to this country.'

Pretty obviously the country belonged to him. He could have pushed the bus off the road if he'd taken his hands out of his pockets. So we started off again. Every now and then the driver would wind his window down slowly. Then he would grope under his seat, produce a newspaper, roll it tightly up with both hands, bend it, and having apparently completed these preliminaries at exactly the right spot on the road, he would hurl the paper over the roof of the bus.

I watched for the paper to descend on my side. It would plop into the grass by the roadside. There it lay, a white speck, brand new, tiny and isolated. For miles and miles on every side the land was twisted and heaved into ranges and hills, valleys and gullies, a gigantic rubble heap which centuries had flimsily covered with grass and bush. There was not a sign of human habitation anywhere. I tried to believe that somewhere, tucked into a hillside there was a house. Someone in the house would come to find that paper every day, and so keep up a kinship with us in the bus, and with Mr Truman and with Princess Elizabeth.

At one stage the bus slowed down and stopped. Only the driver and one passenger knew why. There was nothing on the road, no sign-board, no gate, no mail-box – just a place on the road and a place on the map distinguished no more than that it had a latitude and longitude.

A large woman scrambled out on to the shingle. The driver produced a suitcase from somewhere that clanged at the back, and handed it to the woman. She sat down on the bag, solid, capable and expressionless. Someone would be coming to meet her, knowing exactly where to find her. Perhaps she had been staying for a fortnight with her married sister in town, making beds, washing dishes, peeling potatoes – she would be home in time for the milking if they remembered to call for her; if they found her all right.

I looked at the immense earth and the unbroken sky, at a frail fence groping away down the slope, charred and broken tree-stumps puncturing the cleared ground. And I looked at the woman sitting there placid and strong. She'd be called for, I decided. In any case, she'd get home.

The township when we arrived looked somehow gauche and innocent. We pressed into it, bringing as it were the bridled impetus of a hundred and fifty miles. We brought dust and heat and experience compacted into a solid wedge of steel, rubber, glass and human enterprise. We deferred to the township by courtesy. We were too far gone for the township to have stopped us. The people in the streets were too young.

As I was leaving the bare and petrol-reeking barn of a garage I said, 'So long' to the driver. 'Well, that was an experience,' I said, trying to pretend those giddy feet were my own.

'That the first time you've travelled by service-car?' he asked.

'Oh, no, not really. I used to go by bus quite a lot between Timaru and Christchurch.'

He smiled politely like the big-game hunter whose host was telling about the time the canary got out.

Getting to Know You

Joan MacIntosh

When I was getting to know the country ways, the main general store in the Tokanui township was usually staffed with a manager, two shop assistants and an office girl whose job it was to answer the telephone and attend to all book keeping duties. It was to this nucleus of the business side of the country store that I came in 1944; it was here with the grocery orders, bread orders, delivery van and customers that I grew to know something about country people. It was a rewarding experience.

So very different this, from my office work with a city footwear firm where I had dealt with the code numbers of slippers, gumboots and fashion shoes for stock returns, and handled a cash receipt balance which always trebled the entry accounts. In the country store, the bookwork was mainly credit accounts as only a few of the township householders worked on a weekly wage. While the majority of accounts were paid monthly by cheque, many of the big farm holders settled their accounts annually.

As I worked at the high wooden desk extending almost the entire wall of the office, a farmer, dressed unfamiliarly in his good suit, would call and ask, 'Can you make up a figure, Joan?'

Though I'd faithfully sent him a detailed statement every month with the mounting account rendered total, I would lift the big ledger from the safe and copy out monthly totals for a period often from eight to fourteen months. After checking the grand total, which indeed did look grand even in those days, I'd hand over the pen. A flourished signature across the page brought in the mail a few days later, the cheque from the stock and station firm clearing the backlog of figures from my ledger.

I was often tempted to think that most farmers had only learnt to write their signature, so often was I handed the store account and the cheque book and asked 'to fix it'. This free and easy trust was so different from the almost suspicious attitude to cheques handed in to the city firm.

When I'd filled in the butt end of the cheque form, I trailed the owner about the store to get the necessary signature filled in. Once a nearby storekeeper forgot who'd collected a bag of sugar a day or so beforehand. He decided to charge it to everyone he could recall as having been in the store that day, expecting to find the recipient this way. Only four out of the twenty charged, enquired about the sugar entered on their account!

Over a period of time I learnt to know all the ledger names almost intimately, to

1974, *Never a Dull Moment*

know the ones who ordered regularly, the careful family orders, the bachelor orders, the sawmill orders, the fishing port orders, farm orders, the ones who paid unquestioningly, those who paid immediately, the ones who had to wait for the cheese factory cheque to settle accounts, and those who paid so much a month and let the balance pile up till it became impossible to meet the figure. So many of these became Bad Debts columns at the back of the ledger, though even there they held surprises, and several were able to be written up as paid in full.

So many items entered on dockets had halfpennies in the figure and it was quite a feat to carry these across to a column total, then add correctly to a full total. One customer reprimanded me for an error of one halfpenny in addition, making me so nervous of his account, the figures used to blur as I checked and re-checked.

Sometimes it wasn't hard cash that settled a farm account – sacks of wheat and oats, potatoes, rolls of bacon and fresh eggs received on delivery day in the van often left a credit to carry forward.

It was a most difficult time for the customers and the country storekeepers when war-time rationing was in full swing and many long standing customs had to be dispensed with. I bore the brunt of some of these. When an account was paid the receipt was accompanied with a bag of sweets or a couple of packets of cigarettes, whichever best suited the payee. How well I recall how my brothers and I would hang about our mother when we knew she'd been to pay the store bill … that free bag of lollies was a real treat.

But during the war, with tobacco being in short and irregular supply to retailers, and tins of sweets no longer coming with the biscuit order as discount, the shortages were passed on to the customer. So many did not understand, and often when an account was paid and pleasantries at a standstill, the farmer still waited hopefully for his perk. Many a time I saw the store manager furtively hand out a packet of cigarettes from his own rations or reach for a block of chocolate to save my growing embarrassment …

As office girl I also had a store job of making up the orders. The van from Invercargill brought the warm fresh bread out twice a week and this was taken further to the outlying districts by the store delivery van. Wrapping paper had also been in short supply, so customers provided bread bags. These varied from flour bags with pencilled names and sugar bags with labels, to beautifully embroidered starched linen bags. Most people sent in a bundle and as they were received, rolled them up, and sent them back with the van. On the bread list card were also weekly orders for fresh compressed yeast and I weighed this out from pound blocks of yeast. One housewife made home-made bread twice a week for a family of eight.

Being rather a townie still, I often made blunders in taking orders, much to the amusement of the rest of the staff. Answering the telephone one day, I was asked, 'Have you got any grapes?'

'Oh! I am sorry. We don't have them.'

'Well, can you get me one? I want a good strong handle on it.'

'I think you'd best ring a fruit shop in town,' I suggested.

'I'll wring your blasted neck if I get any more lip like that from you, young lady!' came the irate reply.

I didn't know that a pronged digging fork had a cousin called a grape.

Then I took a very important order for two hundred well-seasoned post holes to be delivered by rail to the Tokanui siding. I solemnly took down every detail given on the 'phone and handed the slip to my boss!

Being a general country store there seemed to be everything sold from sack needles, baby goods, bulk goods and horse covers, to packets of Sykes drench for cows. During the shortages occasioned by the war years, much stock that had been collecting dust in the bulk store, was gone through and met a ready demand. Wallpaper stacked in the rafters was eagerly sought after and rolls of elastic vanished by the yard over night it seemed.

When I worked in the store office we had Wednesday half holiday and worked Saturday till late night. In the city I'd worked a Friday late night and the Saturday morning when the shops closed to re-open Monday. While Saturday in the country was *the* day for shopping, it was overshadowed by the Mondays when the stock sales were held. Into the township came trucks, cars, horses, drays and a few gigs, and the shop assistants were usually rushed off their feet with bulk orders and casual buying, while I used page after page in the receipt book, and on colder days stoked the open fire in the office and made endless cups of tea.

Saledays often brought added diversions, such as the time a local wag dropped oil of aniseed, a most attractive scent to animals, on the cuff of the storekeeper's trousers. Every time he went out to pump petrol, the hordes of dogs sniffed at his legs till he fled inside from the jibes of those in the know.

In more serious vein were the hermit tramps who lived and worked 'just sort of somewhere' and hitched a ride in to the township for stores and tobacco. With sugar bag knapsacks slung up with knotted twine, they preferred the slide door entrance out the bulk store part and would amble about the stock shelves stacking the pack with tins. My job was to go and secure the door if I saw them come in and usher them out through the shop where the 'self help' goods were duly charged, though once the culprit kept on walking and went straight on out the shop entrance and was nowhere in sight when I reported this audacity to the manager

Few of the residents in outlying areas had a telephone so the twice weekly call by the store delivery van was the lifeline to the township. Besides the orders collected, were messages for the Post Office or Garage and I would attend to most of these. Forms for new ration books, Postal Notes to be placed with accounts and posted, stamps to be purchased, the note for the carrier … all helped me to learn of the little problems of outback country living. The little sadness of the housewife who wrote beside the pair of silk stockings ordered on her grocery list, 'Please charge these as a bag of flour.'

Quite often an item on a grocery list would read, 'Please send one pound worth of silver change.' In most cases it was parcelled up and sent, and charged to the monthly account. Later, when I had four school children looking for banking money for school savings books and small monetary items, I longed for the return of this handy service from the general store.

The Snow Down South

'Nor'wester' (Roland Clarke)

At least two good things came out of the big snow. I can now bore the next generation with my story, as I have been bored with stories of the great snow of '45. And, better yet, the TV aerial has gone bung …

We took some overseas visitors to their plane on Sunday, August 7, and went on to dinner with my cousin in Christchurch. We had taken our visitors to our favourite ski-field and up to Mount Cook, when the weather had been perfect.

'Is it always as good as this?' they asked me.

'Too right,' I said.

Over a brandy we heard that there was four inches of snow at Methven. I put a call through to Max and decided not to try coming home. Just as well, my neighbour, Les Roberts, spent a night in his car on the Mayfield Bridge.

Next day was a shocker with a howling southerly and the poor devils down country were in the middle of lambing. The number of slinky skins from dead lambs went up from 700 to 20,000. They didn't have a chance.

The snow started 12 miles down country and we quite obviously couldn't get home, so followed a grader as far as Mount Somers at an average of two miles an hour. But even the grader couldn't clear the way home, and we spent the night with Jim and Betty Kerr.

It was a wet snow and all lines were down. Wooden poles were snapped right off and metal ones were curtseying with their heads in the snow. Even fences were smashed, including my brand new Flexi-fence that I built right on route 12, to give the neighbours something to criticize. We set off the next morning, me driving a tractor and the wife holding on hard in the lambing tray. We only just made it and met Max and Tom Withers [next-door neighbour] at the gate.

'How are the sheep?' I asked.

'Haven't been near them,' was the reply.

I nearly hit the roof, reckoning that I'd have been buzzing round in the blizzard all the previous day, which would have been the worst possible thing to do. Tom and Max had discussed the problem and, quite rightly, done nothing. As a result all my sheep were mobbed up giving shelter to each other and we were able to get hay to them all that day. Not that it was all that easy. A single tractor hadn't a chance and we hitched

13 September 1973, *New Zealand Farmer*

two together, using a wire rope with a truck tyre to ease the jerks. We had a good 26 inches of snow here, which was just within the capabilities of the two tractors. In fact, in one place we had to snow rake a path for them. A couple of miles away there wasn't a fence post to be seen.

There were plenty of stories of dreadful losses flying around at this stage, mainly in pre-lamb shorn sheep. Alas, many of them were true. Some poor fellows lost upwards of a quarter of their ewes. The height of misfortune was the farmer who, very properly, shedded up his ewes, only to have his shed collapse on top of them, killing them all. Or the joker who came to find his garage collapsed and then sacrificed his car to free his tractor. Half a mile down the road the axle broke.

It looked very bad, and we were talking in terms of losing 500 ewes. Now, there are two ways of looking at this: as a disaster, which helps no one, or in optimistic terms, and I really prefer the latter. The important point was not the prospective loss, but the incredible fact that I would still have 3900 sheep. Maybe I had been cheeky running just on eight sheep an acre, but I would still have seven an acre and I'd darned soon be up to eight again.

Once Tom and I had started thinking like this we were away like a box of birds. Mind you, I couldn't always understand him, he's a master of basic Anglo Saxon. The first four days were plain hard work. We treated the two farms as one unit and it took our team of three just to get the hay out – two tractor drivers and Max chucking out the hay. We really began to win on the Saturday. I rang consultant John to thank him for bringing up Ketol [for sleepy sickness in ewes] and milk.

'Do you know where I can get a bulk grain feeder?' I asked.

'Are the roads clear yet?' he replied.

Two hours later, after a drive of 70 miles, he arrived with Don Armstrong's beautiful big grain feeding trailer. Straight away we got into organizing a system of getting the barley out of the silo without an augur, as it needed an electric motor. John was ably assisted by my stockbroker, and the Exchange would have been proud of the result; jacked up from a derelict hen house, No.8 wire and the cocky's friend, bindertwine.

Now I would have been one of Napoleon's marshals in an earlier age – he always picked lucky men. This is the first year I've used grain and all my stock were accustomed to it and were delighted to see it on the snow. I fair poured it into them; expense was no object. And to confirm my status as Canterbury's luckiest man, I had an unused silo of grain, 1000 lovely bushels, and I'll need most of it. The most efficient way to feed grain is on snow. The ewes stand in the wheel tracks like well-bred young ladies and eat the grain off the tablecloth of virgin snow. They forage for every last speckle and, of course, the grains are very easy to see against the snow.

We were short of hay, owing to the dry season, and got in touch with the disaster committee at Methven. They got me some beautiful lucerne – like giving an old man beef after a diet of gummy old rams. I only hope it won't spoil them for my meadow hay next year. We had the most fantastic help from all sorts of people. Federated Farmers' set up an operations centre in Methven, in Pyne's store. They directed the Army and the hordes of volunteers, like the Shearers' Union and the Ashburton Jaycees. Our local stock agents were flat out getting their stock mustered and sent down country. The Greenstreet WDFF sent up hot meals and John Leitch carried a pump round the district to fill people's water tanks. Ritchie Muirhead appeared one day with a trailer and took away a load of dopey ewes. David Bradley came up and helped us drench those with sleepy sickness.

I'm telling this as my story, but it's typical of the wonderful help we all got. And what a wonderful job our wives did. I had three hot meals a day cooked in homemade billies on the open wood fire. Three courses at night, I may say.

We were lucky with losses, under 50. Tom did better. He lost about thirty sheep, and two stone!

A Rural Experience of the Napier Earthquake

E.J.V. Barry, as told to his daughter, Jane Foster

The day came sultry and sweltering like those before. But it didn't look like rain, which mattered most with hay due for raking as soon as the dew dried.

Morning chores came first. Eighteen-year old George, a farm cadet, milked the house cows and fed the dogs and hens while I brought in the day's supply of wood. In 1931 there was no power in that district 40 miles north of Napier, and the range had to be lit, however hot the weather. It was a good range, which I had installed myself when I built the house. My experience as a builder was useful when I took up back-block sheep and cattle land after the First World War.

It would not, I decided, be a heavy day. Later in the week we would all be hard at it with horses, hayforks and wagons, and fervently wishing it done. The lad was soon operating the hayrake and I was lining things up for the harvesting. The older children had not gone to school. Tomorrow would be time enough for the six-mile journey by buggy.

I was in the house when the first rumblings came. The building rocked crazily; it seemed to bounce on its foundations and china crashed. Through the window I caught a glimpse of hills rearing upwards and yelled 'OUTSIDE!'; the children scuttled. I helped Nell, with the baby in her arms, down the swaying steps. As she joined the three little girls, crouched in the middle of the lawn, she gasped, 'The boys! The sandpit, I think …'

Sure enough, there they were. I scooped up a bucket of pumice sand as a nasty thought struck me and rushed inside again. The firebox was agape and burning wood lay on the floor amid the litter of broken glass and papers from the mantelpiece. The sand smothered it successfully and I added water for good measure.

When we were all together on the lawn it stopped for a minute and started again. 'Yes, a quake …' I remembered George, and looked over the fence to see him perched on the hayrake behind two bolting horses. They galloped the length of the paddock before he could bring them to a snorting, lathered halt.

'They bolted,' he said, 'I don't know why.' Then his pale face went a dull grey as he realized it was the earth itself moving.

'An earthquake,' I said again. We managed to unharness the frightened animals and sat down. Beyond the hay paddock the two house cows could be seen running wildly,

1981, *New Zealand Farmer*

tossing their heads. The nightmare shaking stopped but we all stayed silent, recovering. Nell roused first, hoping there was some food fit to eat. I retrieved the baby's bottle, unbroken and nearly full, from his cot.

The kitchen and pantry were a shambles and the storeroom even worse. As on all back-block farms of the time, perishables were home-produced, and there was no electricity, radio or telephone. Our stores came in three-monthly and the contents of the open shelves had been flung to the floor. Tea, sugar, flour, oatmeal, rice, golden syrup and all the rest were hopelessly mixed. A four-gallon tin of kerosene (for lamps) had burst open and literally sprayed everything. So had the big safe door where milk had been setting cream in wide, shallow pans. They were upturned on the floor, but meat still hung on hooks. A big tin of preserved eggs and jars of fruit and jam added to the jagged chaos.

We eventually rescued enough for a day or two. Shocks of varying severity kept occurring but none as bad as the first two. We established the family in George's tent, while he and I made beds in an old haystack nearby. The tent had a wooden floor and half-walls so was safe and reasonably comfortable. No one fancied the house, though no structural damage was apparent. The woolshed too seemed unharmed, except that the heavy sliding door had been wrenched off its runners and lay some chains away. There was cracking in the earth but none where it endangered the buildings.

I set up a campfire near the tent and Nell resurrected an old camp oven. Made of heavy iron, wide, shallow and circular, it was fitted with a handle like a billy, a lid, and three short legs so that it could be set over a low fire, or covered with hot embers and earth, hangi-style. I then climbed the high hill behind the house and was relieved to find that the other three houses in the settlement seemed all right. Two of the families were away and I could pick out all members of the third through binoculars.

After consideration, three days after the main quake, it seemed more dry stores were the top priority. Tremors were now slight and less frequent, and about mid-afternoon, I set out on horseback for the nearest store eight miles away. I took an adze just in case, though I did not expect trouble en route, except possibly going round the bluff. There was a slip covering the road for about a quarter of a mile, but it wasn't difficult to clear a track. I led the mare across. She was a fine animal; trained for the Mounted Rifles, but the Armistice reprieved her. We were firm friends, Belle and I. At high places along the road I could see a pall of dust or smoke away to the south, Napier-wards, which worried me. Nell had her two sisters there and lack of news was a nagging unease. The hotelkeeper-cum-storekeeper met me as I dismounted.

'All well out your way, Ben?'

'Yes, and here?'

'No one hurt, thank God, but the lines are dead and there isn't a safe chimney in the place. You're just the man we need.'

Over a beer I learnt why. The hotel occupants would continue meal-less unless I could do something with the kitchen chimney, now a pile of bricks. I got in some digs about my iron chimney at the farm and set to work, using, among other things, the top of an iron tank. A usable flue was finished before dark and I shared the dinner everyone had been so anxious about.

With the track round the slip in mind, I delayed departure (complete with stuffed saddlebags) until moonrise. Luckily it was a clear night, but the track looked narrow and uncertain in the pale light. I was acutely conscious of the yawning blackness below, and the surface seemed less firm. I told myself it was nerves, until Belle behind me became restive, but there was nothing to do but go on. To borrow the airman's eerie term, we were past the point of no return.

Then it came! Almost without warning the slope convulsed beneath us, and the world became a terrifying, topsy-turvy confusion of noise, dust and instability. Somehow I held on to the reins and we staggered desperately on, climbing, always climbing, as the earth crumbled away beneath. Boulders screeched past, adding to the dreadful roar, and to my panic. (Weeks later I saw them at the bottom of the ravine, and the trees they had stripped of bark in passing. Still I wonder how we got through. Some boulders were immense chunks of solid rock weighing all of 40 tons, while any of the smaller ones could have settled me without pausing in their headlong plunge downwards.)

My limbs must have kept on working after consciousness had gone, because I woke to quietness, lying face down on the road. I became aware of drops of water falling on my neck and the legs, just in front of my face. Belle was standing over me, sweat rolling off her belly, quite still except for her violent trembling. I lifted my head. Moonlight shone coldly on to the familiar road home. The scene was sharply black and white, and somehow unreal in its ghastly serenity. Clouds drifted gently across the starlit sky, but back the way we had come, so frighteningly close, was a sheer cliff face where the track had been, and before the track a 12-foot road. I sat up and shuddered. It was some time before we could complete the journey, short and safe though it was.

Three days later a returning neighbour paused briefly at the gate with the message: 'Napier's demolished'.

Pastimes and Occasions

In its initial stages an anthology can be a lot of fun, partly because the anthologist is eagerly anticipating the sort of material that's certain to be found within specific subjects. Accordingly, for 'Pastimes and Occasions', I looked forward to poetry and prose that celebrated the tradition of Agricultural and Pastoral Society shows. Based on my experiences in country rugby teams and those of friends who played netball or hockey on courts or fields adjacent to sparsely marked and intermittently dunged paddocks, I anticipated many stories of rural team sports. I also expected to find vivid descriptions of district sports meetings, gymkhanas and many other events that are or were an integral part of a district's year, including unregistered race meetings held far from town. The latter were very much local affairs and usually for horses from that area. I did come across one fragment describing a meeting in Northland, where a younger man of the district decided to hire a jockey to ride his horse in a steeplechase event. Sadly, the rider fell at the first fence but the owner had the good fortune to be nearby and, having ridden the horse to victory in the past, he off with his jacket, and rode it into second place.

But for many of the events and pursuits, I either looked in the wrong places or the material I found wasn't suitable for this collection. A & P Show societies, for example, are very good at commissioning histories of themselves. Alas, commemorating a major milestone by means of a chronological procession of facts is not very rewarding for readers from other districts, and fails to celebrate the rich store of incident and humour that surely lies beneath the surface of a century of annual shows.

Never mind, there's plenty to be going on with: a district picnic, calf club day, barn dances, two very different cricket matches, the arrival of 'the mill' and the opening of a new hall. The Women's Division gets coverage, as do the younger set in 'The Young Farmers' Club Experiences a Blackout'. The latter is from Fiona Farrell's prize-winning novel, *The Skinny Louie Book*, and, not surprisingly, this piece and the segments immediately preceding it have been in just about every New Zealand anthology that has appeared since the book's publication in 1992. For that reason I felt I shouldn't include it but found it impossible to leave out. You see, I can't remember whether it was the Kennington Hall or the Myross Bush Hall that the lights went out in. Although it could have been Thorn … no, it can't have been Thornbury because Paddy Keown the Riverton constable wouldn't let couples disappear into the car park during a dance. It might have been the Irwell Hall or perhaps that woolshed near Ngahinapouri … Wherever it was, I know I was there.

Of all the rural activities that have had regular coverage in written form, sheep dog trialling is probably the best, served by writers such as Peter Newton, Ian Sinclair and, I suppose, myself, in both books and the *New Zealand Farmer*. Much of the material penned has been of a human and entertaining nature, and that's very much the criterion I've used for selection, so that result lists, match reports or ghost-written 'autobiographies' miss out. So, when it comes to all my years as a country footballer there's little to stimulate my memory, though there are some things you never forget, such as the challenges that went with my membership of one rugby club in Southland.

This was rural rugby in the raw. There was just one team, which competed in the junior or second grade. Other than a set of jerseys and plenty of enthusiasm, we had no facilities: no changing rooms – we stripped in and around the cars – or showers; we took home varying amounts of the paddock we played and practised on. The field was a southerly slope or slow hill, with sufficient gradient to ensure that, despite the prevailing winds, south or sou'-west, if we won the toss we always played downhill in the second half. After the game the visiting team would be treated to Tiger Tea, Kennington cheddar and salty Snax biscuits in the local hall, with the food sparingly arrayed on newsprint-bedecked trestles. Around them in awkward stance were grubby and often bruised young men, aged from 16 to 24, waiting for the haltingly delivered speeches to finish so they could get down the road and on to their preferred lubricant, Speights.

Weeknight training is a special memory. We didn't have any lights. To avoid practising Blind Man's Bluff, a rough roster was worked out so that at least two vehicles were parked on either side of the paddock to provide some sort of manageable glimmer; the white rugby ball was at least two decades away. There was, of course, one major drawback to driving a 'floodlight': the battery could become as flat as a city club's playing field. But that was all right – when there wasn't sufficient charge to restart the engine, there were plenty of forwards about to push it. Unfortunately they always insisted on applying the necessary shove in a downhill direction. 'We've enough bloody scrum practice for one night, thank you,' they grumbled. Downhill they pushed and, as a rule, the vehicle would choke and smoke itself into life before it hit the eight-wire fence at the bottom. The next challenge was a U-turn, then a run up the touchline – well clear of the playing 'surface' – to exit through the 12-foot gap in the roadside gorse at the top. It's a sad fact of Southern life that winters can be soggy affairs and rare was the car that made it to the road without requiring further human aid – in other words, being pushed the whole damn way. At some stage the forwards would go on strike until we, the backs, put our 'bloody backs into the job!' We did.

Our luxury-free club ensured that we really enjoyed our rugby and became a fit and versatile bunch. Versatility was often a necessity as, with limited player resources – a Friday night ball or 21st birthday could decimate the playing strength – we backs could find ourselves packing down on Saturdays too. Fortunately, we knew how to shove.

The Wrath of God

Tommy Cowan and Valerie Cowan

Picnics were one form of real enjoyment. On a nice Sunday everyone in the district would hitch up their gigs and buggies and head off somewhere for a picnic. One of the favourite spots was Kapara, especially when the raspberries that grew along the riverbank were ripe. Everybody would enjoy picking all the berries and then tuck into a big picnic lunch. Next day the ladies were not to be seen, they were all busy making up the jam. Another good picnic spot was up the Makakaho Valley, as far as the junction, and sometimes we would head for a really beautiful place at Lake Rotokahu, but that was not so accessible and was for horse riders only.

One New Year's Day it was decided to have a gathering on a local farmer's property down by the river. Nearly everybody in the district turned up and were busy getting the food laid out, when the owner of the property came and said that he had a batch of ginger beer made up. As it was a new recipe, he wanted some of them to come and sample it. Some of the men went over to the house and started sampling, and it didn't seem that long before they were all talking flat out and skipping about having the time of their lives. Gradually the others went over to see what all the hilarity was about, and before too long there was a large and happy group of revellers.

We youngsters couldn't understand why we weren't allowed to sample the new ginger beer recipe, but we were given lemonade so were quite happy. I can still remember the astonishment that we young ones felt at the sight of 'Old Unc', the leader of our camping and pig hunting trips – whom we all looked upon as a paragon of good behaviour – frisking around and singing some ribald song from his army days in France. Then one of the men tried to jump a ditch and fell in. This was all very puzzling indeed.

After some time the ladies sent word over that the picnic lunch was ready and as the ginger beer supply had run out, the men made their way back. The lunch was laid out in baskets and on trays and everyone sat around tucking in. It was very hot and nearly all of the men who had sampled the ginger beer started to doze off. All of a sudden there was roll of thunder and then, with no further warning, it began to hail. What a terrific hailstorm it was, and in no time everything and everyone was covered in a blanket of hail. It lasted for half an hour or so. When it eventually stopped, a bedraggled bunch of picnickers started to hitch their horses up and head for home, after a somewhat disastrous New Year's Day picnic.

1997, *Pigs and Me*

The real disaster, however, came a few days later when the awful truth became known; the 'ginger beer' had come from the Waitotara Hotel. The labels had been washed off and it had been passed off as homemade ginger beer. A pall of gloom settled over the district for some time after this event, and some of the older people were quite sure that the hailstorm was sent as a judgment on us all.

The Honey Tree

M.H. Linscott

Father was buckling the saddle on old Monty the horse, but his mind didn't seem to be on the job at all. He kept gazing up into the sky as if he were looking for an aeroplane, only there were no aeroplanes in those far off days; what he was looking for were honey bees. Presently he called, 'Em, Em, where are you? Ah, there you are. I want you and the others to come here for a minute.'

With a few yells and 'Hey boys, come quickly', I managed to get my eldest brother, known as Sol – short for Solomon – my youngest brother Mike and small sister Daisy, to leave their various pursuits and come hear what Pa wanted to talk about. When we were called up like this it usually meant that somebody had been into mischief, an inquiry held and punishment dealt out. Very justly, according to our parents, but quite unnecessary by our way of thinking. This time it was different.

Father said it was time we had more honey and it was his intention to look for a honey tree in the bush. There are usually big old trees whose branches have been broken off by the wind, leaving big scars or holes in the trunk. These get full of water and rot, till they are quite deep. They dry out in time and make nice cavities for the bees to use as hives, and once they make a honeycomb it always attracts other bees. Even if a hive dies out, completely new swarms of bees will find the place and set up new hives, so it goes on indefinitely; once a honey tree, always a honey tree.

Father wanted us to be what he called 'spotters', to watch the bees to see which way they flew laden with honey or, should I say, pollen. When a bee is looking for pollen he flies low, going from flower to flower, till he has all the little pollen bags on his legs full to bursting point. He has a little rest, then flies off like a helicopter: up into the air and straight for home. If you think it is easy to spot which bees are homeward bound and which bees are only out for an airing, you are wrong, it's very difficult. We followed one bee found from place to place or, in our case, from clover to clover, and he took so long to fill his bags he finally got tired and went to sleep! So we got little stalks of grass and gave him a flick to wake him up and, at this, he took off so quickly that it was impossible to sort him out from the other high-flying insects. When we told this to Pa he laughed and told us to lie flat on our backs, on the shady side of a tree, look into the sky and watch the general direction of the traffic up there.

Did you know that on a hot summer's day there is a big traffic problem up there in

1975, *The Honey Tree*

mid-air, about level with the chimney tops or a little higher? Simply millions of insects are flying back and forth at a great rate. No signals, no nothing! Just, 'Whoops brother, sorry' and on they go. We watched the sky until our eyes refused to work any more.

It was hopeless, till Sol got an idea. He was good at bright ideas. That was why we gave him the name of Solomon. 'About these bees,' said he, 'we must all say the same, as Pa is bound to ask us all separately, so we will all say that they were flying towards the bush on our farm.' He went on to explain that if we said they were flying to the bush, Pa would say, 'What a pity, I don't think I can spare the time to go so far, not just now anyhow.'

When the time came, we all said what Sol had advised us to and were a bit surprised when Pa said, 'Good, you are beginning to learn, they're bound to be in our bush, and not very far away.' After a short consultation with mother, he said that the 'bee hunt' would take place tomorrow.

Father was the big hero of this dangerous expedition, and like all wise leaders, he made lots of preparations. First, he got a hat with a wide brim and without any holes in it. He then draped a large piece of net over this to keep the bees from his eyes and ears. Mother tied pieces of string round his shirt sleeves, just above the wrists, to keep the bees from crawling up his arms. His trouser legs were done in the same manner – Pa took no chances with those bees.

While all this was going on, Joe, the boy who helped around the farm, could be seen coming over the hill at a great pace. We scanned his face so eagerly that we read the good news before we he actually said a word. Sure enough, he had found a likely looking tree. He said it was very high and full of holes halfway up. He thought it might have a hive up there in one of the holes. Pa would have felt better if he had not mentioned more than one hole. He had his own methods of getting the honey away from the bees, and one hive at a time was about all he could handle.

We gathered up all the gear, which included a tin full of rolled up oiled paper that had been sprinkled with sulphur. This was the anaesthetic that put the bees to sleep – some of them permanently – while the honeycomb was removed from the hive.

Father led the way with Joe and Sol. They carried the axe and saw and all the important things. Mother, who was small, cheerful and optimistic, carried two milk buckets to carry the honey. I carried the lunch, while Mike took the tea billy. Little Daisy ran alongside Mum carrying her doll. No one expected her to carry anything else, do she ran up and down the line telling us all to hurry, because she wanted honey for her tea.

'Honey,' quoted Father, 'just a little honey for her royal slice of bread.'

Joe led us to the tree, and Father studied it from all angles, and we studied him – we could almost read his thoughts. Surprised at seeing such a big tree, then concerned at all the holes, though bees were coming out of one of them, he said, 'I think it can be done, hand me that rope.'

Luckily there were plenty of other large, branchy trees growing close to the honey tree, and he was able to climb one of these. With Joe's help and our prayers, he succeeded in getting the rope round the tree just near the hive, and what a job it was. He got up there with all the necessary gear, and after much anxiety on our part and no little swearing on his, the bees got the first whiff of the smoky anaesthetic. That was their first dose, they received the next one when the tree was on the ground.

It took quite a while to fell the tree and administer the second dose. While this was going on Mother took us to a safe place and boiled the billy for lunch. At last we heard the crash of the falling tree and in a few minutes Father and Joe arrived looking very pleased with themselves. After lunch we went back to the tree and Pa put the hat and gloves on and summoned up enough courage to put his hand into the now almost silent hive, and start pulling out the honeycomb. What a joy it was too! Large pieces of comb, all golden and dripping with honey. We were glad Mum brought the buckets, as they were both filled with lovely bush honey, slightly darker than clover honey. 'The real McCoy,' Father used to say.

We walked home and Mother put the honeycomb in milk basins to drain and we ate all we could hold, not even waiting for the bread. I was so concerned, lest I should accidentally get a bee in my mouth, I did not see the one that was crawling over my chair. Well, not until he stung me on the knee. Mother had to remove him, and I cried a bit, but the pain helped to ease my conscience about what we had done to the poor bees. I asked Sol how he felt about it, and he said, 'Have another spoonful of honey, Em, and forget it.'

Father must have felt a bit mean too, because of the fallen tree, as next morning he said 'I must go to the sawmill and get some timber to make a nice long ladder, so I can reach the hives without felling the whole tree.'

He was as good as his word, and the next honey tree we found was invaded by our family quite a few times. It remained standing and the bees recovered, to come back as lively as ever.

'Hey! The Mill's Coming!'

Peter Dunbar

The boys of the district followed the progress of the threshing mill from farm to farm for several weeks before their own place was blessed. On a clear day the trail of smoke into the early autumn sky showed for miles. (From the downs behind Lyndon 'a smoke' often could be seen at Culverden, twenty miles away.) Then, nearer home, the toy machines could be seen on a distant paddock, tucked in beside a group of shapely stacks which diminished one by one as the mill moaned on the wind, a new mass of yellow straw growing nearby.

As we rode to school our horses ran with ears pricked at the new sound and smell on the breeze across the paddocks. Occasionally when youthful riders met the noisy red-and-black monsters on the road, a diversion up a side road was sensible. Many a cheerful engine-driver, however, would bring his gargantuan caravan to a dead stop to let a snorting horse and a gigful of grinning country kids go safely by.

A mill in the district was big news at school, and at home fathers were pestered constantly about the date when threshing would begin. What bliss when the mill chuffed, clanked and creaked through the gateway to become one's very own. For sheer joy the day the mill came was even better than Show Day, or the day of a sub-union rep. match. Oh pray it would be a Saturday, or at least late in the afternoon after school …

The road by the gate was slightly downhill, so that when the chuff, the rumble and the singing note of the flywheel were heard, the whole caravan seemed to come bearing down in thrilling magnificence to the boys who ran shouting down to the gateway.

This was the best moment of all – the sight of a mill-train under full steam.

First the engine, gleaming black and gold in spite of the dust of the road and paddock, with governor and flywheel spinning madly. The driver alert, his head darting from side to side, ready to spin his wheel at the sight of dog or child. A more phlegmatic fireman, lounging on the other side of the platform, steam enough in hand for the manoeuvring ahead.

The great red mill coming so close behind seemed to overrun the engine, its folded elevator reaching forward over the engine canopy. What a monstrous machine this was – as big as a house and as red as the stable. The iron wheels graunched and rang on the shingle; from the mill itself came a deep-throated shaking rumble.

Third rolled the bunkhouse, almost as big as the mill but homely in a red

1974, *Our Open Country*

weatherboarded way. Perhaps a face elbowed up from a bunk to a small window, and almost certainly cookie, leaning in the open doorway smoking, was already casting his eyes around for some loose dry wood.

In all, power and mass combined, it was the stuff boys' dreams are made of.

Often yet another wagon rumbled along in the train, a wheeled hut for spare gear of all sorts, with perhaps an extra bunk or two. The only free-moving unit of the whole outfit was the humble watercart, romantic enough in its gypsyish way. This was usually a horsedrawn dray equipped with pumping gear and a 400-gallon tank. The waterman's task seemed a simple matter: he must have the water on hand when the engine demanded it, but the rest of the day was his own. At least, so it seemed. You never saw a water-cart in a hurry, though you often heard peremptory whistles echoing appealingly across the stubble. The driver seemed to match his horse in somnolence, usually perched, legs dangling, on a shaft near the horse's rump. The nearest creek or waterhole might be several miles away, but the day was long and pleasant.

And so the mill reached the farm after some tricky manoeuvring through gate and gully; the extra man at his wheel depressing the great folded elevator to pass under a wire or tree.

And then at last the mill in action. Here, with the engine dug in facing the rear of the mill, the enormous belt crossing and recrossing in a figure of eight from wheel to wheel, the mill groaned and sang so that you had to shout to be heard. High upon his platform the feeder knifed the sheaves loose as they passed from the stack into the jaws of the mill, while at the grain chutes perspiring 'baggies' toiled with needle and twine, carrying the sewn bags to a growing pile with an awkward, stumbling run, clasping the bags to stomach and knees. The elevator alone was worth watching for hours, as the straw passed up in uneven rafts and flopped forlornly at the feet of the stacker on his yellow mountain, or fluttered down at an angle in a breeze. The laths on the canvas carrying-belt clattered unceasingly, even above the din of the mill.

Small boys so often were warned off the actual working area, but much more free and easy was the bunkhouse, usually left for convenience and shelter near the homestead. Here endless conversations went on with cookie, while, as a favour, he allowed boys to peel spuds or sweep out the cookhouse wood chips, or perhaps pound some dough just for the feel of it. A smell of carbolic soap circled out from the cut-down kerosene tins on the grass, and inside at the bunk end the manly smell of tobacco, and well-used blankets, old working clothes and old socks. And around everything the smoke from the stove and the fragrance of the next meal cooking.

Today's youngsters smell the dust and oil and rubber of a header harvester, and lie awake hearing the rhythmic throbbing that continues late into a summer evening, but few have known or will ever know the sum of the joys that leapt to mind when boys of not so many years ago heard the shout: 'Hey! The mill's coming!'

Calf Club Day

John Gordon

Calf club day is one of the really big occasions in a rural school's calendar. At Waimiha School in the central King Country, it means no lessons, and showing off your current pet amid all the fun of the fair. The day begins with assorted vehicles in the playground unloading pet lambs and calves, plus every other creature you could think of. It's nothing to see a child sitting the back seat of the family car with a plump, well-shampooed lamb on its knee or a small goat tripping daintily down from the cab of a Land Cruiser. There are also car trailers or utes with a trio of gates, hastily strapped together with rural sellotape, baling twine, and a calf standing in the middle with a resigned look on her face.

For the children this is the culmination of some months of effort, rearing and training their pets. Understandably there's a strong emphasis on lambs and calves with two classes for each. One is for condition, care and grooming which, for lambs, means preparation akin to wool scouring on the hoof. The other class tests a child's ability to lead and control its charge round a course that includes a gate, for lambs, and a bridge, for calves. Lamb handlers face an extra and somewhat acidic test when they have to leave their pet with a holder and walk some 20 metres away and call it to them. For the crowd, parents and the rest of the district, this is the best entertainment of all. There's always one that, immediately it's called, runs in the opposite direction! Some go half the journey and then stop for a couple of minutes, keeping the poor child, to say nothing of Mum and Dad, in a state of pleading suspense. Then, point made, it walks calmly to its relieved boss. Other lambs need only one nervously falsetto cry of 'Snoweeee' to bring them to a bleating run and straight into waiting arms.

There are classes for other pets too – two hens, a duck, a parrot, two possums, several rabbits, some cats, a few ponies and goats of assorted shades and sizes. As an extra there's a prize for the cutest pet, an Angora rabbit, though everyone gets at least a certificate. And to bring that seemingly unavoidable touch of the classroom to proceedings, the pupils prepare written projects on their pets or other animals. These, embellished with various forms of artwork – the probable and the improbable – are judged by Waimiha's retired storekeeper, Snow Harper. With the aid of apparently rose-coloured spectacles, Snow ensures that no child receives a judge's comment that's less than 'good'. Some are very good.

1987, *People, Places and Paddocks*

Minnie
by Marc Mason, aged nine

People ask me, 'what kind of goat is that?'
I tell them:
'Her name is Minnie, she is my best pet'
– she is a kid.
'She chews string and paper, pumice and plastic'
– she is curious.
'She likes to climb and balance'
– she is courageous.
'She drinks milk with glucose and cod liver oil'
– this is nutritious.
'She was found lost in the forest'
– she was bamboozled.
'She likes to jump and dance and skip'
– she is hilarious.
'Her coat is shiny now, it did have lice'
– she was lowsy.
'She will grow into a nanny and eat thistles and blackberry'
– this is useful.

Rosie and Sonny Kereopa, from Endeanes' nearby sawmill, run the hangi for lunch, where everybody pays good, fund-raising money for the meat and veg they've already donated. The afternoon is more a fun fair, with a variety of rides, games and the special privilege – 10 cents for three throws – of chucking wet sponges at their teachers. This puts the seal on a great day, the day of the year at any country school.

The Battle for the Nodding Thistle Shield

Field Candy

The Indian cricketers might have gone home, but it was test fever all over again at Ohauiti this autumn when two eccentric looking teams lined up to battle for the Nodding Thistle Shield.

The rallying call had gone out some days before when every settler received the following circular in his mailbox.

OHAUTI SETTLERS' ASSOCIATION
3rd ANNUAL CRICKET MATCH
FOR THE NODDING THISTLE SHIELD
COCKIES v GRAZIERS

Honours are even in this hotly disputed sporting event so this
should be a tense and dramatic affair. All able-bodied men and
women, and those whose bodies used to be able, should be
preparing themselves mentally and physically for the match.
See you next Sunday in Jock Riddington's front paddock.

Jock is a placid and generous cockie who accepts the annual invasion of his farm philosophically. He has no choice: he owns the flattest paddock in the district. Like some breeds of sheep, our cricket ground is renowned for its easy-care qualities. Certainly no groundsmen are employed in its upkeep, groundswomen perhaps, but certainly not groundsmen.

Our ground is mowed at irregular intervals by Jock's dairy cows. They tend the grass reasonably well but there are certain consequences which players must come to terms with. In running for a catch it is prudent to keep an eye not only on the ball, but also underfoot. Much as we appreciate Jock and his bovine greenkeepers, it is unfortunate that in all Ohauiti no sheep farm exists with a paddock flat enough for cricket because, as everybody knows, sheep have a much daintier way of doing things.

The two teams, Cockies and Graziers, live and work in the same district, but at very different altitudes. The Cockies and their cows inhabit the lower and easier land nearer Tauranga, while we Graziers farm sheep in the higher reaches of the region.

Players are easily identified by their colourful and arresting tee-shirts. The Cockies'

---

25 June 1981, *New Zealand Farmer*

flaunt a large dairy bull, standing full frontal on his front legs. The dairymen (and women) wear this vulgarity with amazing grace. Depicted on the Graziers' shirts is a hedonistic ram saying to a bashful female: 'Where in the flock have ewe been?'

The shield itself, built of the finest galvanised iron, is finished in glowing copper brown and any resemblance it may have to a dustbin lid is purely coincidental. At its centre is an exquisite painting of a nodder in full and glorious flower, and around its circumference are inscribed the words, grossly misquoted, from Robert Herrick:

> Gather ye nodders while ye may,
> They'll only be worse another day.

The nodding thistle does well round here, sometimes growing as high as a horse. Recently, a prize was awarded for the biggest nodder, and it went to a grazier with a choice specimen nearly 3m high.

This year a plague of settlers came out of the hills and the valleys and the gorse to engage in cricketing combat. Each side found themselves with 26 players of both genders. Such heavy stocking rates required a special set of rules, and these were explained before play began.

The teams: To be made up of any number of men, women or similar. Everyone can bat but only a dozen or so may field at any one time.

Batting: Compulsory retirement at 20 runs. No boundary hits; all runs must be run. No batsman may be dismissed until he, she or similar, has hit at least one ball, whether runs result or not. (This rule tends to slow the game down, some batsmen being bowled two or three times before registering a hit. Its great value is that it makes everyone feel wanted.)

Bowling: Eight ball overs. Every male, no matter how awful, must bowl – females optional. No bouncers to be bowled at superannuitants. Any bowler kicking down the stumps, shouldering the umpire or bowling underarm, will be thrown down the nearest offal hole.

Umpires: Umpires to count better than last year. They are also to refrain from taking catches and participating in run-outs.

Subversive tactics: The Cockies are to discourage their kids from galloping their ponies up and down the pitch just before the Graziers go out to bat.

It is a good idea to win the toss and this the Cockies did for the third year in a row. Looking at the treacherous sheen on the cowpads in the outfield, they wisely elected to bat. But they failed to drive home their advantage, making enough ducks to start a commercial flock. Their best moment came when one of their batsmen slogged a ball into the dark and prickly depths of a barberry hedge, allowing him to compile the fastest 20 runs in the history of the game. Even with this effort the Cockies were all out for 102 runs.

Graziers batted, and without the need to dispatch the ball into a hedge, won easily, passing the Cockies' total for the loss of only 24 wickets.

The records show that the Graziers have won the Nodding Thistle Shield two years out of three. While the rivalry is intense during these contests, afterwards no one really cares about the results. Along with nodding thistles, the people of Ohauiti are alive and well.

Representative Cricket

Ralph Lowry

1925 CRICKET – Moawhanga v Wellington Provincial XI. Venue, Moawhanga cricket ground, matting over grass.

It was Sunday and a one-day match. Wellington were at full strength. Moawhanga were Moawhanga, plus A.P.F Chapman, Captain of England, and Dr R.H. Bettington, Captain of New South Wales. The day was perfect. Everything was perfect. Mick Horton was ordered to bring two hogs heads of beer and place them on the end of his lorry tray with taps turned towards the players. A very good lunch was provided and served by Whiti and Madge Batley, better host and hostess one could never find.

Wellington won the toss and decided to bat. Our bowlers: Gerry Rotherham – my cadet at Ohinewairua – the school boy cricketer of the year in Wisdens, 1918. He was at Rugby and champion 100 yards schoolboy in England and had been playing for Wellington Province at cricket. Had he not turned up in his tails on the Wellington Basin Reserve he would have made the N.Z. side. Other bowlers were Bettington, Jim Whittle, Tom Lowry and Ian Parkes. We got them out by 2.30 for 180.

We went in to bat, with Percy Chapman and Bettington as openers. They made 100 and then Tom Lowry and Gerry Rotherham passed the Wellington total of 180. We all proceeded to the home of the Batleys and we had a magnificent supper, drinks and music. The Wellington team having a marvellous pianist, and Whiti Batley was also most proficient.

1985, *Taihape: Be Happy, Die Happy*

Country Member

Dawn Hayes

Before the little man came in
he took off his boots,
and,
just in case,
wiped his socks on the mat.

Look at him they said
bought up Jennings' place
and now he thinks he's one of us.
    Only a navvy'd work
    that place back
    into shape

He's trying to buy my bushbit
One said

They all knew
One needed the money

Rock bottom price too, One said
but I suppose I'll have to sell,
too big, really, what I've got

That's right
    they said

The little man wiped his mouth,
went out and put on his bumboots

He'll get us all in the end
One said
Likehell they unisoned
    still,
they were counting on their fingers
the number of days
to the next shooting season.

1975, Wetbush Fire

Down the Hall on Saturday Night

Peter Cape

I got a new brown sportscoat,
I got a new pair of grey strides,
I got a real kiwi haircut,
Bit off the top and short back and sides.

Soon as I've tied up me guri,
Soon as I've swept out the yard,
Soon as I've hosed down me gumboots,
I'll be living it high and living it hard.

I'm going to climb on to the tractor,
I'm going to belt it out of the gate.
There's a hop on down the hall, and
She starts sharp somewhere 'bout half-past eight.

Hey, look at the sheilas cutting the supper.
An' look at the kids sliding over the floor,
Look at the great big bunch of jokers,
Hanging round the door.

They got the teacher to belt the pianner;
They got Joe from the store on the drums;
Yeah, we're as slick as the Orange in Auckland
For whooping things up and making them hum.

I had a schottische with the tart from the butcher's
Had a waltz with the constable's wife;
I had a beer from the keg on the cream-truck,
And the cop had one, too, you can bet your life.

Oh, it's great being out with the jokers,
When the jokers are sparking and bright;
Yeah, it's great giving cheek to the sheilas,
Down the hall on a Saturday night.

1964, *A Book of New Zealand*

The Young Farmers' Club Experiences a Blackout
Fiona Farrell

In the valley the Young Farmers' Club summer dance is interrupted by a blackout halfway through the Military Two. Couples stand arm in arm in the dark while Mort Coker tries the switches and the fuse box in the kitchen. Someone has a look outside and shouts that the whole place is black, it must be bird strike or a line down up the valley. In the darkness body blunders against body, giggling. Then Ethne Moran finds a torch and the beam of it squiggles over faces caught wide-eyed like rabbits on a road. Someone brings in a Tilley lamp. The band attempts a few bars, deee dum dee dum who'syerladyfren, but stops because no one seems to be interested. They stand about instead talking, and a few couples are edging away to the dimly lit corners.

Then Ethne, who has organised the supper, claps her hands and jumps up onto the stage. 'Come on,' she says, lit by the Tilley lamp and holding in her outstretched hands a strawberry cream sponge. 'No point in letting good food go to waste! Give us a hand, Margie.'

Margie Pringle brings out the sausage rolls and finds her a bread knife and Ethne kneels by the lamp to cut the cake into triangles, cream spurting beneath the blade. Side on her white dress is transparent and Ross Meikle watching thinks she's a cracker. Big breasts, curving stomach, long in the leg, and good teeth nice and even, with that little gap at the front.

Ethne looks up. She hands him a piece of cake, then leans towards him and bites his ear very gently leaving her broken imprint in soft flesh. 'You do something to me,' she sings in a buzzing whisper, 'that electrifies me.'

So they go outside into the warm night where it turns out that she isn't all that struck on Bevan Waters after all, that she'd fancied Ross all along. On the back seat of the Chev she proves moreover to be astonishingly inventive. So that together they execute with ease a whole series of manoeuvres which Ross had previously discounted as possibly risky, definitely foreign and perilously close to deviance. Ross thinks as a result that it might be worth dropping Margie Pringle who was getting on his nerves anyway with her lisping sweetness and that he'd be better off with Ethne who was bossy, God knows, but had a few clues.

Meanwhile, within the hall, Warren Baty is confessing that it was his ram that had got through the fence and in among the Cooper's stud Romney flock last winter, and

1992, *The Skinny Louie Book*

Jim Cooper, a whole season lost, is saying never mind, no lasting harm done. And Alasdair McLeod is telling the Paterson brothers that it was him who nicked their chainsaw; he'd come over one afternoon when they were out and borrowed it and he'd meant to give it back but they'd made such a fuss calling in the police and all that he hadn't felt he could face it and he'd be round next day just to get the bloody thing off his conscience. Miria Love is telling Joan Shaw that she doesn't like the way she conducts Women's Division meetings and Pie Fowler is telling anyone who'll listen that she can't stick the valley, they're a bunch of snobs who've never let her forget for one minute that she's a townie and she'll be off back to the city just as soon as she can settle things with Bill.

Around the walls hang the valley teams since 1919, lined up for the photographer, thighs spread, fists clenched, unamused by the extraordinary goings-on in the darkened hall: under the influence of the night, sausage roll in one hand, beer in the other, the young farmers appear to have been overwhelmed by truth. The room is buzzing with honesty and for some the accompaniment is love and forgiveness, for others bitter recrimination. There seems to have been a sudden rise in the temperature. 'Remember the morning after,' the valley teams counsel, stonily. 'In the morning will come the accounting.'

The Last of the Barn Dances

Jack Lasenby

Our district was a fairly quiet place. Now and again, a farm passed on to the oldest boy; a daughter went to training college, or did a bit of nursing, came home, and married a farmer. Nothing much changed; memories were long. So, when Mrs Watson gave birth to an idiot, most of the women in the district said it was no more than she deserved. But then things hadn't had much of a chance to settle down since the season before when Jimmy Watson ran his sharemilker off the property with a gun.

Mind you, some people felt sorry for the Watsons, after a while. The child was a bit slow, and they didn't seem to know what to do with him. So, people gave them a hand out, here and there, and the boy grew up and went along to the local school where old Miss Jessop would keep him off the Watsons' hands from nine to three. But even old Miss Jessop said she couldn't do much with the boy, not that he gave her any trouble, but just sat, she said, and did nothing.

Well, that was when Old Billy Newton and his wife stepped in. Their two boys had died in the war, and Old Billy and his wife were getting on a bit, but they reckoned they could do something with the kid.

People said the Watsons were quick to agree, just too quick. In any case, the boy changed hands, a bit like a dog. He took to Old Billy at once and followed him around the farm like a dog. He was at his heels everywhere he went: to the saleyards, down to the store, across to the neighbours', the boy stuck close to Old Billy. And it was funny, he perked up a lot, he looked brighter, he spoke to people. Old Mrs Jessop said he was a different boy at school, and she even thought he might have a few brains.

The Newtons had done a lot of good over the years, helping others out, but what they did for the Watson boy surprised us all, especially those who'd said that Old Billy and Mrs Newton were past bringing up another youngster. 'A pity their own boys couldn't have lived,' somebody said, 'instead of the halfwit …' but nobody would have dared say it to Old Billy's face, and, gradually, the boy began to be accepted as belonging to the Newtons.

On bus days, he'd ride down to the store for the papers and the mail, and he'd take home the bread and anything else Mrs Newton wanted. He was still quiet, but he would speak if somebody spoke to him. It wasn't much of a township: the store, post

1982, *Landfall*, Vol. 36, No.1

office, garage, hall, and church, but there were always a few people hanging around when the bus came in.

Well, one day, the kid came down to the store, and young Colin Flighty and his lot were waiting for him. There'd been a story going the rounds that the Watson boy had been seen in Flighty's pigsty – getting stuck into one of the pigs, so young Colin reckoned. He said he'd caught him in there with his trousers down, caught him on the job, so he said.

Nobody believed anything much that the Flightys said, but that day when the Watson boy came down to the store, young Colin Flighty started snorting and honking at him, and all the other young chaps joined in. The Watson kid went red, turned his horse, and took off up the road with young Colin and his mates chasing after him, throwing lumps of metal off the road, and shouting, 'Pig! Pig!'

Old Billy got to hear of it. He had a talk with the boy and put the word round the district that he'd been having a crap in the pigsty, that's all. Yes, it was a stupid place to do it, but he liked watching the pigs, and he'd been caught short while doing just that. Lots of kids used to climb over the fence and watch Flighty's pigs; their sties were close to the road, too close some said. Anyway, Old Billy said he believed the boy, and he made it clear he expected others to believe him too. The story gave a few people a laugh, time went by, and it was forgotten.

Then a big wedding came up; weddings were always a big thing in our district. The Duncan girl was marrying the oldest Simpson boy, Rob. They'd finish up owning one of the biggest farms for miles around.

The wedding itself was a big affair, and the wedding breakfast, which was held in the hall, but every last person in the district must have been invited to the barn dance that they held up in Duncans' woolshed that night. It was a great turn-out. They'd brought the piano from the hall, and the local dance band played. The big woolshed had been cleaned out and was decorated with ponga and nikau fronds. All the youngsters were there from miles around, dancing and sneaking a beer or two; and all the older folk were there, the women helping with the food, the men drinking whisky.

The wedding breakfast was a rich feast, and supper that night in the woolshed was another. Mrs Duncan was known as a great manager, and the whole countryside must have provided food that night.

It was spread out on long trestle tables borrowed from the hall, and you just helped yourself. The dancers surged round the tables, filled their plates, and sat on the benches and bales round the walls. Men stood in groups, intent upon a joke somebody was telling. Here and there, a couple nestled in the half-dark. Then Mrs Duncan noticed the Watson boy hanging back, and she called to him.

'Come on Tommy, here's a plate. What would you like? There's turkey here, and that's a goose. Have some ham, or a slice of beef. Would you like a nice piece of pork?'

And somebody, one of the young fellows, snorted a couple of times, and young Colin Flighty called 'Pig! Pig!' He reckoned later it wasn't him, but everybody said it was.

It all happened so that a lot of people heard it, and there was a long silence. Then the Watson boy said out loud in his flat voice:

'I did not fuck that pig!'

The young fellows doubled up and headed for the doors. They were spluttering and about to let go when Old Billy's voice cut across the woolshed.

'You did not hear that!' he said crisply. 'Nobody heard the boy say a thing!' He stepped forward, stood by the Watson boy, and looked round the woolshed.

The older people started talking and passing their plates. Young Tommy Watson was helped to food by Mrs Duncan, and the barn dance went on. Everybody agreed it was a great success.

The Duncans' was the best barn dance in years, people said, just like the old ones, they reckoned. In fact, it was the last of the barn dances. Young chaps got cars after that, and they'd travel miles into town to go to a dance. Some of the older people who can remember them say we lost something when we gave up the barn dances.

The Opener

May Williamson

The special committee for the official opening of the new hall was seated round the dining room table in the comfortable, expensive home of their chairman. Upon buying the farm he had immediately built this fine new house on the hill, that hid the shabby old homestead, used now to shelter tractors and implements from the weather. And his stock had long since trampled into the ground the hundreds of lovely daffodils, once planted under the old oak trees.

As the chairman sat at the head of the table, he felt proud of the changes he had made in this little, backward district.

'And now we have settled everything but the opener,' he said. 'Whom shall we get to do that?' His tone left no doubt in the minds of some committee members that he had already decided.

'Someone special,' agreed the secretary.

'Why?' said Millie Mushett, clicking away with her busy knitting needles.

They all looked at her, and the chairman wondered yet again at her presence on this committee. He had questioned her being there right at the beginning, but had been told that when they had the old hall, she had always had a say in everything. She was one of the oldest settlers and was quite harmless, they said. Now, he began to wonder. He looked at the woman, with her untidy grey hair and sloppy tweed coat, and she looked back at him in the same cold, fierce way. What blue eyes she had – blue as hard steel.

'Why?' he repeated, 'because this building's important, that's why.'

'What's important about it? It's only a hall.'

The secretary braced himself for yet another tussle. He felt the beginning of another headache behind his eyes; it was that blasted clicking of those accursed needles. He lit yet another cigarette and watched the smoke drift spitefully down and wrap itself around the minister's wife, who immediately began to cough.

'What did you have in mind?' the secretary asked the chairman, avoiding the who or whom, because, unlike the chairman, he was never sure which was correct.

The chairman's face became animated again. 'The Prime Minister,' he said.

The committee held its breath and then came the chorus, *The Prime Minister!* It could not have been better done if it had been rehearsed a hundred times.

---

22 May 1969, *New Zealand Farmer*

The chairman beamed in satisfaction. 'Yes, the Prime Minister.'

'Who's he?' It was Millie again.

The chairman took a firm grip on himself. 'Mr Holyoake, of course.'

'Never heard of him. What's he ever done for our district?'

The pain in the secretary's head exploded in a blinding flash. He thumped out his cigarette on the elaborate ash-tray and looked at it lying there, burst at the seams, and only half smoked.

'Let's not get all political, Millie,' he said quietly, wanting to shout. He turned to the chairman, 'If you think you can arrange this –'

'Well, the whole point is, Keith will be in this area at that time. If we have the opening about 11, wine and cheese I thought, it could be managed.'

The clicking needles stopped suddenly with a frightening silence. It was as though the whole world had ceased turning and was listening and waiting. Millie Mushett put down her needles and opened her mouth.

The secretary rushed into speech. 'Then I move that our chairman approach the Prime Minister. Someone second that? Thanks. Shall we declare this meeting closed?' He looked at his watch and noted the time in the minute book. The chairman pushed back his chair and rose to his feet.

'Wine and cheese, you said, didn't you?' Millie said. 'What about my ham sandwiches?'

'They won't be necessary.'

'Rubbish, we always have them.'

'This time we won't.'

'We'll have them all right.'

'I said no, Miss Mushett.'

'We'll see,' said Millie.

The long anticipated day for the official opening of the new public hall was fine and sunny. This was just as well as the chairman had issued orders that everyone must stay out on the parking lawn until the ribbon was cut. He and the secretary would go down at 9 o'clock and put out the wine and cheese, then lock the door and put the white satin ribbon across it. No one, but no one, was to enter the hall until the Prime Minister cut the ribbon and stepped inside.

The people of the district were thrilled with the chairman and his city ways. The women dressed as though attending a Royal day at Ellerslie, and the men donned their wedding-funeral suits. They began to gather early and the sight of them standing elegantly on a well-cut lawn, at the side of a country road, might have made passing motorists wonder, except that the occasion had been well publicized in the town paper. Even the children were let out of school for the event. In fact, everyone was there … except Millie Mushett.

Millie was busy making ham sandwiches from the ham she had cured herself, just for this occasion. Spread liberally with mustard, she had piles and piles of the big squares; she did not believe in cutting them into little fingers or triangles. She had been at them since shortly after 9 o'clock, when she had gone to the hall and hidden in 'the ladies', while the men did the wine and cheese. When Millie heard the cars arriving outside the hall, she knew it was time to prepare the tables. So she moved the 'silly cheese' and put her lovely sandwiches in haystack shapes between the glasses and the bottles.

When the new clock above the new front door to the new hall said 11 o'clock, outside it was suddenly hushed, with only one voice speaking. Millie wiped her hands on her big, grubby white apron, picked up her carving knife and walked towards the door. She shot back the lock, opened it, slashed the clean, white ribbon with her greasy carving knife and said, 'It's open. C'mon in.'

The Women's Division of Farmers' Union
Alice Mackenzie

The Women's Division has been a boon
To many a farmer's wife,
For now she meets her neighbours
And has more joy in life.

There are lessons given in cooking
And how to do repairs;
How to ice a Christmas cake
And upholster worn-out chairs.

We are shown how to use up waste,
Create carpets out of rags,
And all the useful things to make
From humble sugar bags.

And we would all go to the meeting,
With notebook and a pen,
If someone gave a lecture
On how to manage men.

1948, *Poems*

The Good Old Days

Peter Newton

I got into conversation with a chap last week and he recalled a certain day at the Oxford dog trials. I remembered it well. It was back in the 'good old days', when the game wasn't taken quite so seriously, and a bit of skylarking seemed to be the accepted thing.

I was at Grasmere Station, up the Waimakariri, at the time, and I had taken the day off to go to Oxford, with my old mate, Reg Ferguson. Reg had mustered in those parts for some years, had the Bealey pub then, but times were still pretty hard (this was just before the last war) and he still kept a dog or two and gave us a hand out on the station. Neither of us was any great threat to the heading events, but Reg had a little Reg White's Toss dog called Brave that could put in a useful run, and I had a dog called Ned, by Bob Innes' Lloyd, that I thought wasn't bad. In any case, what ever our dogs did we were pretty sure of having a good day's outing. We did too.

I've forgotten just how Reg's Brave went, but I got away to a bad start; the judge had a brand new car and as I went out for my run, Ned widdled on it. I didn't expect that would be much help and, sure enough, as I came back past the car after my run, the judge was sharpening his pencil. That's a bad sign and I decided that I might be better occupied over at the bar. Jack Spenser who had the West Oxford pub at the time, ran the booth and he treated us extra well.

The event finished early in the afternoon – I believe it was Bill Ross with a dog called Don Minor who won – so to fill in the day they held a musterers' race, up to the top huntaway poles and back. Needless to add, that didn't help much. All hands needed a reviver after that and, as a matter of course, the winner had to cut out his winnings. It was worth a quid and the 'shout' only cost him two, so he couldn't growl. We were well wound up by this time and after the crowd had drifted away, old Jack capped things off by making us a present of what draught beer was left. It's not very often that you get it for free, so we made the most of it.

I'd better not mention the judge's name or some of his family might take to me. He was a man of round the 60 mark, but still loved his bit of fun and, nothing loath, he joined in with us. We got him as full as a bull and, just to show there was no ill feeling, finished up by bundling him in the boot of his car.

Not content with that, we decided that what was good enough for us was good

23 December 1965, *New Zealand Farmer*

enough for the dogs. We picked out those that hadn't fared too well with their runs and poured a few beers down their throats. When they were properly primed we tried them out on a run, and reckoned most of them went better than they did when they were sober. It might be worth trying; we figured it only cost about half a dollar [2s 6d] to get a dog drunk.

By the time we finally got away, Reg and I were in pretty good order and rearing to go. We had our dogs – four of them all told – tied on the back of Reg's old V8 truck and just before we got to Sheffield we ran into a cocky with a mob of ewes on the road. Not wanting to run over any of his sheep, Reg leaned on the horn and, just before we reached them, we started the dogs barking. We cleared the road all right! The lead of the mob took off as though all hell was after them – we reckoned they were touching 30 [mph]. We turned off the main road half a mile or so after that, and the leaders were still going full bore. We reckoned those sheep must have been fed on oats the way they could stay.

The old cocky was wheeling a push-bike and had no dog. As soon as the hooley started he just made one leap onto his bike and took off for the lead – he didn't even have time to turn the handlebars down. He was no chicken that bloke, but he could certainly push a bike. When we finally disappeared round the next bend he was still going strong, and so were those ewes.

They say that troubles never come singly and, sure enough, just as we reached Springfield we got into more bother. One of the old residents, also with a pushbike, was bringing his half a dozen cows down the road. Just as we reached them our dogs, to our horror, jumped off the truck and took to them. Within seconds there wasn't a cow in sight; with flying tails they scattered in all directions, over fences, into flower gardens and everywhere. The last we saw of the old chap, he was standing in the middle of the road putting the boot into his bike. It looked quite a good sort of a bike too! Reg and I couldn't sleep that night, we felt so sorry for that old bloke.

We pulled into the Springfield pub just after that and when we came out, an hour or two later, the dogs were all there, as happy as Larry. They looked as if they'd enjoyed their day out as much as we had. All the same, on looking back, it might be just as well the dog trial game is taken a bit more seriously now, than in the good old days!

One Trial After Another

John Gordon

There are few competitive pursuits as rural as sheep dog trialling, which means that wherever you are, you're surrounded by great scenery. In time you take for granted that trialling is a passport to some amazing country, both the courses themselves and the back roads and overland passes you travel to reach them. Among the most memorable for me is the magnificent drive between King Country's Tokirima and Taranaki's Whangamomona trials on a mellow February evening. This stretch includes the winding, riverside and bush-clad Tangarakau Gorge, the rough-hewn limestone tunnel leading on to the Tahora Saddle and then a switchback road, with a view of sawtooth ridge after sawtooth ridge disappearing into the sunset. The journey to Tututawa a couple of mornings later has its moments too, especially the first rays of sun on Mount Taranaki, through the mists that linger round the Pohokura and Strathmore saddles.

Heading to Kaitieke's trial grounds, by turning west near the Raurimu Spiral, there's a magnificent view of that bush-enveloped valley nestling in the Whanganui River catchment. The drive between two of that club's courses would also have any tourist bus stopping to disgorge its passengers and boost Kodak's profits. To get to the long head, the track follows a clear and busy river and then crosses another as it tumbles and twirls through a limestone chasm to marry up with the former. What makes it even better is that the long head course would be worth crossing a desert for anyway, so travelling by the babble and blether of the creeks, surrounded by bush, birdsong and the moist gleam of a misty morning, is a real bonus. In my own centre [dog trial association region], the trip up SH52 from Masterton to Waipukurau is one of the last, back country, non-tourist drives in the country. Its 214 kilometres wanders in and out of valley after pleasant valley and, most important, interconnects with six different trial grounds.

In the South Island, one of my most memorable journeys was early one autumn morning through North Canterbury to the Waiau Club's trial. It was one of those days when everything seemed as close to perfect as it could get, especially the tonings of the turning leaves, the menu at the cookshop, the company and the huntaway sheep. Even one of my dogs attained the mantle of perfection … for a while! Later that day, the overland drive towards SH1 and Cheviot – 'down the Leader', as the locals say – ready

---

1998, *Three Sheep and a Dog*

for that Cheviot's trial next morning, was another reminder of how good it is that we don't compete in town. Similarly, coming off the Pigroot into the Maniototo, with the promise of two or three trials to come, is always a great feeling, as is approaching Mount Nessing's grounds, near Fairlie. From the turn-off at Albury to their headquarters below the foothills of the Rollesby Range, the road and farm track climb 300 metres just to get to their huts above the Opawa River. As a rule, what follows will be a searing hot March day, typical of inland Canterbury but, towards its end, the air will become cool, clear and relaxing. By evening you can be sitting by a boulder-strewn stream, watching huntaways shift half-bred two-tooths up a steep face, with nothing more to worry about than your next run.

Next day it's the Levels trial, on the other side of the broad valley, and from their hunt courses, which seem to start halfway up the Brothers Range, you look back to yesterday's location. In mid-afternoon sun the detail on the tussock-clad hills is lost; it's just a warm blur of tan and gold – sheep and dog country, all the way west to the Southern Alps.

The sights, animal instances and quirks of tradition that contribute so much to the special world of sheep dog trialling wouldn't exist without the most important ingredient of all, the people. Remove any practising triallist from dogs, sheep and hills and, as long as there was someone in the vicinity with the same interest, he or she would be as happy as a pig in mud. Happier still, if a dog or two were sniffing round a cluster of rural vehicles with weather-beaten faces nearby, squinting into the hills and yarning at the same time. Some of the best memories I have are of the people and what they've given me in the way of companionship and support.

I've also been fortunate to see the top competitor and dog combinations of the last two or three decades in action, all of them providing unforgettable moments. There are other times, too, that a triallist never forgets. There's that very personal five- to fourteen-minute moment that starts when the dog leaves for the sheep and, as it unfolds, becomes something that you dreamt about, but never really dared to expect. The more it continues, the more you determine not to let it go, becoming increasingly aware that this could be the one, *the* run. More and more you and your other self reach out across the flat or up the hill, to steady and steer the dog to maintain what, so far, is the closest you've ever been to perfection. There are a couple of flaky moments as nerves, a dry throat, then a hasty ewe, cause heart flutters, but it all holds together, steady and true. You go through the last moves and commands almost as an automaton, without drawing a breath, and the other world to which you seem to have ascended is suddenly broken by the reality of the judge's call, 'Right!'

It's over. You show no emotion, and certainly don't look at the judge. Then call the dog off, praise it and walk away – while at the same time becoming increasingly aware that you might just have pulled it off. Still stoic and betraying no emotion, you walk past the judge's hut and say 'thank you', avoiding any eye contact. Behind the hut and out of sight, you stop, heave a huge sigh of relief and nervous release, tilt your head back, bend your right forearm, clench your fist and say 'Yeess!' Now, *that* really is dog trialling, and why we travel the length of this land looking for the perfect run.

The Single Shepherd

David Geary

They'd played a lot of darts
in the single man's quarters.
Filled an old exercise book
with scores. Social Studies
wasn't his strong suit.
'R' versus 'L'. Page after
page. He's Leonard. I asked
'Who's this 'R' guy?'
'No, mate, that's my right
hand versus my left.'

1998, *New Zealand Listener*

Nga Puke (The Hills)

John Broughton

ACT 1

Scene 1: Nga Puke: a hill country sheep farm. 1st September 1939.

Angie walks in through the audience. She carries an artist's easel, stool, sketch pad and a cane basket containing paints, pencils, brushes, her lunch and a thermos flask. She surveys the view, picks a spot and sets up her easel and stool. Angie paints the landscape before her.

Waru: *(He is standing among the audience)* YOU STUPID BITCH! What the hell do you think you're doing?

Angie: *(She looks up startled. Where is the voice coming from?)*

Waru: I said, what the hell do you think you're doing? *(Waru storms onto the stage, he is furious.)* Jesus Christ! I dunno! *(He turns his back on her and whistles.)* Get in behind, boy – that's it, that's it. Keep it going. *(Whistle)* Easy now. *(Whistle)* WINSTON! … On the side, Winston … Not that bloody side. Winston, over here you bloody mongrel! Jeez, Winston! That's it boy, easy now. *(Whistle)*

Angie: AAAh … um, er 'scuse me.

Waru: Shut up you! *(Whistle)* Keep it going, on the inside, boy. Don't let that one bloody get away! WINSTON! *(Whistle)* I'll bloody skin you, Winston. That's it boy. Good one, Winston.

Angie: Ah, could I …

Waru: I'll deal with you in a minute, girlie. That's it Jake, get 'em all in. And give that bloody dog a boot while you're at it. I'll be down in a sec. Now girlie, what the hell do you think you're doing?

Angie: Don't 'girlie' me!

Waru: I'll say what I bloody well like. Well? Who said you could come up here?

Angie: I just wanted to paint. The view from up here is incredible. It's just beautiful.

Waru: I know it's bloody beautiful, but that don't answer my question.

Angie: I just came up here.

1992, *Nga Puke (The Hills)*

Waru: Even I can bloody see that. You might try asking first.

Angie: I'm sorry. I didn't know who to ask.

Waru: Well you see that farm house down there. You might start by knocking on the bloody door.

Angie: I said I was sorry.

Waru: Bloody hell!

Angie: Do you have to swear all the time?

Waru: I don't bloody swear!

Angie: I didn't think anyone would mind.

Waru: Mind what?

Angie: Me coming up here.

Waru: Didn't think anyone would bloody mind! Jesus! Just look what ya bloody done!

Angie: What? Where?

Waru: KERRISTE! She doesn't even know what she damn well went and done.

Angie: Look, I'm sorry if I've caused any trouble. I'll just pack up and …

Waru: Now you see that down there – you know what that bloody is? The long wire thing with the bits that go up like that. That's a bloody fence. And you see that funny bit in the middle with the other bits going this way and that? That's what we call a bloody gate. And you know what happens when you leave the God damn'd gate open? My bloody sheep get out! That's what!

Angie: *(She laughs quite loudly)*

Waru: And it ain't no bloody laughing matter!

Angie: *(She laughs even louder)* God, you're funny when you're angry.

Waru: Jeez, a cheeky bloody hooer!

Angie: Your nostrils quiver on both sides. Have you ever noticed?

Waru: Now look here you. Just take your bloody stuff and …

Angie: There it goes again. Look at that. Quiver, quiver, quiver.

Waru: I said, get your stuff and …

Angie: You've got a great nose. Did you know that? I'd love to paint your nose.

Waru: And make sure you shut the bloody gate behind you.

Angie: In fact I'd love to paint you. C'mon, what do you say. Would you sit for me?

Waru: God-All-Bloody-Mighty. Don't you ever give up?

Angie: No.

Waru: You're a bloody stayer, I'll say that for you.

Angie: I don't give in easy.

Waru: So what are you doing here anyway?

Angie: Painting.

Waru: What?

Angie: The landscape. It's just amazing.

Waru: You one of them, what-you-call-it, artistes?

Angie: Artist. That's what I want to be. I was nursing but I finished that and went to art school.

Waru: An artsy-bloody-fartsy type.

Angie: Watch it, you cow-bloody-cocky.

Waru: Hey fullah, it's sheep, about four thousand of the buggers, less one or two thanks to you.

Angie: Oh the gate, I am really very sorry about that.

Waru: Well you bloody should be. I've enough to do around here as it is.

Angie: I guess I didn't think.

Waru: So don't let it happen again.

Angie: Does that mean I can come back up here then?

Waru: Well, let's see what you've been doing.

Angie: I only started it this morning.

Waru: Hey, that's not bad. Not bloody bad at all.

Angie: You think so?

Waru: Jeez, you got the cabbage trees looking, just like cabbage trees.

Angie: Thank you.

Waru: And there's the valley. That's Dog Leg Creek.

Angie: Dog Leg Creek?

Waru: 'Cos it's as crooked as a dog's hind leg.

Angie: Oh, of course.

Waru: Put the wool shed in down there. And that's Nga Puke.

Angie: Nga Puke?

Waru: Nga Puke, The Hills. That's what Nga Puke means, the hills.

Angie: This place?

Waru: This farm actually.

Angie: You own this farm then?

Waru: Too right, fullah. Well, the Ol' Man does.

Angie: So it's a family affair then?

Waru: You could say that. Goes back a long way.

Angie: And I suppose it'll be yours too, one day?

Waru: We're just the kaitiaki, the guardians of the land. Toitu te whenua whatungarongaro he tangata.

Angie: What's that?

Waru: Nothin'.

Angie: Oh by the way, I'm Angie. Angela Duncan actually. But everyone calls me Angie.

Waru: Okay Angie, I'm Number Eight.

Angie: Number Eight?

Waru: Waru. Waru Thompson. That's what Waru means – Eight.

Angie: Oh, I see.

Waru: But me mates all call me Number Eight.

Angie: Number Eight, isn't that rather unusual for a name?

Waru: Nah. It's after the fencing wire. Number Eight fencing wire. Good for anything, fix anything. Like me.

Angie: Well Number Eight, how do you do.

Waru: Kia ora there, Angela, er Angie.

Angie: Angie, that's better.

Waru: I kind of like the sound of that, Angie.

Angie: I'm glad. So Number Eight, you think you're a bit of a dab hand then?

Waru: Oorr, 'specially on the footy field. I play at number eight there as well.

Angie: Last man down. Now that I have to see.

Waru: I was even born on the eighth of August. That's why the folks named me Waru.

Angie: You know, to the Chinese, the number eight is very lucky.

Waru: I'm not a bloody Chinaman!

Angie: I didn't say you were.

Waru: Jeez! First of all she lets half me bleedin' sheep out, then she calls me a bloody Chinaman.

Angie: I did not!

Waru: Bloody hell, what next.

Angle: There, it's beginning to go again.

Waru: What?

Angie: Your nose, quiver, quiver, quiver.

Waru: It is not.

Angie: It is so too.

Waru: Well so what if it is?

Angie: It's funny.

Waru: It's my nose.

Angie: I kind of like it, your nose.

Waru: I didn't come up here to waste my time talking about my ihu.

Angie: Don't get mad again.

Waru: I'm bloody not.

Angie: Yes you are.

Waru: Jeez, you'll end up in the creek if you're not too careful.

Angie: Just you try it.

Waru: EEE, get you.

(*pause*)

Waru: So where are you from then?

Angie: Dunedin.

Waru: Dunedin eh? Jeez, you're a long way from home. What are you doing up here in the Bay then?

Angie: I'd never been up here before. I just wanted to see this part of the country, and maybe do some painting.

Waru: You're very good.

Angie: Thank you.

Waru: I mean the painting.

Angie: I know.

Waru: In fact, very, very good.

Angie: It's very kind of you to say so. Would you like some tea?

Waru: No thanks. I've gotta get down. Jake'll be wondering where I've got to.

Angie: The tea's nice and hot. I've got a thermos.

Waru: Besides, I've wasted enough time as it is.

Angie: Date scone? I made them myself.

Waru: I've got two more runs to check before it gets dark.

Angie: Are you sure you wouldn't like some tea?

Waru: Course I'm bloody sure. We're right in the middle of lambing.

Angie: Can I have permission then, to finish the painting?

Waru: I guess so.

Angie: Thanks Waru, I mean Number Eight.

Waru: See that you shut the bloody gate behind you!

(Exit Waru. Angie sits at her easel and resumes painting)

Boys will be Boys

The gentle art of gorilla gardening

Louisa Herd

James Heriot, in one of his famous vet books, observed that farmers are notoriously bad gardeners. Mr Herriot understated the case. Farmers are bloody appalling gardeners. This does not apply to rural women. The farmers' wives in our district run a thriving garden club and several, notably my cow cocky boss's neighbour, have elegant *pleasances* that would have Maggie Barry gnashing her teeth in envy.

These dedicated ladies snip, prune and cosset their plants into superb displays – on sandy, drought-prone soil that makes the surface of Mars look like best potting compost. They know the names of the most exotic flowers, subscribe to all the gardening journals and are always ready with cuttings and advice to new horticultural chums. In short, these women are Genuine Good Gardeners.

But the blokes? Oh dear! Winter, combined with the lull between drying off the cows and the start of calving, sees the emergence of the Gorilla Gardener, *Homo roughasgutsus.*

The Gorilla Gardener, having ignored his fruitful plot since last year – except to spray Roundup on the edges of the paths – looks around and decides the plants are taking over. Jeez, mate, the red-hot pokers are marching up the drive, the agapanthus are executing a swift outflanking manoeuvre round the rockery, and the plum tree is mounting a coup against the shrubbery. Time for a bloke to do summink, quick!

To Gorilla Garden in true rip-shit-'n'-bust style, you only need one tool. It's pricey – a good one will set you back about five hundred bucks – but without it you can go sit with the girls. This is serious stuff, not for sissies. Be a man, get a chainsaw. Pull that starter cord and hear that throaty roar. Brrmmm … Brrmmm … BRRMMM! Now chop the bejasus out of all the vegetable matter in your garden.

Watching my otherwise quiet, mild-mannered employer in the throes of chainsaw fever is novel, like perving on Clark Kent in the phone booth, pulling his grundies over his pantyhose. Chainsaws are boys' toys, like electric guitars and gas-guzzling V8s. You never see a woman with a chainsaw, though I did once see an advert for a leading brand in which a Nordic bimbette was shown doing a spot of tree pruning, dressed in cut-off jeans and a Wonderbra. The effect was akin to seeing a huntaway in a rhinestone collar.

Need a tree shifted? That Japanese flowering cherry never did too well over by the rockery, did it? Maybe it could be transplanted out the front, beside your Purple Herba-

January 2001, *Growing Today*

ceous Border. Get a bit more sun, soil's a bit better over there too. And it's only a small tree. Should be able to dig it out and put it in a better 'ole. Save your back and do it the Gorilla way. Easy peasy! Pull the tree out with the tractor then put it in the new spot, which you excavated earlier with your front-end loader. Fill in around the roots with the loader bucket and the job's all done, and you never got off the tractor seat.

At the end of a couple of intensive days of Gorilla Gardening, your plot should be tamed, all shrubs reduced to little stumps and all unknown greenery ripped out. A touching fact about farmers is that whilst they can tell the difference between perennial ryegrass and poa, cocksfoot and Timothy, and are on intimate Latin name terms with clovers red, white and subterranean, they don't have a clue about ornamental plants. I discovered, chatting to him whilst raking up the chainsaw debris, that the boss had been seasoning his lamb roasts with lantana, in the mistaken belief that it was rosemary.

Before cracking a celebratory cold one, there's a last wee job before your Gorilla Gardening session is done for another year – a final *frisson* of fun that will appeal to the closet pyromaniac dwelling in all men. Load the huge piles of rubbish onto the tip trailer, dump it in a back paddock and have a big bonfire. Coupla good glugs of diesel and up she goes. Whoomp!

Boy, I could write a book about it, do a TV series even.

Forget your gentle, pretty, Maggies, your sensitive bespectacled Bugmen. How about Jonah Lomu's Garden Programme? Guest Gardener this week is David Tua, with some exciting tips on pruning, plus Jonah and the All Blacks transform a boring vegie plot. Sponsored by Caterpillar Earthmovers. Jonah uses a Husqvarna chainsaw and a Case tractor ...

Reality

Reality is a condition we seem to refer to only when there is a problem, or a whole series of them, that makes life seem totally grim and unhappy. But periods when everything's 'as good as gold' are equally real and, therefore, very precious. There are, though, plenty around with a Jonah perspective – and I don't mean the rugby player – who, in the middle of agreeable weather and decent prices, are likely to come out with cheery little asides such as, 'You'd better make the most of it. Sooner or later – probably sooner, if our bloody luck's anything to go by – the whole thing'll turn to custard.'

The underlying emotional state of the average New Zealand farmer (male) is one of fatal realism – or real fatalism. After all, it would never do to get too excited about anything. Such scepticism is not the sole preserve of farmers but few in the world can do it better. Some years ago *Punch* published a cartoon depicting farmland so badly flooded that only the tops of the fenceposts were above the waterline. On a rise to one side stood a couple of farmers taking in the scene, with one turning dolefully to the other and observing, 'This flood's receding so fast we'll probably be in for a long drought.'

Down on the farm, reality means the facts of life which, apart from animal reproduction, include a host of seemingly inflexible situations. As a phrase, I have always preferred the grim-jawed 'The ways things stand, we're going to have to face facts.' Then there's the time-honoured, 'The long and bloody short of it is …' Both are eminently suitable when all and sundry need a reminder that the current problem 'isn't going to go a-bloody-way, unless something's done about it!' Many a writer has made much of the comic situations that arise from apparently insuperable problems, and none more so than Frank Anthony, whose *Me and Gus* stories are the epitome of unemotive Kiwi humour. When he recorded and fictionalised his experiences, Anthony celebrated the tussles and tedium of life on his uneconomic dairy farm, noting in an unpublished jotting, 'The great pleasures that are to be gained from relating personal tales of great difficulty'.

The best description I've encountered, uttered by a farmer facing grim reality, came from Tony Sheild of Bank House in Marlborough. In my book, *People, Places and Paddocks*, his account of how he coped at the height of a two-year drought, around 1979 to 1981, showed both distress and discipline:

It was devastating to your morale and it really was a severe drought. …I used to get out of bed each morning and say, 'I'm going to get through this day. I'm determined to finish this day and that's as far as I'm going to think!'

There are many ways of accepting and then coping with 'how things are'. In many cases this means a compromise, and if that becomes too complicated, well, this extract from a Field Candy essay, 'Reality', deals with the dichotomy that is livestock farming better than anything I have read.

It is true that I live by nurturing the young and newly born; yet after all the careful tending I must kill in order to survive. Life gives me pleasure and purpose but death gives me profit. Sometimes it is difficult to distinguish between the two. At other times it doesn't seem to matter.

If this section does anything, it reminds us that farming is not just green hills, daffodils and white, fluffy lambs in spring, and golden tints, ripening crops and well-conditioned stock in autumn. These things do exist and are certainly part of why we live and work in the country and love the life. But part of that affinity comes from the fact that farming has its grim side and recognising, then mastering that reality – or, in extreme cases, simply surviving it – gives a sense of achievement and strengthens the bond that ties people to their land. The following pieces describe human hardship and consider both slaughter and survival. In essence, though, they do not testify merely to isolation, grim frustration and senseless slaughter. Rather, they celebrate the difference between town and country, and what living and working in the New Zealand countryside really means.

Different Worlds

Jim Morris

Riding the river
Looking for a ford,
Water high and dirty
After days of rain.

Floating log
Startled horse,
Hits soft spot
In deep water.

I slide from saddle
Grab flailing stirrup,
Hooves churning
Downstream rushing
Boulders tumbling
White waves dancing
Wild eyed gelding.

Through luck
Pull out on sand bar,
Shaken, panting,
Thankful, pale.

Looking skyward
Way above,
See jumbo jet
Sydney bound.

Silken businessman
Orders a gin.
Monogrammed handkerchief
Wipes caviar from chin,
Away it winged
Like some great silver dart;
I rolled a wet smoke –
We're worlds apart.

1997, Different Worlds

Isolation

Joan MacIntosh

When I think of our tar sealed road all the 50 miles to the city and the reliable car we have, it makes our circumstances of 25 years ago seem as if I were talking about the pioneer days. It took over 40 miles of rough gravel road, thousands of potholes and desert proportions of dust to reach the nearest stretch of seal and our Whippet sedan was far from reliable. I cannot imagine our Holden stationwagon allowing its windscreen to slide out on to the bonnet and subjecting itself to the indignity of having it secured again with a piece of wire from a fence. That would be like asking the Chef at the Ritz for fish and chips.

Having a baby 25 years ago in the backblocks of the southern districts presented many problems. The nearest doctor was seven miles away after he'd travelled nearly 40 miles to hold surgery hours three days a week, so it was usual to attend a city doctor and book in at one of the several maternity homes at that time. There were also registered midwives who attended with a doctor, a birth and after care in your own home. This is what I chose for my first baby. I consulted an elderly doctor and arranged with a nurse to attend me at my mother-in- law's home. I only met the nurse on one occasion. She gave me a list of requirements and instructions for setting up the bedroom, and in answer to my query, 'When will I know to come to town?' she replied, 'There's plenty of time to think of that.'

Certainly this was late July and the baby was expected in January. The doctor told me to come back in a few months time. Home I went and searched everywhere for books and magazines for information about having a baby. I found two things which stuck in my mind: 'having a baby is not an illness. Do not treat it as such' and 'enjoy the pre-natal months'. Another said, 'try to cat nap as much as possible between pains', 'relaxation is most important during labour'.

I concentrated on the first clause and despite many peculiar discomforts as the months went by I carried on as usual on the farm and in the house and prepared a layette for this very important addition to our home. Close friends sometimes questioned the January date for the birth, as I was quite a size for my stated time, but my doctor always sent me off with reassuring words.

One morning, when we had visitors, the cramping pains I experienced were so bad I kept having to leave the room until the spasms passed off. Next day we drove to a

1974, *Never a Dull Moment*

neighbour's place to use the telephone to ring the nurse and tell her about my troubles. She advised me to tell the doctor when next I visited him if they persisted. This visit was set to coincide with Christmas shopping in December. I was never to keep that appointment.

My father-in-law, Pop, came out to stay and we began the annual shearing. We did this with blade shears then and it was my job to pick up, skirt and roll the fleeces. During the day, I was having pains again and sometimes they were so bad I had to lie down on a sack on the floor of the shed till they passed off. I look back in incredulous wonder at the number of fleeces I handled that day. My husband and Pop were through a doorway busy shearing and couldn't see my ups and downs so they were as unaware as I that anything was wrong.

About six o'clock I dashed to the homestead to prepare a dinner while the others went off to milk our cow and attend sheep and lambs at the shed. It was then that I discovered I had a 'show' … this was to be the warning sign my friends had said, and here it was! But I couldn't believe it. I was two months ahead of time, perhaps nearly three if this was my sign. I carried on peeling vegetables and setting them to cook. Then a niggle crept in. Suppose I do have to go to town? I hauled out my suitcase and checked over the contents. They were all there.

'See that you have everything washed and packed by your seventh month.'

I planned to have our evening meal, then motor over to Mrs B. to ring the nurse and seek her advice first. I rushed out the back door to get more firewood and a second 'sign' exploded about my feet. There was water everywhere. This really shook me and I realised I was about to have the baby. Being brave wasn't one of my strong points and I went roaring and yelling from the house to the cowshed where I met my husband coming up with the milk. He was equally as startled, but he backed out the old Whippet car, collected my suitcase and me and set off to B's leaving Pop to get his own tea. Our neighbours were finishing their tea and when I told my tale there was instant reaction.

'You sit in that chair and don't you move. I'll do the ringing to town. Have you had any tea?'

Excitement had taken hold of me, above any fear I felt, and I couldn't think of food, but Mrs B. hastily filled a plate with cold meat slices, scones and buns which I fed to the father to be as he drove to town. Our car wasn't put to the test of rushing me to the doctor for our good friends insisted we use their car. It must have been a nightmare drive for my husband and my neighbour who was able to bring little more than a bottle of dettol and some clean linen with her. Every ten minutes or so I'd collapse on the seat in a spasm of pain and in between I chattered like a Pollyanna about how marvellous it'd be to have the baby for Christmas … this was the fourth of December.

When we arrived in town there was consternation and confusion at mother-in-law's.

The nurse couldn't attend as she was already caring for two patients and two more were due; the doctor couldn't come as he was confined to bed with influenza. I was dumbfounded. Every time I groaned with a contraction it seemed that the now crowded house emptied out and then slowly filled again. A message came … I was to go to public hospital.

I then added to all the upset by refusing to go on the grounds that they'd get the baby mixed up and no one would be able to come to see me. Protesting, but comforted by my Aunt Lil's kind assurances, I was led to the car and taken to the hospital. A young house surgeon came out and asked how far apart the pains were. These had closed in to only a few minutes apart, but he said, 'Good. Arrangements have been made for you to go to St. Helen's. You'll have time to drive across there.'

How I blessed dear Saint Helen, though I knew nothing about her at all. It was like a reprieve and I entered the St. Helen's Maternity Training Hospital happily and willingly. An hour later I gave birth to a tiny baby son and surprised everyone by having another son a few hours later. Twin boys! My delight was so evident I don't think the nurses had the heart to tell me anything other than that they were very premature. My twins were headline news around both families and mothers and husband came to see me that afternoon. They were called away to see the Matron and soon the sad news was out. The little sons were barely viable and had not responded to the oxygen tent for more than a few hours and had died. Everyone was extremely kind to me at St. Helen's but no one could assuage the dreadful emptiness as I left with my suitcase, the new shawl still inside.

The Winner

May Williamson

On this particular evening, and with a cold gale hitting my face, I should not have been walking across the bull paddock of a Northland farm, on my way to feeding the pigs. No, I should have been down in Wellington getting ready to meet the Governor-General's Lady. And I should have been dressed in a beautiful evening gown and wearing long white gloves. It was the long white gloves that tickled my fancy: but this is what the instructions said – 'Members of the New Zealand Women Writers must wear evening gowns and long white gloves.'

Well, I hope they have a good time down there. Too bad I won't be there, because I am the winner of the Donovan Cup for Poetry and it is to be presented to me tonight at this grand affair.

I dipped the plastic bucket into the drum of pig skilly and as I raised it the gale took the bucket and tossed the contents all over me. The whey ran down my face, through my hair and settled on my arms. Defeated by the gale, I struggled back up to the cowshed. 'Behold the winner of the Donovan Cup for Poetry,' I said, 'and look, yes, long white gloves and all.' I held out my arms. The white skilly had soaked into my old scarlet jersey, and covered my hands.

Had we been characters in a romantic Mills and Boon, this is where the hero would have stepped forward and held the woman of his dreams to his heart, stinking and all. But this wasn't fiction, and what the hero said was: 'You'd better go and have a bloody bath.'

1985, *When Women Write in Northland*

All for Ayrshire

M.L. Allan

Efficiently Richard checked the AB book. Two cows for Ayrshire, he mentally noted. Hang on, old Binz was bringing three.

'How many cows have you?' he shouted.

'How many does it look like?' came the reply.

Richard muttered to himself, 'Typical, two in the book, find another one and forget about writing her up.' Resigned to the inefficiency of the New Zealand farmer he loaded up his pipettes with Ayrshire semen. Binz had the cows into the first yard of the old walk-through shed. Richard stood waiting for Binz to bale up. Two were waiting patiently but a third gave Binz a little trouble. Richard prized his stockmanship and felt it best not to start until all the cows were in the bales.

'Come on old love,' said Binz. 'That's the old girl. Get in there, go on.'

Then the old voice tensed, 'Come on you old bitch, think you'll have me on, eh?' The cow dodged around the yard with Binz busy trying to force her into a bale. Binz's temper was on the up. 'Get in there,' he shouted. Richard smiled; he was feeling superior. Binz promptly gathered up a piece of alkathene from the heap of litter that surrounded his cowshed. As he turned back towards the yard the rebellious cow strode in to the first bale.

Richard's smile widened. 'All for Ayrshire then?' he questioned.

Binz spluttered, then in a composed manner replied, 'Yes, all the cows for Ayrshire, Richard.'

Richard inseminated the victim of Binz's verbal assault first and then spent a little longer on the Ayrshire heifer. Binz watched all this and said nothing. Then, as Richard walked towards the third animal, eager to complete his work, Binz said caustically: 'So you're a Pom, eh?'

Richard was feeling very superior now. He looked at Binz as he delved his gloved arm into the rectum of his last patient. 'I would be more inclined to say Englishman than Pom,' he retorted.

Richard seemed to be having trouble finding the vulva of this particular beast. He started to unfold the skin beneath his glove, thinking he must have scooped the vulva up as he inserted his left hand into the rectum. The animal stood patiently.

Binz smiled. 'No, I'd say Pom. I think an Englishman would know when he had his hand up my pet steer.'

1980, *Top Yarns from the New Zealand Farmer*

Lambing Beat

John Foster

(On the farms, we know it's dawn when the birds begin to sing.)

Pause after the peak – stop, to count the dead and dying,
The living that's left.
Dog tired, dog's tired.
Sock's wet, neck's wet.
Rain's heavy on the roof,
      And you'll be with it all, until nightfall.
A thousand petty grievances,
      Doing a job that is never altogether satisfactory,
Just your best.

(On the farms, we know it's spring when the mud dries up.)

(1970) 1999, *Selected Poems*

Bobby Calf

Barry Mitcalfe

I drove down last summer's road
did not see the calves at every gate
boxed in, blaring to the pitiless square
of absconding sky, did not hear
yesterday's pet, too little to eat
on its journey to my back, my belly, my feet

1978, *Uncle and Others*

Sweet Dieseline

Tom Landreth

Where the Mack trucks, there truck I,
From Whangarei to Bluff I ply
On gravel roads and tarsealed highways
City streets and country byways,
From busy port to lonely station
Shifting freight across the nation.
Where cops and cameras strew the way
I keep a legal 80k,
But bowling down State Highway One
I'll tailgate cars and do a ton.
Diesel fumes and stock excreta
Leave my trail a lot less sweeter,
You'll realise as I pass by
That, where the muck tracks, there truck I.

1998, *Speaking Tongues in the Wide Wilderness*

Scientific Management
David Ray

At Balclutha in the South
of the South Island far from Europe
and with a hand's curve of earth
in between, we breeze past
a freezing works. The concept
is clear. The sheep come in
by train through a great gate
that someone opens on signal
and when it is very busy –
thousands processed each day –
it is left open for the trains,
boxcars one after another.
And then it begins.
The sheep are not told, of course.
Wool to one bin, tallow of bodies
to another. But the sheep
have no gold in their teeth
nor rings on their hands.
It is Sunday and the long docks
are clear and no smoke drifts
from the stacks. Yet we speed up,
thinking of friends.

1993, *Wool Highways and Other Poems*

Loading the Bulls

William Owen

The cattle race extended from the yards, crossed the beach and the few feet of tidewater, then canted upwards to fit the scow's loading port. The Captain stationed Clarrie and Sid on either side of the ramp which led up to the port while Burney was sent as prodder for the beasts coming out of the yards. The Captain himself, and the mate, arming themselves with long poles, mounted the wide boards which formed the tops of the pens. Skoon was assigned a roving commission, to assist the flow of stock around the deck, to seal off the pens as they filled, and to keep Jocko supplied with the ropes he required. Jocko's job was to hornrope the bulls, position them bow to stern so to speak, and snug them tightly to the pen rails.

'Right, Tommy,' the Captain called.

'We're all set. Give us a couple of quiet ones first.'

'By jingo, that's a hard job,' Tommy sang out. 'We give you a couple of polies to start.'

'Righto. Watch them, lads,' warned the Captain. 'Keep them moving when they come down.'

Following a commotion in the yards the first bull, belaboured still from behind, appeared at the head of the race, baulked for a moment, then lumbered uncertainly down. In short order, several others followed. The first, assisted by Clarrie and Sid, whose billies aimed at the tender vertebrae above the juncture of the tail, clambered up the race and thundered onto the deck. Jack and the Captain, poking with their poles, guided it around the centreboard case . This bull was more bewildered than fierce. In a trice Skoon had it positioned. Jocko slipped a noose about its neck, for it was a naturally polled animal, half hitched the rope around its snout and tied it to the rail. Only then did the beast really begin to object to its treatment. Straining against the rope, it gave out a muffled roar and threw its hindquarters about the deck in a skittering dance of rage. But it was too late. Other beasts were being forced into the pen. Jocko gave the tethered bull an almost bone shattering clout which caused it to jump crashing against the cabin side, the Captain squeezed a further beast in and Skoon leapt down and dropped the planks into place.

'We are lucky with that first fella,' the Captain shouted. 'Got them going nicely. Give us some more, Tommy. Anything now. Whatever you can get into the race.'

1974, *Tryphena's Summer*

Work for Jocko and Skoon began in earnest. There was no way other than by brute strength to position these bulls. Both men wielded their billies, kicked if the flanks came within range, even twisted the tails if opportunity afforded. To turn a beast around, Skoon laid into the haunches while Jocko tugged at the hornrope and at the same time clubbed to the head. The bulls bellowed and slavered at these indignities but could do little in such close confinement.

As the beasts came aboard in greater numbers, the thundering of hooves on the deck, the roars, the shouts of the men, rose to a crescendo.

'Keep them going. Keep them going,' the Captain's voice cried above the uproar. 'We've got two pens full. We're going well.'

The Captain was everywhere above the pens, one moment leaning far over the loading race to rap an animal which baulked at the ramp, at another, nose whacking a beast which tried to turn back, the next, poking a bull which hesitated to join its fellows in a pen.

'Tommy's got them coming first rate. Just hitch them down, Jocko,' the Captain advised. 'We'll get them all aboard and neaten them after.'

By this time Jocko was sweating heavily from his exertions. He had completed the first two pens and was well into his third.

'Get Tommy to slow them down,' he answered. 'I've got most of these properly tied.'

'He's got to keep them going,' said the Captain, moving away. 'If he stops, he'll have a job getting them going again.'

'Just do as I've told you,' he said, over his shoulder. 'I want to get them aboard.'

'Right,' said Jocko. 'Come on Dutchman. Let's fill these goddamned pens.'

He threw down the rope he had been holding and jumped down to the deck. 'You'd think I didn't know my goddamned job,' he snarled up at Skoon.

The shout which issued from the yards at this moment was above the normal roar of the loading.

'Watch this one,' cried Tommy. 'He gave us a lot of trouble but we got him.'

Burney cheered as the grey bull appeared and rocketed past him. The men tending the lower part of the race cheered as the bull approached. Swaying from side to side, bumping the rails, it shot down over the sand. But at the sight of the tidewater in front of the ramp, it stopped.

'Give it to him. Keep him on the move. Get him up that ramp,' the Captain shouted.

Sid and Clarrie prodded and clouted and the Captain, leaning from above, swung his pole into the race and drubbed the beast's hindquarters. But the bull would not budge. It resorted to its peculiar mutter, to a spreadeagled stance that not even a tractor would shift, and to a retaliation in which it hooked and smashed at the rails.

'Reach in and poke him in the stones. See if that'll shift him,' the Captain said.

Jocko was working in amongst the bulls.

'Better come up, I think,' Skoon advised. 'A bad one coming.'

Jocko did not deign to reply. Had the others observed him, they could not have but remarked that he was pretty to watch. It was dangerous work, but it was nothing to Jocko. He moved among the beasts, keeping to the flanks, close in, rolling with their movements, gentling them, prodding them, tapping them into position. They knew he was there, but the bull which turned to regard him received a sharp rap on the jawbone to reward its interest. In a few minutes Jocko had them closed up.

'Righto. Help me put these pen bars up,' he called.

Skoon began to pass the planks down and Jocko fitted each into its slot. Suddenly, involuntarily, dropping one of the boards, Skoon cried a warning.

'Look out, man,' he shouted.

Jocko must have noticed the momentary lull in the flow of beasts onto the ship. Engrossed in closing up the third pen, he could not have been concerned by it. At Skoon's shout he turned, caught no more than an impression of that which confronted him, and sprang for the top rail. The bull, squealing with pain and rage at the attack on its testicles, had plunged onto the deck.

'Look out. Up on the rail, man,' bellowed the Captain. His warning was a second behind Skoon's. He had not seen that Jocko was working down on the deck. Jocko's leap was not quick enough. From its entry onto the deck, the bull did not stop. It was across the deck before a breath could be drawn in. It rose off its forelegs a little, hooked, buried the horn under the stock handler's ribs, jerked from the neck, and sent the man flying to the opposite side of the ship. Jocko staggered up and this time took a frontal attack. With this attack, he uttered his first, agonised cry. Perhaps it was this cry which electrified the Captain into action. Or perhaps it was the next awful punishment, which, surely, no man could survive. Knowing the exact reach of its horntip, the bull calculated its lunge, spitted the man again, lifted him up, held him like a bale on a hayfork, then shook him loose.

Desperately, weakly, futilely, Jocko attempted to come close to the bull. A shotgun was kept in the wheelhouse for just this kind of emergency. Except against a shark or two, it had never been used. Racing across, amazingly agile over the pentops, the Captain grabbed the weapon from its rack, scrabbled for shells, rammed two into the breach, raced back, aimed and fired. Even then he did not shoot to kill. The cartridge discharged to the top of the head, at the moment of the blast the fur on the bull's poll flew off, revealing a flash of white bone, the bull jerked back, then stumbled, stunned.

Dropping the gun, the Captain sprang to the deck.

Gasping, Jocko was endeavouring to rise. His eyes stared at the Captain in a gaze which did not see. The bull was also trying to regain its feet. It shook its head slowly in a drunken, circular movement. Its poll was a bloodied mass and blood poured into its eyes.

The Captain grasped Jocko under the armpits.

'Help me up with him, lad,' he appealed to Skoon. 'He can't move on his own.'

Together they carried him aft, past the watchers who had raced down from the yards following the shotgun's blast. With Sid's and Clarrie's assistance the shattered man was hefted gently up and laid on the catwalk.

The Hydatids Officer

Michael Henderson

Speeg Inglish,'said Colley Main, 'f'cries ache!'

'Dead, *dok bilong yu*, Bounce he dead?'

'Deered as a doornail, carput –'

'*Olaboi!* He good alive time last before, sure –'

'Beads me. Buried 'm yestidee, deerder'n cold muddon – '

'Yes day?'

'– todoy, gawn termorra –'

'*Em tasol*, that's it. *Wan* the less,' said the Hydatids Officer, looking around the yard in the drizzle: Sarge under the truck in the hayshed, Loam by the wood heap under the tankstand, but no sign of Bounce in the dank jungle of waratahs and netting, mouldy sacks, mildewed tyres, moss-grown drums, rusting corrugated iron, curried chainsaws, paint tins, traps, goatskins, the lopsided rainwater tank overflowing on the corner of the shed – another foot of mud and a few more dogs and it'd be a toss-up between Wewak and Madang. In the undrained quag and ooze, septic and faecal, he could hardly be more at home –

'When we've god rid of hidaddydids an' sheeb measles, they'll fine somethin else ter keep youse bastids in meat, never yer moind –'

'Meat?' said the Hydatids Officer, writing DEC'D by Bounce's name.

'The Director of Annymal Helf is a bleedin Commie his'elf. Ride up yer alley, the bleeder, red as they come, red as beedroot –'

'*Mi no gat rong, olsem mi no pret,* I no fault, so I no perturb perturb.'

'Shid,' said Colley Main. 'When were you born? Yestidee?'

'Yes day? The day Masta Bounce he die? *Dok* day?'

'Yair, the doy me dorg doyd.' Wrists like the shoulders of dogs that had seen a few too many scraps, full of scars where the hairs wouldn't grow. *Man em i bikpela,* he's big, thought the Hydatids Officer. *Het diwai, bikmaus,* and pinbrained, the bigmouth –

' 'ard yagger fer dorgs. 'Ard enough wiv out youse nosey Parker bastids stiggin ya stiggy beaks in. Plush four-wheel machines an' all, by cribes you're a pag a namby pambies iv ever I seen one, beads an' all.'

'Nam, Nam be pam be?'

'Oil soy,' slobbered Colley Main. 'Ev'ry wog I come across these doys 'as a cushy

1991, *The Lie of the Land*

jawb for the gawvermint, an' they're all remanded or remarried too, the whole load of 'em, the bliders, fer god's ache! There order be a law against it!'

'*Tapos yu no wok, yu no kisim pe*. You no work, you no get pay –'

'Kiss yer arse! How gum they call yer a offy sir? Where's ya yoonerform? Eh?'

'Form?'

'Dorgs doan hack yoonerforms. An' humins doan hack pigmy freaks givin 'em the creeps, friggin cannybulls –'

'*Maski palenti tok-tok –*'

'You'll never 'ave a road noimed after yer, ya know thad?'

'– nevermind talkie-talk.'

In the sun shower, the Hydatids Officer was lost in the farmer's shadow.

'Like me, fer instunce,' said Colley Main.

The Hydatids Officer looked up, and up, holding his clipboard.

'A road, I said,' said Colley Main.

'*Em i tri kolok sitret*, it's three o'clock –'

'Boy, are you bastids thick! *MAIN*! – Main Road, see? Ha blardy ha!' shouted Colley Main, swatting his thighs.

'*Mi laik i go nau*, I go now. *Tapos yu no wok –*'

'Shoim about thad dorg, a dorg like thad, tough as tannylised timmer. Wooden give a tinker's cuss fer *these* blardy mongrels, the pod-liggin bastids!' He let fly, and Sarge and Loam slunk off behind the four-wheel drive, from which the radio crackled and spat like gorse in bloom.

The Hydatids Officer gestured across the ridges and gullies of bush and scrub, puce and dun to the saddle and the Pass. 'River safe cross, *brukim wara?*'

'River? Huh!' derided Colley Main. 'The *creek*? Peas of cake!'

'Roadway *malmalu*, river –'

'F'cries ache!' shouted Colley Main. 'Thad creek's a peas of piss, 'ow many toims der I 'ave ter tell yer?'

The Hydatids Officer squeezed his birthstone. 'You for true?'

'You'll be orf like a dirdy shirt!' Colley Main thumped the tyre on the bonnet. 'Oil wadge ya through me rifle scope, ha blardy ha!'

Sick as the Sepik, uric and xanthic along the bilious banks, spewing over the ford. *Mi no laikim dispela samting.* He removed the fan belt, tied his oilskin across the grille and, clenching his juju, headed into the froth, the bow-wave troughing collusive and glaucous around the bull bars.

The water sloughed over his shoes, over the gear lever, and as the spare tyre dematerialised and the engine clunked and expired along with the radio, he saw his list swirl out of the capsizing cab:

HOLLY ✔
BRICK ✔
CHIP ✔
MOSS ✔
SARGE ✔
BOUNCE DEC'D (Natink em i dai pinis)
LOAM ✔
TOSS
SNOW
LOCK
BLUE
RAZZ
MIDGE
BROOK

He fetched up on the riverbank in a mangle of manuka, retching diesel. When the spasms subsided, he methodically cut, barbed and sharpened a stake. Then he stripped, leaving only the bloodstone around his neck. Naked, he knelt and scooped up clay, caking himself from ankle to scalp. He pared a smaller piece of wood, and with willow bark bound it to his penis.

Lek bilong mi-dai. Klosap mi bin-dai. My leg's numb. I nearly died.

The last thing he discarded was his watch. *Wara* resistant, my foot. *Ingilis i kranki*, my foot is the same as my eye, a piece of cake is the same as a piece of piss.

Below the ford, the four-wheel drive was on its back in rainbows of oil, its black feet in the air like the cow jammed up under the opposite bank.

He tore out a forelock, rinsed it clean of clay and looped it, looking through his uprooted hair, amaranthine in the last of the watery sun. Then, blood turning hyacinthine in the clay on his forehead, he pulled the noose of hair into a knot around the sun and said, 'Watch O *san,* and I will spit the meat of a pig.' Then he blew and spat upon the sun and threw it into the river, saying '*Mi no kaikai no mi no slip,* I no eat and I no sleep. *Kilok in-dai pinis, paia in-dai.* The clock has stopped. By the grass of my head, until I excrete long pig, O *san,* my stalk is torn from the corm of my fathers.'

He headed off the track, *brukim bus,* circling back through the bush, tasting the river, the clay, the blood, ichor. *Olaboi!* he cried as he loped and limped along, *OLABOI!*

In the scrub at the edge of the clearing, Bounce came bounding, nosing his bloody feet, red as beetroot. '*Yupela i-go pas,*' he said, jabbing the dog with his spear. 'You go ahead.'

Death in the Hayfield

Maureen Doherty

Today, a moment ripened so fast
it took my breath away
up to the birthplace of the stars and back again.
I'd found a pheasant's nest two days past
hidden deep and sure within the grass,
my dreaming feet had nudged her there
sitting as still as mare's breath on autumn air.
I spoke low and left her
peacefully in her warm brown camouflage –
unmoving except for the slow golden blinking of her eyes.

Today, I came once more to that place in the valley
amongst the river's blue meanderings
and the cicadas singing full throat in the trees.
I topped the wind-flung ridge
and heard the tractor's muffled roar
and saw the broad swathes of shaved green
with the grass lying, dying,
waiting for the baler's neat regurgitation.
One small grassy island still remained
where I knew she hid;
transfixed I stood and mutely watched
the monster round her roar
… still she did not rise, I held my breath,
the tractor passed right by her very beak
trailing its wider mower blades behind
and then she rose,
crying desperately into a world of blue.
Shielding my eyes, I watched her fly
speck-like into the sun.

The man had stopped for smoko,
the paddock done. His dogs and tractor
silent under the trees.
I found the nest and gently stooped
to where her smashed eggs lay
and then I stood, head bowed
in greater sorrow still –
for beside her eggs, her two legs lay,
clean cut – just like the hay.

1987, *Antipodes New Writing*

The Initiation

Brian Turner

Use a decent length of no. 8:

make sure you get it in deep, right
to the back of the burrow
if you have to.

Push and probe
until you feel the bastard
trying to squirm out of the way

then when you feel you've got it cornered
shove it in
and twist like hell

until you've got the bastard
really wound up
tight (it'll

squeal a bit) then
pull it out slowly
like you were pulling a lamb
from an old ewe's cunt,

then grab it
and break the bastard's neck,

the foreman said.

It wasn't *that* easy.

1978, *Ladders of Rain*

Ferreting About

Dan Davin

The surface of the day was as still as if there had never been men. The few sudden spurts of breeze sprinted over the young oats in silence, glowing briefly on their green with the wax-like gloss of a buttercup or the inside of a poppy. In equal silence overhead the white, separate ships of cloud sailed under the sun.

Watching them, John lay on his back, his hands clasped under his head. The few sounds that reached him were those that can be heard only in quiet, as the flick of an insect on the surface of a pool could not be heard without the silence it marks rather than destroys. His ear could distinguish them without his needing to look: the sheep in the next paddock cropping the new grass; a thrush moving about in the dense, dry prickles of the gorse hedge; a lark high up somewhere encouraging the sun; blades of grass straightening themselves with a tiny jerk after having been pressed down by his elbow; Paddy's tense breathing where he lay with his ear to the ground; the beating of his own heart.

'It's time there was a bolt,' Paddy said.

John straightened up on one elbow and stopped chewing the grass stalk in his mouth.

'Give them a chance,' he said. 'They probably feel a bit sluggish. Think how you'd feel if something came busting in on your Sunday snooze. You'd need time to get your pants on even if it was after your jugular.'

He took the piece of grass out of his mouth and looked at it. Then he bent it double and let the ends come slowly apart. A glassy pane of saliva formed in the angle. He held it to his eye as they used to do when they were kids and looked through.

A rabbit appeared in the tiny, triangular window. John dropped the stalk but did not otherwise move. The rabbit paused, looking at him.

Paddy was lying with his ear against the earth, oblivious to everything except sound.

The rabbit and John went on looking at each other. Its eyes were dark, wild with life hunted. Its sides moved in and out quickly. The fur on its chest rose and fell. A finger of breeze lifted a tuft on its back, showing the bluish grey.

John swivelled his eye slowly right to his rifle. His lock on the rabbit was broken. As it began to move, turning with a faint scutter of dust, he reached for the rifle, and twisted on to his stomach. By the time he had his eyes to the sights the rabbit was safe in the further hedge.

1949, *Roads from Home*

'Well, I'll be damned,' said Paddy. He had looked up just in time to see the rabbit disappear. 'I wonder where that blasted dog's got to. Just like one of Uncle Tim's dogs to have vanished when he's wanted.'

Paddy ran over to look for the place the rabbit had sprung from. John followed him. 'It was here,' he said. 'Look, there's the pop-hole.'

Neatly hidden under a Scotch thistle there was a small hole. The grass round it hung over and they had missed it when setting the nets.

As they were admiring it Pompey's triangular face looked out at them. He rested his two yellow forefeet on the edge of the opening. There were tufts of grey fur mixed with the damp, caked earth on his claws.

'He must have had a fight to shift that fellow,' said John.

Pompey blinked at them, his pink eyes objective and unreproachful. Then he dropped back into the hole.

'You'd better get another net, Paddy. If he's gone back there must be more where that chap came from.'

Paddy pegged the net down and then spread it over the pop-hole, keeping the drawlines free of the thistle. They settled down again to wait.

'One thing I will say for a pop-hole,' Paddy said, 'once you've found it you're pretty well set. They always make for it.'

John just nodded. He was sitting up now, his hands draped loosely over his knees. Ferreting wasn't the fun it used to be when he was a kid Paddy's age. Something had gone out of it. You had a tendency now to think about what the rabbit must be feeling. It was all right for kids and ferrets. They were both wild. Only you got tamer as you got older. You began to see what other people were feeling yourself. And from that it wasn't a very big step to thinking what animals must feel about things. That rabbit had been wild with fear. Fear had followed it across the paddock till it was safe in the gorse, still alive and free …

The ground under him drummed and thumped. Another one bolting. John looked at his brother. He could see the pride in Paddy's eye. Pompey was going to be a winner.

The thumping grew louder. It moved towards the pop-hole. They swivelled where they sat, to watch it. There was a final rush. The rabbit hurtled into the air, taking the net with it. But the peg held, the drawlines ran free. Caught by his own speed, frantically struggling and bunched always tighter by his struggles, the rabbit lay across the broken thistle, a bundle.

Paddy rushed on him, separated the two rings at the ends of the net and opened it. He caught the rabbit by one hind leg and held it while he freed the other, splayed out on one string of a mesh.

'Got you, you beauty.' The rabbit, getting its other leg free, gave a last, raking kick and drew three furrows of blood down the back of his hand.

'You savage sod,' Paddy said. But he kept his hold on the one leg till he had the other also. Then he held the rabbit up by both hind legs in his left hand. He raised his right hand with the palm stiff and the fingers straight and brought it down with a swift, chopping stroke on the back of the rabbit's neck. The wild, dark eyes grew still, more velvety; the ears dropped. Paddy threw the body on the ground. It kicked once or twice. But these were only the echoes of life. The head was lolling on the broken neck. There was blood at its ears.

The ferret's fierce face flickered for a moment in the opening of the pop-hole and then withdrew.

'Isn't that a ferret for you, now?' Paddy said, stooping over the net to re-set it.

'Time enough. He might stick you up yet before the day's out. Especially if there are any younkers about.'

'It's too early for there to be many yet. The frosts were very late this year.' But he was thinking uneasily of those milky-doe skins he had sold yesterday.

'I'm not so sure.'

'Well, anyhow, he's a bloody good worker, you can't deny that. Look at the way he shifted those two. He couldn't have worked better if I'd trained him myself.'

'We'll see. Time enough yet to talk.'

He sat cross-legged and watched Paddy take out his knife and start skinning. One stroke up the left thigh, another up the right. A cut severing the skin from under the tail and joining the first two. Then a foot on the rabbit's hind feet to give purchase, and the skin peeled off like a football jersey. A cut at each of the forelegs, and the skin was tight round the head. A cut there and the wet, bluish-white surface opened, yielding fur. A final tug and the carcase dropped to the ground, the skin came away free in Paddy's hand.

'A good skin,' Paddy said. 'Still got the winter coat, or still had it, rather.'

He picked up the steaming carcase and was about to throw it into the gorse hedge.

'I'd hang on to it, Paddy, if I were you. You might want it to coax Pompey out if he sticks you up.'

Paddy paused. That was sound sense. If the ferret made a kill down the hole and went to sleep on a full belly the smell of a fresh carcase was the best way of waking him up and tempting him out.

But it'd show he didn't have faith in Pompey, to keep it. He whirled the carcase round by the legs and flung it into the hedge. It caught over an upper branch and swung there. A thrush flew out, chittering.

'He won't stick us up,' Paddy said.

John smiled. That was what he liked about Paddy. That, and the fact that he hadn't thrown it very far.

Paddy stabbed his knife into the ground till it was clean, then folded it and put it back in his pocket. He picked up the skin and put it away in the net-bag. Outside the house he was well-trained. He might throw his trousers on the floor when he went to bed but you'd never have to pick up a net after him when he'd ferreted a hole. And lately, Mum said, since he'd got his first suit of longs he'd even taken to putting them on a coathanger and yesterday he'd pressed them, wet dish-towel, spitting on the iron, and all. Which meant he was beginning to take his appearance as seriously as his ferrets. Growing up. John knew the signs. It wasn't so very long, he remembered, since he, too, had strolled up and down Dee Street of a Sunday night and eyed the giggling girls who went by arm in arm.

They sat there waiting for the next bolt. Then John got tired of sitting and lay on his back again. In the restored silence the sounds of quiet came back. Only now the lark was gone and in the sky a hawk hovered, envious at the smell of blood. John turned on his face. As his eye focussed to this nearer infinity he saw how the grass broke up into individual grass-blades and how among them tiny insects, ants, a lady-bird, wandered, labouring, adventurous, and amazed.

> 'Lady-bird, lady-bird, fly away home.
> Your house is on fire, your children alone.'

He set her on the back of his hand and tapped her with his finger. Her wing-case opened, showing the black under the red. With a faint whir she took off. Home?

Pioneer Woman with Ferrets

Ruth Dallas

Preserved in film,
As under glass,
Her waist nipped in,
Skirt and sleeves
To ankle, wrist,
Voluminous
In the wind,
Hat to protect
Her Victorian complexion,
Large in the tussock
She looms,
Startling as a moa.
Unfocussed,
Her children
Fasten wire-netting
Round close-set warrens,
And savage grasses
That bristle in a beard
From the rabbit-bitten hills.
She is monumental
In the treeless landscape.
Nonchalantly she swings
In her left hand
A rabbit,
Bloodynose down,
In her right hand a club.

1976, *Walking on the Snow*

Nor'wester

C. Evans

Here I come
out of the devil's blast-furnace
to shake your trees,
steal your topsoil,
rattle your windows,
lift your tiles,
probe your crannies,
tug your tender shoots,
sting your eyes,
choke your breath,
wrench your branches,
scatter your leaves,
ruin your gardens,
despoil your lands,
searing, forcing, roaring,
killing.
Rogue wind of the Plains
– I hate all growing things –
Nor'wester.

25 October 1973,
New Zealand Farmer

The Dam

Elizabeth Hill

The man watched his wife as she poured hot water from a kettle into the sink. In silence he picked up two kerosene tins and walked out of the house. It was almost half a mile to the only place in the creek where they could get water. The well was dry, and precious little left in the house tanks. The sight of the distant sea teased him as he followed the track through open gates in bare paddocks.

A few bales of hay were stored in the shed for their two hacks; he had sent most of the stock off to the abattoir. Only the nucleus of a breeding flock remained, left to find food and moisture, God alone knew how. They too would have to go before they dropped. If it wasn't for the cattle left in the hill paddock they called the Devil's Punchbowl, they might as well walk off the place themselves.

He filled the tins at the waterhole, bailing out the precious fluid with an old saucepan. He tried not to get any mud, but that was impossible. At least the hole was fenced off from stock, and the dogs tied up so they couldn't go near it.

He stopped at the kennels and topped up their water dishes; then, looking helplessly at his desiccated vegetable garden, entered the kitchen and put the tins down.

The woman had made a pot of tea. She sat at the table, elbows resting, her hands around her cup. A shaft of late sunlight accented the deep red of her long hair, an illusory highlight in the otherwise flat scene. She looked at him briefly once, then poured his tea.

They scarcely spoke to each other now. There would have been only one subject anyway. Whatever they mentioned came back to the inevitable topic of watching animals near starvation and death. Their lives had become like the dust which sifted in round doors and windows.

She put a hand up to her hair, then pulled it away in disgust. Only a week ago she'd said she'd wait until it rained before she washed it, then celebrate with gallons of water. She thought bitterly of her scissors. Perhaps if she cut her hair it would rain. He watched her as he drank his tea, understanding.

Tonight they'd go to bed and lie apart, thinking, staring into the darkness. Tomorrow they must ride over the hill to the Devil's Punchbowl to inspect the dam. When *it* dried up, they'd drive the rest of the stock to town, and that'd be that.

The sun dropped behind the hill, and the great nor'westerly arch in the sky offered

1979, *Landfall*, No.130

less hope than ever. They were too numbed even to listen to the weather forecast.

Morning was the same as every morning had been for months, except that this was the day which would probably decide their future –the day the dam might be too dry for them to stay on the farm any longer. The man got the horses ready in the yards, while his wife came out carrying two water-bottles. He tied them onto the saddles and slung a Greener .303 rifle over his shoulder. Only the dogs appeared to be enjoying the prospect of the exercise, while the horses were cranky, sensing tension. The couple mounted. He whistled the dogs in and they jogged towards the hills.

There was an early morning breeze coming in under the westerly, and the woman could taste the bite of salt. The momentary coolness and whiff of clean kelp soothed them as they gained height, but soon died away. When they reached the lip of the Devil's Punchbowl the uprush of kiln-dry air tore at them, lifting the horses' manes into wild streamers. Now they must ride down over bare soil and crumbling sheep tracks. Everywhere the dried dung.

The woman tried not to think of what might lie at the bottom of the great basin, concentrating on the smooth rhythm of her husband's horse in front, and the patches of white sweat-suds under its tail. Even her saddle was wet with perspiration soaking through her jeans. The reins were slippery in her hands and sweat blurred her vision, but she could see the dam now. Its dregs could barely be called a waterhole. Three Hereford steers were trapped in the dark cone at its centre, held prisoner by suction and their own weight. Seeing the riders, they heaved into galvanic action, then settled down once more as if accepting their fate.

Husband and wife tethered their horses in the shade of an empty hay barn. The man took a coiled rope from his saddle and handed her the rifle. She sat on the ground watching the now familiar scene. The man approached the first wallowing beast, and while it struggled, slipped a noose round its horns. At a given signal the dogs went in, chivvying and barking, goading the animal into a final effort to free itself, while the man strained on the taut rope. The woman was tense, rifle at the ready, planning how she would aim should the rescued steer 'go' the man. They could appear to be almost dead from exhaustion, thirst and starvation, then attack with incredible agility, intent on killing whoever had saved them.

One by one, freed from the mud's grip, the red cattle stood quietly on safe ground, their legs and bellies thickly plastered, fading rapidly from grey to white in the intense heat.

Under the tin roof of the open shed the couple rested, sipping from their water-bottles. The dogs panted heavily, and the horses hung their heads, eyelids closed, tails swishing.

'Well, that's that then. Might as well start moving the herd. It's a long way to town.'

The woman lay flat on her back, not speaking. She was counting the nail holes in the old roofing iron, but she also appeared to be listening. She suddenly sat bolt upright and placed her hand against his mouth.

'Quiet, listen!'

Then he heard it too; that low rumble. Every nerve in his body tensed as he thought of the possibility of the shimmering waves of heat being forced up from the wide hollow by an advancing cold front. Could it be real, or was it just an echo of the thunder in the mountains?

The beige sky darkened and a chillness met their bare arms, pimpling them with gooseflesh. Dusty wisps of hay were torn into the air. A lightning flash was followed by a crackle and thump overhead. Then came that indefinable smell of reviving earth, compounded of suspended elements in the parched soil, all coming alive in the saturated atmosphere. The next roll of thunder was followed by the first splat of rain. In seconds the air was pierced by slanting spears of water.

The woman rose slowly to her feet and began to loosen her auburn hair. With slow, ritualistic movements she took off her clothes, letting them fall where she stood. He watched, mesmerised.

Rain was now hurling itself against the ground, bouncing up in thousands of water spouts, and running off in spreading rivers. Thunder ricocheted continuously along the rim of the bowl. Lightning exploded in the swiftly rising air currents.

The woman's skin glistened as she began to dance, moving rhythmically, trance-like into the storm. Her long hair draped her shoulders, and she lifted it to the deluge, combing its soggy strands with her fingers.

His clothes fell beside hers, and he was dancing through the streaming curtain towards her. Together they laughed and spun, touching, separating, but always aware of each other. Unspeaking they joined hands, and with water deluging them their laughter rang as they reached the shelter of the shed where rain threaded through nail holes in the roof and their horses waited patiently.

Only their audience of cattle remained in the storm, red and white faces staring from the amphitheatre, while life-giving water soaked muddied hides and the dam began to fill.

So easy

Pat White

you wake, and suddenly
winter is at the back door

it's so fucking easy
this time heavy clouds have moved
east from the Tararuas, and
the bastards know their business
two days steady rain

too little, too late …
Christ knows! Bog Irishmen would
see the joke, the Krauts dig a drain
the Longbush cocky, he
turns from the wind to light
a smoke – aged, hard, meaner
for the season that has been

1999, *Drought and other intimacies*

The Past and the Passing

For a so-called young country we have quite a rural past to look back on, along with the remaining sights and symbols of earlier days. The most obvious of these are the farm buildings, in varying stages of disuse and decay, that nestle beneath macrocarpa or poplar or have been infested by elderberry and fern, but can still be glimpsed as you shoot past at 110 kilometres an hour. These remnants, important though they may be, are merely structures; the real history lies with those who built and worked in these sheds and yards and lived in the nearby huts and steadings. The sight of rusty iron, slanting weatherboards, mortar-less bricks and broken rails can cause some to stop and remember other days and different ways. They call it nostalgia, though nothing tangible ever came of it, other than many of the stories and verses in the following pages.

None of us have to get very old before we start reminiscing about good times and, as the years advance and the memories accumulate, it becomes a very comfortable means of escape from a more awkward present. Not surprisingly, though, we are inclined to drop the uncomfortable bits. This convenient failing was neatly summed up by Marion Rowan in a piece she did for *Open Country*: 'Looking back, Sundays were always fine, and it was always summer'. But seasons pass and some of the material in this section is about rural folk in the autumn of their years who have found themselves living in the city. Some, men in particular, have found coping with their estrangement from the land very difficult. A trio of well-known New Zealand writers, Amelia Batistich, Barry Crump and Owen Marshall, show different aspects of the transition from country to town, youth to old age.

For my part I remember back in 1987 filming a *Country Calendar* profile on the legendary Bill Chisholm, for over 35 years manager of the huge and formerly overgrazed and rabbit-devastated Molesworth Station in inland Marlborough. Our task was to film this great man of action 10 years after his retirement and take him back to the station to describe his early days there and recall later achievements. We also looked at the life of a man who, by dint of the government's retirement policy – the station was administered by the then Lands and Survey Department – had been forced to retire to Blenheim.

That film took us into some of the greatest mountain country in the world: expansive upland basins, daunting, gaunt and grey peaks and historic manmade sights such as the Tarndale Homestead and the Red Gate Hut. And wherever you looked in that early summer, there were cattle, mobs of them, thriving on hock-high pasture that no one could have dreamt of when Chisholm took up the reins in the early 1940s. Despite those upland images, my most enduring vision of that time was down country and human: 'Big Bill', beneath the same 10-gallon hat he'd have worn on Molesworth, seated on a pushbike, pedalling the back roads round Blenheim. Waddling behind was his companion corgi – the faintest imaginable link with the posses of mounted stockmen and packs of cattle dogs that once would have followed in his wake.

The ride was a morning event; just as regular was Bill's post-lunch snooze. This, which filming did not defer, took place in a little room at the back of his garage. There, gently snoring on his day bed, beneath photos of cattle crossing rivers in mountain valleys, lay one of New Zealand agriculture's legends. It was a scene that embodied both the past and the passing.

Mutton

John Newton

Through the glassless window frame
a breeze. The quiet week after shearing.
In the press is the season's last bale,
the mob needs shifting,
a gate needs swinging,
there's a morning's work shovelling under the pens
where the blood and shit
that's drained through the wooden slats
re-emerges as pumpkin tucker.

This, the original shed, has held up
as long as the place has been farmed.
It threatens to leave us on every wind.
The roofing iron is no longer red
but the colour of rust. The weatherboards
are no longer the red they were painted
but the colour
of woolsheds seen from the road,
seen from the hill, known by heart.

A sack needle, wide as a spoon, stitches
a cap on this last batch of bellies
and leavings. The slow
ticking fall of an axe
drifts through the gaping frame;
the sea-breeze freshens; the next
mutton, knotted
in cheesecloth, sways
nostalgically over the catching pens.

1985, *Tales From the Angler's Eldorado*

Boots
Field Candy

There were always boots steaming haphazardly across the back verandah, a muddy, disorderly fleet which ranged in size from quaint little cockleshells to much larger launches and runabouts. Overlooking the wallowing armada were two ocean-going vessels, Mona the mother ship and me, a reluctant and ineffectual fleet commander. We would survey the gumboot squadron with a mixture of resignation and despair. More often than not these lesser ships lay capsized or in collision, their hulls encrusted with mud and dung.

Every command to spruce up, to clear the decks, met with only desultory success. It was usually left to the mother ship and me to wade in amongst the beached boots to set them on an even keel and arrange them in some sort of formation. How was it with small boys that there was usually as much mud on the inside of their gumboots as on the outside? The feet that emerged from them were not always easy to look at; the effects on the olfactory senses were even more difficult to bear.

The years passed. The feet grew and so did the size and cost of the replacement gumboots. The space on the verandah grew even more congested. Were there enough rubber trees in Malaysia to keep us going? The time came when my own boots began to go on undisclosed voyages of discovery, often when I needed them most. Some day, I raged, I would get even with those sons of mine. Some day their boots would be big enough for me to wear. That day never came.

What did come about was that a shiny new pair of boots berthed at the back door. I rubbed my hands together in vengeful anticipation. I'd take those boots on a maiden voyage to the cowshed. I arranged them into launching position but upon stepping into them I was engulfed by their immensity. It was like plunging into a couple of funnels. I made to get the voyage under way but was nearly brought down by the size and weight of those dreadnoughts. Revenge was sour.

Once I was a tall ship among lesser ships. One by one the lesser ships grew to over-look the old mother ship and me. One by one they weighed anchor and steamed out of their home port: to a distant city, to Australia, to Europe. Only one small 13-year-old frigate rides at anchor in the harbour, our most recent launching. Apart from his gum-boots there is order and emptiness on our back verandah. Now we look back with affection upon the former chaos of capsizes, collisions and mud. We may never again see the entire fleet at anchor in home waters.

1988, *Every Living Thing*

276

When Jean Deans Raced the Train
'Blue Jeans' (Ross McMillan)

Last night the hills were blue and black
And fresh from top to toe.
This morning like my head – alack –
They wear a crown of snow.
When autumn days are red and gold
And all the world is still.
It makes me think of days of old –
Jean Deans and Curly Bill.

You've never heard of her of course –
No reason that you should.
But no one ever sat a horse
Or rode it like she could.
A slender girl with chestnut hair
And eyes like summer days,
She always had a smile to spare,
And gentle winning ways.

And from her home, three times a week,
She'd ride across the plain.
And stop awhile at Barnens Creek
And wait there for the train.
A whistle from the crossing gate,
The throbbing of the rail,
Would mean that old 'twelve-thirty-eight'
Was coming with the mail.

A plume of smoke around the curve –
Her hand and head went down.
With plucky heart and steely nerve
She'd start the race for town.
Across the creek and over hedge
And ditch and fence and rail.
Past Bob Brown's henhouse on the ledge
And past his old cow bail.

Past the gum trees standing guard
Along the river bank.
And past the sheep and cattle yard –
And past the water tank.
Up to the siding ran her mare
With flying tail and mane –
And how the passengers would stare
When Jean Deans raced the train.

The old grey headed engineer
Would give a whistle blast.
Fireman, a grin from ear to ear
Would 'sling' the coal in fast.
And second class, and first class too
Would cheer with might and main,
Oh what a sight it was to view
When Jean Deans raced the train.

She had a sweetheart on the hill,
A true son of the land
And everyone liked Curly Bill
Out where the high hills stand.
When came the call for Bill to sail
To war so far away,
She never failed to meet the mail
And race the train each day.

For letters came across the seas
From strange and foreign lands.
They came from where the tall palm trees
Grow in the sunburnt sands.
From Egypt, then the Dardanelles
To tell of tears and pain.
Till no one waved with happy yells
When Jean Deans raced the train.

She came though thunder clouds would roll,
She came in sleet and rain.
It seemed as if her heart and soul
Were wrapped up in that train.

Beside the rails she'd whirl and wheel,
In one wild frantic ride,
Then homeward down the road she'd steal
The mail bag at her side.

Billy fell at Chunuk Bair
Where many brave men lie.
In all the bloody battles there
No others climbed as high.
A savage struggle in the dark
To take the top and stay.
But with the dawning, still and stark
The New Zealanders lay.

And though the seasons turn and turn
And though the years drift by.
And nations fight and never learn –
And men grow old, like I,
The one day in my life I'd name
That caused such bitter pain –
The day that Jean Deans never came
To race the train again.

2000, *The Country Bloke*

One of Our Aircraft Failed to Return

Patricia M. Saunders

In the squadron you will be replaced
by another young officer,
open-faced
with a good nerve,
dash of initiative
eager to serve. …

… And in the mess
another such
gay and modest will confess
there are often moments when courage fails
in spite of purple ribbons
and comrades' tales. …

… Only on these acres of green
pasture-land dedicated by your forebears
could your passing mean irreparable disaster
to the woman who loved you, the horse you rode,
and the dog who called you master.

1948, *Arena*

The Old Kitchen Table

Jim Henderson

Let's pay honour to the old kitchen table.

Sister Hilary and her schoolteacher Alice, coming in from school up the hill in freezing winter, 2 ½-mile walk each way, thawing out, clasping mugs of hot soup.

The stuffing on that table, of Christmas poultry beneath the hanging red mistletoe.

The cutting, on that long table, of scores of thousands of sandwiches, invariably roast meat, chopped egg, or tomato – even salmon was regarded with some suspicion, for midday tucker, by the farm folk. Early breakfasts for the men going out on the hills. The smother and leak of bottling fruit, sauces, the rare plucking of quail for casserole with bacon.

Up there, up the Takaka Hill, I had my own little flock of turkeys. Alas! Alas! My turkeys were taken from me, and banished to the back of the farm to punish me for vileness and vandalism. The turkeys became wild. Sometimes they provided a tasty roast.

One great day, Hilary and teacher Alice took turkey sandwiches to school, weak with anticipation. As they set out, my brother Ron halted my sister.

'Don't you tell any of the other children what's in your sandwiches. Some of the men working on the hill might fancy a roast turkey too. Not a word to anyone.'

The shearers gathered around the table in shearing time, the tremendous meals they'd earned and deserved. The women proud there were no holdups. Faces like a Dutch painting in oils …

Over 70 years ago. Mum ironing, yes ironing Bob Huganon's back through brown paper, to cure his lumbago. It didn't. Everyone apprehensive, especially Bob, prone on the long table.

And the endless ironing of endless avenues and avalanches of sheets, and so on. The hell of homework there, night after protesting night. The old kitchen table, scrubbed white over more than 70 years … oh, the thousands of meals, the miles of pastry, preparing cake mixtures, rock cakes – mountains of rock cakes – sponges, and Mum's endless cavalcade of the big fruit cake she called Black Joe.

Birthday cakes … icing … cream puffs … cutting out biscuits. Bathing the baby on the table, gurgles and splashes …

Every day except Sunday, the green canvas mailbag emptied on it, the modest cas-

1989, *Jim Henderson's New Zealand*

cade, the weekly thump of the *Auckland Weekly News,* the bigger thump, twice yearly, of the Bournville tin of chocolates from saved cocoa tokens.

Nearly 80 years back, a dear woman, Mary Mearing from Edinburgh, who, with her husband, George Mearing, had come from marriage in England to this Takaka hilltop believing it was a fruit farm.

Dear Mary was very embarrassed on this kitchen table. A stranger came into the kitchen without warning. This was 1911. There on the table lay Mary in only her petticoat, while young husband George was scraping all the biddybiddy burrs off her petticoat … the burrs were a curse in those days, hard on sheep and lambs, some of them even blind from it.

The faces of all those good and open and true workers … and teachers like clever Elva Baigent from Wakefield.

Good old Dad, Herbert Henderson, absent-minded, up with the men about 3 o'clock one morning for a special morning muster, Dad half asleep and intent on explaining the various beats and work of the day. He amazed everyone by walking round the table and carefully pouring the tea onto each man's porridge.

I chased my brother Ron once round and round that table with a big carving knife, determined to kill him. Unsuccessful.

So you see, of course, it wasn't really a kitchen table at all, or not just a kitchen table. It was anything and everything … or nothing. It witnessed the best in us and the worst in us, the highs and lows of our everydays.

Whether an object of derision or delight, never underestimate the sly versatility of the extremely ordinary kitchen table.

Squatters' Rites

John Gordon

Dunny, privy, longdrop or loo: whatever name you knew it by – and never the urban title, 'toilet'– this outpost of the past stands as a monument to the time when the words, 'I'm going for a walk', had a very personal meaning.

The decline of the 'wee house' began when the Korean War reached its peak. Wool prices soared, and the rites of squatting became – like their incumbents – flush. At the first sign of a healthy cheque, rural women plumped for porcelain and plumbing, along with other long-awaited home aids and improvements. No more for them the chilly dash on wet and windy nights or listening to the imagination-stretching noises a slab and corrugated structure could make – just as the moon came out to cast a threatening shadow in the wrong place. Then there were the nocturnal nasties that could creep over a hand or thigh! And the never-to-be-forgotten time that the farm's last Clydesdale came to the back corner to give its neck a damn good rub. The whole valley was able to share the power and pitch of that squatter's fright!

For many a farming man, though, the dunny's disappearance meant the end of a regular a.m. ritual. Out the back door he'd come, pause at the hathook, hobble into his gumboots then amble round the side of the house and on down the path to the back gate. For those of us who came later, it was necessary to open, close and snib the gate noisily, allowing he who had stolen that morning's march to defend his position – 'I'm in here!' Then, confident that any wool gathering from within would have ceased and that the seat would be warm, you leaned back on the gate and waited. Here you could enjoy the freshness of the morning. Cast your eyes over the flat and check that all was where it should be; that the bullocks hadn't broken through their break in the chou' and that the ewes were on the right side of their fence in the swedes. Birds were listened to, the crisp crystals of the dew observed, and various scents sniffed. Remembering, of course, that a well-aired privy was always devoid of odour – no need to use the can of a thousand visits in the great outdoors.

Siting a wee house was as important a rural planning task as the line of a farm lane or positioning a new homestead. It had to be placed so that you could sit with the door open to a wide vista, yet remain unseen from nearby windows, sheds and shelter-belts. If the weather dulled the view or came in the open doorway, the door could be closed and reading caught up on. Windowless though privies were, their gaping slabs, cracks

1985, *New Zealand Journal of Agriculture*

and knotholes provided plenty of light. Perhaps a book or paper you'd brought with you or one of the resident collection that lay dog-eared in the corner of the all-purpose shelf. Occasionally the wording on one of the squares of news or magazine print, impaled on a wire spike or threaded on a baling twine loop, would catch your eye. These were always ripped just where the story was reaching its climax or the name of the guilty given. In more complete form, a long running survey of rural reading habits showed that pastoral periodicals were more often read in the wee house than the big one.

Although the time spent in here was often the only truly reflective and relaxed part of the day, squatters weren't incommunicado, as they were usually well within earshot and, when necessary, could be called on to participate in three-way telephone conversations. In other circumstances visitors could be received, though not seen; they stood at the stern quarter. Many a farm worker received his daily instructions from a polished pine-wood throne.

Some male members of the old school found this daily pattern impossible to break. Years after the installation of housebound plumbing they still took a morning walk, regarding the new facilities as 'the ladies'. Sadly, nowadays, there aren't many gents left.

38 Years

J.M. Kerwin

Farming was different when I first started. I don't just mean aerial top dressing and three-point linkages. These of course have made for great changes, but it's more the little things like church on Sundays, holding the crank handle the right way, and the neighbours. It's hard to explain. I wouldn't swap anything for what I had then. The church was always more social than religious for me, wouldn't have a Model A on the place and my next door neighbour's been Harry Miles for 38 years.

It'll be a long time before I forget my first meeting with Harry. The cows were giving me sheer hell. What with bloat and mastitis, I was run off my feet for three weeks. Nothing fatal for the cows, just enough to take twice as long over milking and up all night with sick animals. Sometime during all the confusion the next door farm had been sold and the new owners moved in. I'd heard about it of course, knew their name and that they had a young baby.

When I first saw Harry he was doing a fencing job on the paddock across the creek behind my yards. His red boiled face shone with sweat as he rammed the earth around a post. I wandered over to introduce myself and have a look at the job he was doing. After the introductions we both started to roll a smoke. Looking at his post I got such a shock I nearly dropped my fag.

'Hell,' I said, 'is that willow?'

'Yes,' he replied, 'it was shading the house too much and after cutting it down, I thought I may as well use it.'

'But it'll grow,' I said incredulously. 'And even if it doesn't, willow will rot away in no time.'

'Oh well, it'll have to do for now, it's about all there is on the place of any size,' he said.

I tried to talk him in to cutting some yellow pine from the government reserve, but he was pushed for time, had to drive his herd on to the place in a couple of days, and wanted a few wires up to keep them on the property.

Thirty-eight years later that fence is still standing. The willow grew all right, but not enough to cause the wires to break, just enough to keep a nice tension on them. The cows browse on them so they don't get too wide, and it must be the wind that stops them getting too tall. They did grow a bit, but Harry just put another wire on the bottom to fill the gap.

I don't give Harry much advice these days; my yellow pine yards have been replaced twice since then.

1982, *Landfall,* No.143

September, 1983

Mapiu, Remembered Roses

Nancy Fox

I never deluded myself that the past was golden,
but I remembered roses.
The house my father built was white and my mother's roses
covered one end.
There would be people, I thought,
the rattle of a dog-chain
and the friendly, inconsequential conversation of chooks …
though perhaps no roses.
There were no roses.
There were no people.
The house was white still, but blind and silent …
windowless, and filled with hay.

1989, *Landmarks: Poems 1937-1987*

Farewell Prickly, Luscious Blackberry

'Grammaticus' (E.M. Blaiklock)

A detail passed unnoticed in the budget, save by the Northland farmers; something which had to come, but it was sad. The common blackberry was listed among the noxious weeds which can claim a subsidy. The farmers of the long peninsula will launch a great assault on the invading brambles, and blackberry and apple pie will be a memory of vanished years.

I agree with all the arguments. Blackberry was fine on someone else's property, but once see a sprouting runner on our own ground and out would come spade and mattock to destroy it. The tangled masses of the bramble, thoughtlessly introduced by homesick pioneers, covered acres of good ground and miles of roadside. You could burn it and slash it, and still it crawled to 'unwind the works of men'.

But blackberrying was good. In those days of empty roads we would find our way to the Wairoa Valley out of Clevedon, where the roadside jungle grew headhigh, rich with thorns and February fruit. We had short lengths of board to place on the springy vines, and make an entrance to the harvest of big black berries. It took an hour to fill a kerosene tin or a big bucket. Then, red with scratches on arms and legs, we would emerge as though from a battle with Kilkenny cats, wash in a clean waterhole, build a safe fire on the river shingle, and picnic as that generation knew so well how to do. A clean stream it was, noisy under the willows. There was another place I remember, no doubt by now purged and weedless, and stripped of its free fruit.

We enjoyed some holidays in a good friend's house on the edge of the Rotorua lake near Ngongotaha. We always chose that magic week when the schools had resumed with sultry February's onset, but with the universities still on vacation ... I would take a large billy and step from the lawn into the lake, limpid and not yet green with pollution. A small promontory and a brake of bracken and young willow made a short wade necessary. Beyond that tangle was a full acre clogged deep with bramble. The soil was pumice and the blackberries not as luscious as the variety from the black, river silt at Clevedon, but good for a gallon or two to mix with apples for a pie. There was cream along at the camp store, and no great effort to make a pie, to eat as the evening waves clucked along the frontage with its pumice beach. The eastern sky turned opal, and the sun dropped behind the black heap of Ngongotaha.

In these Auckland western suburbs, there were blackberries near at hand. The roads

10 January 1978, *New Zealand Herald*

up to the central parts of the Waitakere range had their rich roadside vines before an affluent suburbia bought up the land, and cleared away the infestation. Even the summit road to the top of Mt Atkinson was good for a pie or two.

But all things pass. I suppose old moa hunters told stories to their grandsons of how good it was when hunting was real; to sit by a campfire on the Catlins or Owaka rivers and chew a big moa bone before reckless slaughter killed off the dinornis. It is as much the berrying as the berries that bears the subtle pleasure, that sense of an unbroken link with all the past.

I found blackberries once by a stony little lane in Cornwall, and wondered whether they had been there in the days when Launcelot came riding by ... I stood and sampled the berries with the sea calm around the rocks below. The taste of them flooded my mind with pictures of the stream under the willows, and the still lake, with Mokoia swimming, and stirred a wild longing to be home.

Clarence Pack Team

Frances Blunt

They know their business, and it is to carry
Balancing loads from daylight chaff till sleep.
They know the summer shingle, and the flurry
When water fills the footholds fetlock deep.

These are the experts; when ice is thawing
Thin on the rocky climb above the face,
These take it calmly, step in single turning
Edging well out, to leave the load its place.

If you should meet they are surprised at strangers
Intruding on the known accustomed way,
High on the mountain they are at home and usual,
Save where the plane's roar spits across their day.

The radio sends them, and the planes supplant them,
Bred to their skill they are no less the last.
Stand back to watch the string come down this evening –
Jaunty and tired they file into the Past.

1949, *New Zealand Farm and Station Verse*

We Mustered Sheep Together

'Blue Jeans' (Ross McMillan)

I read it in the Daily Press,
'One William Johnson, single.
No fixed abode or firm address,
Killed by a fall of shingle.'
('Twas just above the shipping graph,
And underneath the weather).
And so I write this epitaph –
We mustered sheep together.

He came from some small Central place,
'Twas Arrowtown I reckon.
He was one of a hardy race,
To whom the high peaks beckon.
For men like he the ranges beg,
And bind fast as a tether,
At Pisa and the Roaring Meg,
We mustered sheep together.

He took the top beat at Cecil Peak,
And outside beat at Walter.
He scaled the bluffs by Devils Creek,
Where other men would falter.
He had his faults – and I have mine –
He liked to booze and blether,
But hard work never brought a whine;
We mustered sheep together.

I'll bend my arm and raise a glass,
He's past his final river.
And mustered out through Shepherd's Pass
And off the range forever.
He'll not hit Queenstown on the spree,
Nor straddle saddle leather;
Last autumn in the Lake County
We mustered sheep together.

1970, In the Shade of the High Country

A Bitch Called Fly

Peter Stewart

It was turning out to be a tough end to the autumn muster. The early bad turn in the weather had continued and now snow was falling. It was nothing to worry about at this stage but was an indication that unless the tops were cleared promptly the old white phantom would throw his chilly cloak over the mountains and let it fall in heavy folds in the valleys blotting out the tracks which led to the safe pastures of the home river flats.

Charlie Carter, short and nuggety, his face as brown as summer tussock, had been mustering for his whole life, virtually – or so he claimed. And everyone reckoned he must be over seventy. Yet he could cover as much territory in a day as any eager young gun.

And his dogs – well, everyone acknowledged Charlie's dogs were good; there was no question about that. There was Tip, still a hard-working all-rounder, even though he was getting on in years – like his master, Charlie used to say with a grin. Jacko, the huntaway, could still bark all day behind a reluctant mob on the hills, or spur them along equally well in dusty yards. Smoke, the young heading dog, already had an eye that was a match for any stubborn old ewe refusing to move until her lambs were ready. And, of course, there was Fly – still the fastest old bitch the station could remember, with one of the widest casts any of the high country dogs ever made. She would still be working the scree slopes when they had cut her feet to ribbons and she'd be the first to lie at Charlie's own feet when the day's work was over, such was her loyalty to him. Charlie often said he'd give up mustering when Fly gave up. And those who knew them thought that would be the case only when they both dropped dead.

Charlie had to admit to himself he was feeling tired this afternoon. He'd been out almost twelve hours now. He had left the hut on Steep Ridge at five in the morning and he was looking forward to reaching the stone-walled sanctuary again. If the snow hadn't started he would be almost there now. But first there'd been the cold winds, then the snow flurries that had made the ewes even more unruly than they usually were after their long, undisturbed period on the tops. They had kept cutting back as he brought them out of Strange River Valley, and the dogs had been up and down the steep hill-sides as they'd fought to keep the mob together.

But now he had reached the valley's end and the sheep were walking more willingly

1988, *Short Stories from New Zealand*

towards the open river flats. The snow wasn't as bad here either. He called Jacko to speak up again and the dog's bark was strong. The mob made an effort, not much, but at least an effort to move faster. It was enough for Charlie to stop and turn his horse back towards Steep Ridge.

He whistled in Smoke, ranging out on the mob's right flank, and then sighed with some satisfaction as he thought of the hut   only an hour away now. Lake, his horse, must have sensed the day's work was over, too, because her pace quickened a little and her ears pricked up

Charlie leaned forward and patted the small mare's neck. Lake Maiden, she'd been named when her original breeders, the Marshalls of Lake Station, had expected a successful racing career for her. But that hadn't eventuated. She was fifteen now, and Charlie knew she was as game as his hardworking little bitch, Fly.

Charlie was conscious of the snow again. It was certainly heavier now that he had rounded the bluff and started the final climb to Steep Ridge. And the wind was stronger too.

Charlie swore quietly, and hoped it would be clearer tomorrow. He only had the south face of old Shoe Valley to sweep and he'd be through. Then it was only a day's drive down to the lower flats and he'd be back at the homestead for the winter … His hut at the homestead had one of those old stoves that heated up like a small furnace … He often went to sleep in the evenings, just sitting in front of it … drowsy and very peaceful …

He jerked himself violently back to the present! Hell! He shook his head, angry with himself. In another minute he'd be sinking into a dangerous sleep. It was the cold, numbing his mind as well as his hands and face.

He looked around quickly. The dogs were trailing Indian file, behind the horse. They were as tired as he was, even Fly, who was, surprisingly, last in the line.

'Come on, Lake,' he urged. 'We're nearly there.'

The mate quickened her pace again, and soon, through the white gauze curtain of falling snow, Charlie saw the lonely trees and, tucked at their base, Steep Ridge Hut. Within minutes after he arrived, his horse was safely stalled in the adjoining old shed but the dogs joined him in the hut to collapse exhausted before the warmth of the blaze that Charlie soon had crackling in the huge, open fireplace.

He had to sit down himself for a few minutes. He hadn't realized how weary he was. Funnily enough, it was his arms that ached with tiredness the most. His legs, in spite of the walking he'd had to do on the shingle faces, were as sound as ever … well, almost. He felt that nagging twinge in his right hip that had bothered him for each of the last three or four seasons, especially in winter. But as the warmth came back into his body, so the twinges gradually disappeared.

Soon he was up and heating the remainder of the stew that he'd made as soon as he had arrived three days earlier. It was only when he sat down to give Fly the regular scratch behind the ears that he realized she was still lying just inside the door, where she'd dropped when they arrived back at the hut. Charlie grinned to himself. It *must* have been a hard day to knock the old bitch out like that.

'Come here girl,' he said gently.

Fly's tail flopped in acknowledgement and she began to struggle to her feet but the movement was laboriously slow and so obviously painful. Charlie stood up and grimaced as another sharp twinge reminded him of his own discomfort. But it was all over in a second. Not so the pain Fly was experiencing. She stood uncomfortably, head dropped and tail still.

Charlie laid her down gently on her side. He knew it would be her paws yet he whistled quietly in surprise when he saw their state. The pads were raw, and, though not bleeding now, they'd obviously been cut for some time yet she'd worked on willingly throughout the day.

He thought about the morning muster. It could have happened on that bad slope where a small mob of cunning old ewes had proved so difficult to flush down the shingle to the main mob. He sighed, and stroked the bitch gently. She responded with a wag of her tail. Charlie told her she'd be okay. He had something to make her feel better. It was as if she were a child … and probably that's how Charlie saw her anyway.

Without standing up he could reach the small brown jar on the bench. It was the same jar he had carried for thirty years, and it contained the same ointment he made before each muster on the high slopes. He rubbed it gently on to Fly's paws now.

'There'll be no work for you tomorrow, my lass,' he told her, and the dog's ears pricked as if she were surprised at the situation.

He told her to stay where she was and after he'd eaten his stew, he gave her the rest of what was in the pot. The other dogs had been ready to move in when they saw what he was offering Fly but a curt command made them stay back. They were led outside, on normal rations, and were left out for half an hour before being allowed in again. Charlie never used to have his dogs in the hut but over the last couple of years for some reason he'd been pleased to have their company at night.

At least it had stopped snowing when he let them in, even if he didn't like the look of the sky. For no reason he shivered suddenly. He knew he should check his horse, but all he wanted to do was close the door, and forget about the mountains and the clouds that were hanging far too low. He threw another couple of pieces of wood on the fire. He wouldn't even bother lighting the lamp tonight. He'd be under his blankets straight away. Before turning in he had one last look at Fly's paws, shaking his head slowly when he realized again just how badly cut she was.

Charlie woke automatically at 4 a.m. His familiar routine was soon functioning – dogs outside, fire started, porridge mixed, billy on, and the two big slices of bread cut.

But today there was a difference. Old Fly didn't run outside with the others. Her paws were badly swollen this morning; the cuts looked nasty. Charlie scratched her behind the ear, and said he'd miss her, but … she'd have to have the day off. When he was ready to leave, Fly struggled to her feet, but he told her to stay. She watched him, almost accusingly, as he left the hut, but her eyes were tired and she remained where she was. It was only the third time he'd had to leave her behind in all their years together on the mountains.

Outside the air was crisp and still. Charlie knew there'd be more snow today. It was as if Lake Maiden felt this, too. The little mare, usually such an eager starter in the darkness of morning, moved reluctantly today, and had even shrugged her displeasure when Charlie threw the saddle over her.

It must have been nearly eight o'clock, when he was well up Old Shoe Valley, that the first flakes began to fall. They were gentle at first, but within an hour the wind had risen and the snow was driving hard at man, horse, dogs, and the sheep which were moving frustratingly slowly along the mountain tracks. By mid-day, Charlie was tired – like his horse and dogs. The mob was still struggling down the valley but at least could be picked up easily tomorrow. Now all Charlie had to do was back-track, climbing constantly, to return to the hut.

But the going was tougher all the time. He'd dismounted to give Lake a spell, but it seemed as if every step brought the knife-like stab in his right hip. He'd run into deeper snow, too, and finally he stopped and took out his ancient thermos. He was disturbed to find there was barely half a mug-full left.

The tea revived him … but just for a short time. Soon the cold was numbing him again and every step became harder. He mounted his horse and urged more effort from her. The snow was thick, driving, blinding, blotting out familiar landmarks. It was a white, mixed-up world.

Tip was the first to give up. It was some time before Charlie realized the old dog was not following in the horse's tracks. He peered back through the snow, but Tip wasn't in sight. Charlie turned Lake Maiden, retracing their path. He came on Tip after travelling a couple of hundred yards. The dog was lying curled behind stubborn rocks that defiantly jutted out of the snow.

It was an effort for Charlie to dismount, and still more difficult to lift the dog on to the horse's back. Why were his arms so tired again? His hip was really playing up now … Why couldn't he be back at the homestead? Mrs Marshall would give him some of those fresh scones she made every Tuesday … or was it Wednesday? Charlie realized vaguely he was back at the homestead with its poplars and gentle willows by the creek. But why were the trees shimmering and why was he so tired? It would be much easier to sit down.

He shook his head and rubbed his eyes. What was wrong with him? He was on the mountain, wasn't he? God! He was tired … and his eyes were painful. Everywhere it was white.

But was it? What was that small, dark dot moving out there? Charlie shook his head again. His eyes were clearer now … and his awareness. Hell, he'd been drifting off again! He had to get moving, had to make the hut before this fatigue, this cold and aching stopped him for good. He was too old for this weather, that's all there was to it.

That *was* something moving up ahead! It was Fly! Surely it was Fly! How the hell did she come to be out here? She was nearer now, making a valiant effort to reach him through the snow. He saw the so familiar eagerness and affection in her every movement.

'Hang on, girl!' Charlie cried. 'We'll come to you.'

And, with a new determination, he straightened up and slapped the horse into movement, at the same time urging his other two dogs to get cracking. He told them they couldn't let Fly show them up, just because the weather had decided to be nasty.

Fly had turned now and was leading some fifteen to twenty yards ahead all the time. The old musterer stumbled up the ridge. He had to stop a couple of times but on each occasion the bitch circled back and he roused himself to follow her again. She seemed to make no tracks in the snow but knew her direction clearly. Charlie simply accepted the fact that she was leading them back to the hut.

And, sure enough, they arrived on it suddenly, a blurred but welcome shape. Charlie's hip was as painful as the devil and his arms were almost numb as he struggled to lift old Tip off the horse. He pushed Lake into the shed, still saddled. Charlie knew he'd have to thaw out before he could stable and feed her properly. His hands were freezing as he fumbled awkwardly with the hut door handle. How had Fly got out?

He stopped in astonishment when he opened the door. The bitch was still lying where he'd left her that morning. He moved quickly to her. She was asleep … and there wasn't a single flake of snow on her! He bent down to scratch her behind the ear. She didn't move. He looked closer, and with sudden urgency felt for a sign of life.

The bitch was perfectly still, and Charlie remained motionless for a long time, too. When he straightened up, the pain in his right hip was intense.

He didn't really notice it. He was thinking of Fly, as he'd seen her, hadn't he, eager in the snow that afternoon. And suddenly he knew they'd both had their last muster …

A Glass of *Prosek*

Amelia Batistich

The two old cronies sit hunched over the table, the bottle of *Prosek* unopened between them. How many times had the two of them, quaffing the local wines, remembered the *Prosek* of home. No wine in the world like it, sacramental wine, wine of memory – to sip of its sweetness again!

'It would make a man young!' Old Petar is talking. 'The blood thins, the *Prosek* never. I remember my old grandfather Petar Petrov telling me how his grandfather got married a third time to a spicy widow at seventy! On his wedding night he downed a whole bottle of *Prosek*, the old devil. Nine months to the day later he was father to twins.'

'It would take more than a bottle of *Prosek*!' Stepan sighed deep in his bones. 'Two bottles, perhaps.'

One bottle or two, there was no *Prosek* to prove him a dreamer. The old widowers made do with what there was: a jugful of Petar's own backyard vintage. You could say that wine is always wine, as blood is blood, but … there is blood and blood.

Blood of youth, fire in the veins. Just to see a skirt swishing by was enough to set it alight. Just as well a man has to work hard in his young days, sweat and empty pockets soon cool him down. And here they are, pockets full enough, the pension coming in regularly, and the damn rheumatics!

'Oy!' Petar says creakily, 'dis leg of mine she's gorn. Been to Doktor, he say, "Man, if I good as you when I be seventy I be all right. Got to expect a man get sore leg. How many miles you walk on that leg?" he say. "Oy! Doktor, I walk plenty," I tell him. "I run too. I jump across the sky. But I no jumping now."

'Doktor he laugh. "You had your time for jumping," he say. 'Now someone else time."

'"An' lay off too much of that vino. Bad for rheumatics. Leave it for me to drink when I come. Here!" An' he give me a piece of paper with all doze prescription on it. Pills for leg. Pills for the heart. Pills for the blood pressure. Pills for the water … .

'I look at paper. "Doktor," I say. "Is dis all a man good for? To be pill swallower?"

'"Go swallow a sword then!" he say. Cheeky young bugga in white coat. My gran'son too.

'Funny, his name Petar, like mine. But I like call him Doktor. Doktor, my gran'son.'

1980, *Top Yarns from the New Zealand Farmer*

Eh, but it was a long time ago, that getting of sons and the sons getting them grandsons. The battalions of memory converge. Two widowers have a lot to remember. Aih! There's Mara and Tera sleeping in their beds of stone, their pictured faces looking so young from the headstones. Rest in Peace, till I come, the stones say, but the two widowers are in no haste to join them. Some living to do yet. Some talking to get through.

'Remember, eh! Stepan! That time on Parenga an' we dig down deep as hell to get kauri gum an you say if we dig down deep enough, maybe we dig ourselves back to Dalmatia?'

Remember. Remember. It is all remember now.

The first farm Petar got for himself. Draining that swamp, ploughing those paddocks, getting out those stumps. Water! How much water in this goddam New Zillan', reckon she floats like a ship.

'Same was for me.' Stepan's turn now. '"Land no good," bank man say, "sour like a bog." But I show him.'

Living in the town and talking all the time of back there. Up North. Sons got farms now. Daughters they marry away. Come and live by us, girls say. Stepan's girls and Petar's, they get their heads together. Nice for you to live close, you been neighbours so long. Clever girls, they fix it, find houses in same street. Funny how a man gets used to his own backyard. But he don' easy get used to living alone. First is Mara, gone. Heart, Doktor say. Then Tera. Now is like in beginning, just two mates to talk back the years. And before them a bottle of *Prosek*.

Who's going to open it? A hand – Petar's – reaches out, hesitates, then curls round the glass. It's like putting your arm round your girl. But kiss her too soon and the savour is lost.

What if the *Prosek* is not as they remember it? Golden grapes drying in Dalmatian sun, their essence captured in the wine as the moth is captive in that piece of kauri gum up there on the shelf. Ah! Those grapes make a picture in the minds of the two men; it's as if both are watching the same spool of film reel back the years. Back in the strength of their youth, they shoulder the piled baskets home from the grape harvest. *Kolo! Kolo!* The call of the dance drums in their veins.

Stepan's hand closes over Petar's. 'Open the bottle!' he says.

The two of them sitting in silence, a glass of *Prosek* in their hands. Sunlight catches the amber glow of the wine, dances like a jewel in its gleaming refulgence. Outside the motorway traffic hums, a blackbird, sated, sings from the fig tree. Let him sing.

But what are we waiting for? *Zivio!* The glasses clink. Petar takes the first long drawn sip, feels the velvet glow warm first his mouth, then seep down through his blood. Answering content gleams from Stepan's eyes – this is the wine they remember.

'No wine like our *Prosek*!'

'No wine like our *Prosek*!'

Another glass then, and another. To hell with pills. That young fulla in white coat, he don' know everything. This is the stuff to give a man.

'Remember old story, Stepan?'

'What story?'

'Story about Bishop when he curse wine after young monks make him drunk, an' he say … an' he say …' Petar can't go on for laughing.

Stepan caps the story. 'He say wine be madness to young and medicine to old!'

The bottle of *Prosek* sits like a moment of truth between them. Medicine to the old – what if this is what they have come to?

Not on your life. The bottle is tipped again, the glasses refilled.

'Is only a story,' Petar winks. 'Now if we had two bottles …'

Journey

Barry Crump

The hand that felled and split the tree
And sank the posts in sand and scree
And strung the wire and battened-up
Now raps the saucer in the cup.

The arm that sprung the hauler-sprag
And slung the axe and strung the stag
And swung the six-horse ploughing team
Now reaches out to play the queen.

The foot that trod the frozen clay
And kicked the winning goal that day;
The foot that once wore hide and steel
Now puts its slippers on by feel.

The ear that once heard the south wind roar
And fling the vessel on the shore,
And heard the names of shipmates read
Now hardly hears what's being said.

The eye that saw the car come through,
The monarch crowned, the ration-queue,
The plastic pipe, the rocket risen,
Now rests its gaze on television.

The soul that since before its birth,
Now weary of its time on earth,
And quickened by a glimpse of light,
Rejoices, and prepares for flight.

1989, *Bedtime Yarns*

Requiem in a Town House
Owen Marshall

Mr Thorpe came off sixteen hundred hectares of hill country when he finally retired, and his wife found a town house for them in Papanui. Town house is a euphemism for a free-standing retirement flat, and retirement flat is a euphemism for things best left so disguised.

Mr Thorpe made no complaint to his wife when he first saw the place of his captivity. She had accepted a firmament of natural things for forty years, and he had promised her the choice of their retirement. Yet as the removal men brought those possessions which would fit into the new home, Mr Thorpe stood helplessly by, like an old, gaunt camel in a small enclosure. Merely by moving his head from side to side he could encompass the whole of his domain and, being long-sighted by nature and habit, he found it hard to hold the immediate prospect of their section in focus.

It wasn't that Mr Thorpe had come to the city determined to die. He didn't give up without a struggle. He was a farmer and a war veteran. He went to church on Sundays with his wife, and listened to the vicar explaining the envelope donation system. He joined the bowling club, and learned which side had the bias. But he could not escape a sense of loss and futility even amid the clink of the bowls, and he grew weary of being bullied by the swollen-chested women at afternoon tea time.

Mrs Thorpe developed the habit of sending her husband out to wait for the post. It stopped him from blocking doorways, and filling up the small room of their town house. He would stand at the letter-box, resting his eyes by looking into the distance, and when the postman came he would start to speak. Bu the postman always said hello and goodbye before Mr Thorpe could get anything out. There might be a letter from their daughter in Levin, a coloured sheet of specials from the supermarket, or something from the *Reader's Digest* which he had been especially selected to receive. It wasn't the same as being able to have a decent talk with the postman though.

The town house imposed indignities on Mr Thorpe: its mean conception was the antithesis of what he had known. To eat his meals he must sit at what appeared to be a formica ironing board with chrome supports. It was called a dining bar. After a meal Mr Thorpe would stand up and walk three paces to the window to see the traffic, and three paces back again. He would look at the knives in their wall holders, and wonder at his shrunken world. He had to bathe in a plastic water-hole beneath the shower. His

1989, *The Divided World*

arthritis prevented him from washing his feet while standing, and he had to crouch in the water-hole on his buttocks, with his knees like two more bald heads alongside his own. He thought of the full-length metal and enamel bath on the farm. Sometimes he went even further back, to the broad pools of the Waipounae River in which he swam as a young man. The bunched cutty grass to avoid, the willows reaching over, the shingle beneath. The turn and cast of the water in the small rapids was like the movement of a woman's shoulder, and the smell of mint was there, crushed along the side channels as he walked.

In the town house even the lavatory lacked anything more than visual privacy. It was next to the living room: in such a house everything, in fact, is next to the living room. Mrs Thorpe's bridge friends could hear the paper parting on its perforations, and reluctantly number the deposits. Mrs Thorpe would talk more loudly to provide distraction, and her husband would sit within the resounding hardboard, and twist his face in humiliation at the wall.

The hand-basin was plastic, shaped like half a walnut shell, and too shallow to hold the water he needed. The windows had narrow aluminium frames which warped in his hand when he tried to open them. The front step was called a patio by the agent, and the wall beside it was sprayed with coloured pebbles and glue.

The section provided little comfort for Mr Thorpe. The fences separating his ground from his neighbours' were so vestigial that he found it difficult not to intrude. One evening as he stood in the sun, like a camel whose wounded expression is above it all, he was abused by McAlister next door for being a nosy old fool. Mr Thorpe was enjoying the feel of the sun on his face, and thinking of his farm, when he became aware that he was facing the McAlisters as they sunbathed on a rug. Mrs McAlister had a big stomach, and legs trailing away from it like two pieces of string. 'Mutton-headed old fool,' McAlister said, after swearing at Mr Thorpe over the fence. Mr Thorpe turned away in shame, for he was sensitive concerning privacy. 'Oiy. Go away, you nosy old fool,' shouted McAlister.

After that Mr Thorpe unconsciously exaggerated his stoop when he was in his section, to reduce the amount of his body which would appear above the fences, and he would keep his eyes down modestly as he mowed the apron lawn, or tipped his rubbish into the bag.

He tried walking in the street, but it was too busy. The diesel trucks doused him with black fumes, and most of the children used the footpath to ride bikes on. The pedestrian lights beckoned him with Cross Now, then changed to Don't Cross whenever he began.

Mr Thorpe took to sleeping in the garage. In the corner was a heavy couch that had been brought in from the farm, but wouldn't fit in the house. It was opposite the bench on which on which he'd heaped his tools and pots of dried-up paint. At first he maintained a pretence of occupation between bouts of sleep, by sorting screws, nails, tap washers and hose fittings into margarine pottles. As his despair deepened he would go directly to the couch, and stretch out with his head on the old, embroidered cushion. It was one place in which he didn't have to stoop. He had an army blanket with a stripe, for he had begun to feel the chill which is of years, not weather. There he would lie in the back of the garage; free from the traffic, the McAlisters, and the confines of his own town house. He had always been able to sleep well, and in retirement he slept even better. He was granted the release of sleep.

Mr Thorpe would lie asleep with his mouth open, and his breath would whine and mutter because of the relaxed membranes of his mouth and throat. His face had weathered into a set configuration, but it was younger somehow when he slept. His wife played bridge in the living room with her friends, or watched programmes of glossy intrigue. Mr Thorpe lay in the garage, and revisited all the places from which he had drawn his strength. Age is a conjuror, and it played the trick of turning upside down his memory, so that all he had first known was exact and fresh again, and all the things most recent were husks and faded obscurity. Mr Thorpe talked with his father again, soldiered again, courted again; yet when he was awake he forgot the name of the vicar with whom he shook hands every Sunday, and was perplexed when asked for the number of his own town house. Waking up was the worst of all. Waking from the spaciousness and immediacy of past experience, to the walls of his small bedroom closing in, or the paint pots massing on the garage bench.

'He sleeps all the time, just about,' Mrs Thorpe told the doctor, and Mr Thorpe gave a smile which was part apology for being able to sleep so well. 'He must sleep for sixteen or seventeen hours of the twenty-four sometimes. He sleeps most of the day in the garage.'

'Ah, he's got a hideaway then,' said the doctor. He used a jocular tone, perhaps because he was afraid of the response to any serious enquiry. Let sleeping dogs lie is a sound enough philosophy. 'You need more sleep when you're older,' said the doctor. He'd forgotten that the last time Mrs Thorpe came on her own account, he'd told her that old people don't need as much sleep.

'And he hasn't got the same energy anymore. Not the energy he once had. His interest in things has gone. Hasn't it, Rob?' Mr Thorpe smiled again, and was about to say that he missed farm life, when his wife and the doctor began to discuss the medication he should have.

He never did take any of the medicine, but after the visit to the doctor he tried briefly to interest himself in being awake, for his wife's sake. He sat in front of the television, but no matter how loud he had it, the words never seemed clear. There was a good deal of reverberation, and laughter from the set seemed to drown out the lines before he caught their meaning. He could never share the contestants' excitement over the origin of the term *deus ex machina*.

A dream began to recur. A dream about the town house in Papanui. In the dream he could feel himself growing larger and larger, until he burst from the garage and could easily stand right over the house, and those of his neighbours. And he would take the town house, all the pressed board, plastic and veneers, and crush it as easily as you crush the light moulded tray when all the peaches have been eaten. Then in his dream he would start walking away from the city towards the farmland. He always liked that best in his dream He was so tall that with each stride he could feel the slipstream of air about his head, and the hills came up larger with every step, like a succession of held frames.

He told his wife about the dream. She thought it amusing. She told him that he never could get the farm out of his head, could he. She said he should ask McAlister if he would like to go fishing.

In the dream Mr Thorpe never reached the hills: he never actually reached where he was walking to so forcefully. But he seemed to be coming closer time by time. As he drew nearer, he thought it was the country that he knew. The hills looked like the upper Waipounae, and he thought that he would soon be able to hear the cry of the stilts, or the sound of the stones in the river during the thaw, or the flat, self-sufficient whistle made by the southerly across the bluffs at the top of the valley.

Abandoned Homestead

Brian Turner

A family lived here   in this homestead
on a terrace   above a wide valley
with a river running down   to a glacial lake

In the distance are mountains   blue and black
and   closer   the river winding
thin and waxy like floss

Dust   droppings   cobwebs   straw
the house is full of signs of uninvited guests
and on a shelf beside the range
I find a piece of wood
inscribed with the words   Agnes Brown toiled here

To my knowledge   there is no other record
of what she thought or said   so we're not
going to know   what she did
when the man she lived with   was riding
the farthest boundaries of the run

and we can only imagine   what she said
to her children   when they left home
headed for the big smoke   one supposes
they drove off   harness jangling   dust
puffing from hooves and wheels   the cart
rocking and bouncing along the track   but
how long she stood there   after the cart
had gone   we cannot say

The summer evenings are long here
and we assume she sat   on the verandah
knitting or reading   watching the ridges
for the shape of a man on a horse
silhouetted against the flare
from the setting sun

More than a lifetime has passed   and the wood
where I sit   on the same verandah
is rotted now   and the evening light's
like panic   on the cracked windows
behind me   and in the west
the sky is tangerine   and the mountains turning black

1989, *All that* Blue *can be*

Contributors and Sources

Thank you to the following writers and publishers for permission to use their material. Every effort has been made to contact the various sources that have yielded the material in this anthology. In some cases this has not been possible. The publishers and I would be pleased to hear from any copyright holders who could not be traced.

The works in this anthology that were originally published in the *New Zealand Farmer* and the *New Zealand Journal of Agriculture* are reproduced by kind permission of New Zealand Rural Press Ltd.

All the works in this collection that were originally published by Whitcombe & Tombs and Whitcoulls Ltd are reproduced by kind permission of Penguin Books (NZ) Ltd.

All the material originally published by A.H. & A.W. Reed is reproduced with the kind permission of Reed Publishing (NZ) Ltd.

Anon.

'The EEC', *How You Doing*, eds Harry Ricketts and Hugh Roberts, Lincoln University Press, 1998.

M.L Allan

'All for Ayrshire', *Top Yarns from the New Zealand Farmer*, Shortland Publications, 1980.

Mona Anderson

Born in North Canterbury, and married to Mount Algidus station manager Ron Mason, Mona Anderson made her name as a high country author, especially with books featuring the station, on the 'other' side of the Rakaia River. Her first book, *A River Rules My Life*, was published in 1963, and became a bestseller. Eight other volumes on farm and station life were to follow.

'The Water-Joey', *The Water-Joey*, A.H. & A.W. Reed, 1976.

Frank S. Anthony 1891-1927

Frank Anthony was brought up on a farm at Whakamara, in South Taranaki. At 17 he went to sea, and later spent three years in the Royal Navy, mostly as a gunner on HMS *Opal*, which was at the Battle of Jutland. Returning to Taranaki, Anthony bought a scarcely broken-in 76-acre property at Midhurst, which he named Opal Farm. After five years there, milking never more than 20 cows and writing articles for 'the weeklies', he sold up and went to England, hoping to make it as a writer. Weakened by a wartime chest injury, he died of consumption in a Bournemouth boarding house.

'My New Heifer', *Me and Gus*, Auckland University Press, 1977. (First published *Christchurch Weekly Press*, 1924.)

E.J.V. Barry

'A Rural Experience of the Napier Earthquake' (as told to Jane Foster), *New Zealand Farmer*, 13 September 1973.

Amelia Batistich 1915-

Born and brought up in Dargaville, she is the daughter of Dalmatian parents, Ivan and Milka Barbarich. He came to the Northland gumfields in 1897 and Milka followed in 1913, though both were from the same little village, Zaostrag, on the Adriatic coast. Amelia Batistich has lived in Auckland most of her adult life and is the author of two novels, two books of short stories and a recent publication that is part autobiography, part short stories.

'A Glass of Prosek', *Never Lost for Words*, Auckland University Press, 2000

Millicent Bennett

'Baa baa baa', *New Zealand Farmer*, July 1969.

E.M. Blaiklock 1903-1983

Born in England, he was quite young when he and his parents settled in Auckland. His father, an engineer, took up a smallholding in what is now suburban Browns Bay. Professor Blaiklock taught Latin, Greek and Ancient History at Auckland University for 42 years, holding the chair in Classics for 21 years. As 'Grammaticus', for 40 years he wrote weekly articles for, in turn, the *Weekly News*, the *Sunday Herald* and the *New Zealand Herald*.

'Farewell Prickly, Luscious Blackberry', *New Zealand Herald*, 10 January 1978.

Frances Blunt, died 1984

Born Frances Acton-Adams at Kaikoura, she was one of 11 children brought up on Clarence Reserve, an isolated station beyond the Seaward Kaikouras. Educated at Woodford House, she later taught there and at Marlborough College. She and her husband farmed another Kaikoura property, Steepdown. A collection of Frances Blunt's poetry, *When Leonardo Painted Trees*, was published after her death.

'Clarence Pack Team', *New Zealand Farm and Station Verse*, Whitcombe & Tombs, 1967.

John Broughton 1947-

A qualified dentist and accomplished playwright, John Broughton has affiliations with Ngati Kahungungu and Ngai Tahu. Born in Hastings, he has been a lecturer in Public Health at Otago Medical School since 1989. He has penned several full-length plays, including *Michael James Manaia*, which was performed at the Edinburgh Festival, and others that have been toured extensively at schools throughout the country.

'Nga Puke (The Hills)', *Nga Puke: A Play*, Aoraki Press, 1992.

Anne Earncliff Brown

Her husband was the director of the Agriculture Department's Fields Division, but the couple also farmed, first in the Manawatu, then South Canterbury, losing that property in the 1922 slump. He returned to the department and she, single-handed, managed a dairy farm for five years. Indebtedness overcome, the Browns returned to full-time farming in North Canterbury. From this property Anne Brown contributed a regular column or 'Calendar' to the *North Canterbury Gazette*.

'The Farmer's Wife': 'Mendel', 'Ending', *North Canterbury Gazette*, 1932-1933.

Heather Browning

Grew up in the Wairau Valley, Marlborough and now lives in Waitaria Bay in Kenepuru Sound. A mother of five and involved in community education, she both paints and writes, and as a member of a local writing group, The Weka Writers, has contributed to their publications.

'Sausages for Tea', *Sleeping Dolphins*, Cape Catley, 1999.

Ormond Burton 1893-1974

Teacher, soldier, writer, Methodist minister and pacifist, Ormond Burton was awarded the Military Medal for bravery in the First World War, and jailed for publicly expressing pacifist ideals during the Second World War. Auckland-born and educated, Burton taught at several country schools and published 17 works of non-fiction, from military histories to treatises on pacifism and many other subjects.

'Bart and the Cows', *Bart, the Story of a Dog*, Harry H. Tombs, 1944.

Rod Campbell 1914-

Born in Poverty Bay, Campbell now lives in Warkworth, after a working life as a stockman, musterer and horse-breaker. The designer of the Rod Campbell Saddle, he also has an international reputation as a faith healer and has published two small books of reminiscence.

'The old way of learning to ride', *At One With Nature*, Rod Campbell, 1994.

Field Candy 1926-1984

Born in Te Aroha, he left school at 15 to work in the family milk business. He later moved to a dairy farm at Ohauiti, in the Bay of Plenty, where he established New Zealand's first walkway on private land. Field Candy began writing in the 1960s and had short stories and articles published in the *New Zealand Herald*, the *New Zealand Listener*, the *New Zealand Farmer* and Tauranga writing group publications. In 1988, his wife, Mona, published a selection of his work, *Every Living Thing*.

'The Constant Help', 'The Khaki Pit', 'Boots', *Every Living Thing*, Mona Candy-Moana Press, 1988.
'The Battle for the Nodding Thistle Shield', *New Zealand Farmer*, 1981.

Peter Cape

Writer and broadcaster, singer and songwriter, Anglican priest and art critic, Peter Cape was educated at Auckland University and St Johns Theological College. The author of several photographic works for children, he also produced several albums of New Zealand folk music and revised J.C. Reid's *A Book of New Zealand*. His CD *I'm an Ordinary Joker* was released posthumously in 2001.

'Down the Hall on Saturday Night', *A Book of New Zealand*, A.H. & A.W. Reed, 1964.

Roland Clarke

Born in Northern Ireland, he saw naval service during the Second World War and later managed a linen flax mill in Ulster. He then emigrated to New Zealand and settled on a farm at Staveley, Mid-Canterbury. From the mid-1960s to the 1980s he wrote a monthly *New Zealand Farmer* column, 'The Month Down South' under the name, 'Nor'wester'. Roland Clarke now lives on a tree crop nursery on Banks Peninsula and still contributes to newspapers and periodicals.

'The Month Down South', *New Zealand Farmer*, excerpts from 1965 to 1970. 'The Snow Down South', *New Zealand Farmer*, 13 September 1973.

Nelson L. Cooper 1916-2000

Born on the East Coast, he left school aged 14 and became a drover. He later farmed on his own account in both Poverty Bay and the Waikato and managed a family property, Broadhurst Station. Much of Nelson Cooper's only book was collated from taped material by his niece, Margaret Cooper.

'Bulls' Horns', *Memories of a Stockman*, N.L. Cooper, 1999.

R.A. Copland 1918-

Born in Feilding, he was educated at Napier Boys' High School and gained his masters and doctorate from the University of New Zealand. A member of Canterbury University's English department for many years, and professor from 1970 to 1976, in the 1950s Copland wrote a series of light commentaries for the *Listener* under the pen name 'Augustus'.

'Yes, to the Very End', *New Zealand Listener*, 1950.

Neroli Cottam 1949-
Born in Canterbury, she has lived on a farm near Cromwell since 1994. She is a member of the Cromwell writers' group and her work has been published in periodicals and collections, here and overseas.

'Shaping Up', *Under Mount Pisa: Central Otago Poems*, Neroli Cottam, 1996.

Tommy Cowan 1908-1995
A keen hunter and bushman, Cowan was born in Awakino and lived for many years in the back country of the Waitotara Valley, then in Wanganui. His tales were told to his daughter-in-law, Valerie Cowan, a former public health administrator who has produced three books of the reminiscences of elderly New Zealanders.

'The Wrath of God', *Pigs and Me*, Cape Catley, 1997.

Joy Cowley 1936-
Born in Levin, she was educated at Palmerston North Girls' High School and Pharmacy College and can list among her former occupations, farm worker, builder's labourer and photographer. A very prolific children's writer, Cowley has written a number of adult novels, published collections of short stories, and edited the collection, *Summer Dolphins*, written by women of the Marlborough Sounds, where she now lives.

'Au Revoir', *Return to Open Country*, A.H.& A.W. Reed, 1967. 'Birth', *Two of a Kind*, Blackberry Press, 1984.

Barry Crump 1935-1996
The 'good keen man' of New Zealand writing was born in Papatoetoe, Auckland, and penned more than 20 books and several collections of yarns and bush ballads. Many regard his first book, *A Good Keen Man*, as a New Zealand classic. A deer culler, goat and pig hunter, fencer and farmhand, Crump was also a successful broadcaster and four-wheel drive demonstrator.

'Uncle Wally's Pacer', *Horses and Horsemen*, A.H. & A.W. Reed, 1974. 'Journey', *Bedtime Yarns*, Hodder Moa Beckett, 1997.

Allen Curnow 1911-2001
Born in Timaru, he was educated at Canterbury and Auckland Universities, where he later joined the staff of the English department. A serious poet and editor of considerable standing, from the 1940s to the 1960s Allen Curnow also produced a weekly satire on current events in verse, under the pseudonym 'Whim Wham'. Several collections of these newspaper columns have been published.

'The Cold Shoulder', *The Best of Whim Wham*, Paul's Book Arcade, 1959.

Ruth Dallas 1919-
The Invercargill-born poet, who now lives in Dunedin, was manpowered into herd testing during the Second World War; the background for 'Milking before Dawn'. The author of eight children's books, several poetry volumes, a short story collection and an autobiography, Ruth Dallas worked on the quarterly *Landfall*, alongside its founding editor, Charles Brasch. For her services to New Zealand writing Ruth Dallas was awarded the CBE and made an honorary D. Litt. by Otago University.

'Milking before Dawn', 'Pioneer Woman with Ferrets', *Collected Poems*, University of Otago Press, 1987.

Dan Davin 1913-1990
Rhodes Scholar, soldier, author and academic publisher for the Oxford University Press, Dan Davin was born in Invercargill of Irish Catholic stock. Although his father was a railwayman, they lived on a smallholding on the city's edge and milked up to four cows. Many of his uncles were Southland farmers and they, and his early years, provided the background for Davin's work set in the South.
'Ferreting About', *Roads From Home*, Michael Joseph, 1949.

John Dawson 1950-
A former Ministry of Agriculture farm adviser on the West Coast of the South Island, he is now an executive with the New Zealand Dairy Group, based in Hamilton.
'Texas Longhorns', *Whitebait and Wetland: Tales of the West Coast*, David Bateman, 1998.

Maureen Doherty 1938-
Born in Timaru, she has lived in various parts of New Zealand and, since 1993, at Ohau Channel in the Bay of Plenty. A member of the Rotorua Mad Poets Society, she has had work published in several collections and a number of periodicals.
'Death in the Hayfield', *Antipodes New Writing*, Antipodes Press, 1987.

Oliver Duff 1883-1967
Born on the Otago goldfields and brought up on a Central Otago farm, Duff went to the Boer War as an 18-year-old. On his return he studied for the Presbyterian ministry but declined ordination and went rabbiting, shearing and swagging, before teaching for 10 years. This was followed by 30 years of journalism; he became editor of the *North Canterbury Gazette*, the *Timaru Herald*, the *Press* and the *New Zealand Listener*. Oliver Duff retired to a small farm in Canterbury and as 'Sundowner' recorded life there in a *Listener* column, 'A Shepherd's Calendar', which later became a book of the same name. He wrote two other books.
'A Shepherd's Calendar', *A Shepherd's Calendar*, New Zealand Listener, 1953.

Eileen Duggan 1894-1972
Poet, essayist and journalist, Eileen Duggan was born in rural Marlborough and gained an MA in history from Victoria University. Ill health put an end to her teaching career and for over 40 years she earned her living as a writer, including editing 'Pippa's Page' in the *New Zealand Tablet*. Between 1922 and 1951 five volumes of her poetry were published.
'Twilight', *Poems*, Allen & Unwin, 1937.

Peter Dunbar
' "Hey! The Mill's Coming" ', *Our Open Country*, A.H. & A.W. Reed, 1974.

C. Evans
'Nor-wester', *New Zealand Farmer*, 25 October 1973.

Fiona Farrell 1947-
Playwright, poet and novelist, Farrell was born in Oamaru and educated at Otago University and in Toronto. She has had five stage plays performed and several on radio, and has published volumes of poetry, short story collections and two novels. Since 1993 Fiona Farrell has lived on a farm at Otanerito, on Banks Peninsula.
'Sheep', *Sport* 19, 1997. 'The Young Farmer's Club Experiences a Blackout', *The Skinny Louie Book*, Penguin Books, 1992.

John Foster

An accomplished muralist and printmaker, John Foster has been an artist since 1973. He lives with his sculptor wife, Pat, on a farm near Wellsford. Foster's works have hung in over 50 exhibitions and others are on display in his own woolshed-gallery. He is also a writer, illustrator and publisher.

'Lambing Beat', *Selected Poems*, Silverhill Press, 1999.

Nancy Fox 1913-

Born in the King Country district of Mapiu, Nancy Fox has lived in Auckland for many years. She describes herself as 'A teacher, from a family of teachers'.

'September, 1983, Mapiu, Remembered Roses', *Landmarks: Poems 1937-1987*, Griffin Press, 1989.

David Geary 1963-

A playwright, he was born in Feilding and educated at Palmerston North Boys' High School and Victoria University. He has had several full-length plays performed since 1991, including *Pack of Girls*, *Lovelock's Dream Run* and *The Learner's Stand*. David Geary has also contributed short stories and poetry to journals, anthologies and periodicals.

'The Single Shepherd', *New Zealand Listener*, 5 September 1998.

Tim Gilbertson

He farms at Waipawa in Hawke's Bay, as have generations of Gilbertsons before him. He is currently leasing out most of his property and concentrating on developing an olive grove and tourist operation on the remainder. His monthly column, 'Gilbertson', has appeared for several years in the fortnightly farming and agri-business newspaper, *Rural News*.

'Gilbertson: Tourist venture earns more aggro than EBIT', *Rural News*, 22 May 2000.

John Gordon 1944-

Writer, broadcaster and casual shepherd of southern rural descent.

'Drama at the Yard', 'One Trial After Another', *Three Sheep and a Dog*, Reed Publishing, 1998. 'Calf Club Day', *People, Places and Paddocks*, Lansdowne Press, 1987. 'Squatter's Rites', *New Zealand Journal of Agriculture*, September 1985.

Patricia Grace 1937-

Born in Wellington of Ngati Toa, Ngati Raukawa and Te Ati Awa descent, she was educated at Wellington Teachers' Training College and Victoria University. She taught in Northland and later moved to Plimmerton where she brought up seven children and continued to teach until 1988; she still lives and writes there. Patricia Grace has published books of short stories, adult novels and children's fiction. She was awarded the QSO in 1988 and a year later made an honorary D. Litt. of Victoria University.

'Between Earth and Sky', *The Dream Sleepers*, Longman Paul, 1980. 'Spring' ('A Way of Talking'), *Waiariki*, Longman Paul, 1975.

W.H. Guthrie-Smith 1861-1940

Born in Scotland, Herbert Guthrie-Smith came to this country as an 18-year-old. In 1882, after a two-year cadetship on New Zealand sheep stations, he and a cousin took up Tutira, in Hawke's Bay. In time he bought his partner out, developed the station and became a respected naturalist. He wrote five books on natural history, including the classic, *Tutira*. In 1924 Guthrie-Smith was made a Fellow of the Royal Society, one of very few without a university education to be thus recognised.

'The Rise and Fall of H.G.-S. and A.M.C.', *Tutira: The Story of a New Zealand Sheep Station*, William Blackwood, 1926.

William Hart-Smith 1911-1990

English-born, he arrived in New Zealand as a 12-year-old and lived in Auckland. He first worked as a radio mechanic, then in Australia as an announcer and copywriter. Following war service he became a freelance writer then returned to New Zealand where, from 1946 to 1954, he was an adult education tutor in South Canterbury. William Hart-Smith wrote six volumes of verse and contributed to publications on both sides of the Tasman.

'Harvest', *Harvest*, Georgian House, 1945.

Dawn Hayes 1928-

Born in Weymouth and educated at Christchurch Girls' High School, she was first published in 1948 in the *Auckland Star*. Her work has appeared in many papers and periodicals since then, including the *New Zealand Farmer*, the *Listener* and the *Australian Journal*. A Whangarei resident, Dawn Hayes was owner-manager of a real estate firm and has published one volume of verse.

'Country Member', *Wetbush Fire*, Pegasus Press, 1975.

Jim Henderson 1918-

Born and brought up in Takaka, Jim Henderson became one of the most identifiable rural communicators of his generation. His radio programme, *Open Country*, was a weekly must for many listeners and led to the publication of five books of the series' contributed articles; these amounted to nearly a quarter of all the books he either wrote or edited. Columnist, broadcaster, war veterans' champion and author of the classic, *Gunner Inglorious*, Jim Henderson lives in Auckland.

'The Old Kitchen Table', *Jim Henderson's New Zealand*, Grantham House, 1989 (First published *New Zealand Times*.)

Michael Henderson 1942-1998

Born in Nelson, he was educated there and at Canterbury University, where he studied law. He was first a diplomat, but turned to writing and in 1975 the novella, *The Log of a Superfluous Son*, was published. Michael Henderson's short stories have appeared in publications around the world and his first collection, *The Lie of the Land*, in 1991. His second selection, *The Small Change of Silence*, was published posthumously in 1999.

'The Hydatids Officer', *The Lie of the Land*, John McIndoe, 1991.

Louisa Herd 1964-

Born in Scotland, she came to New Zealand in 1987 to work as a podiatrist. Since 1994 she has worked on a small dairy farm near Wellsford in Northland. Louisa Herd writes for magazines here and in Britain and, through Massey University, is studying extra-murally for an applied science degree.

'Boys will be Boys', *Growing Today*, January 2001.

Elizabeth Hill 1920-

Born in Napier, she was first a radiographer, and began her writing career as a freelance journalist. *Landfall* and several other periodicals have published her short stories, and she has written one book of non-fiction and another of fiction.

'The Dam', *Landfall*, No.130, June 1979.

Noel Hilliard 1929-1996
Born in Napier and educated at Gisborne High and Victoria University, Hilliard became a journalist, and later chief sub-editor of the *New Zealand Listener* and editor of three *New Zealand Heritage* information series. He was, too, a schoolteacher, farm worker and full-time writer who wrote five novels, two short story collections, one children's book and an account of his travels in Russia.
'Off to School', *A Piece of Land*, Robert Hale, 1963.

Amanda Jackson
Born in Mangakino and raised in Napier, she married a schoolteacher and spent 25 years in Hawke's Bay and East Coast country settlements. She trained late as a schoolteacher herself, 'But I sign myself as "writer" now'.
'Harsh Mistress', *Growing Today*, December 2000.

Karalyn Joyce 1964-
A poet and writer from Pleasant Point in South Canterbury, she has an Advanced Diploma in Fine Arts (writing) from Whitireia Polytechnic. Her work has been published in the *Listener*, *Takahe*, *Grace* and other New Zealand periodicals and anthologies.
'Love Poem to a Farmer', *New Zealand Listener*, 10 March 2001.

Philip Kenway
Born in Birmingham in 1861, he came to New Zealand in 1883 to join his brother in Poverty Bay, where they developed Kiore Station. He returned to England in 1906 and wrote two autobiographical works and one on Social Credit policy. A Quaker, Kenway drove his own ambulance in France during the First World War.
'Of Cooks', *Quondam Quaker*, Cornish Brothers, 1947.

J.M. Kerwin
A dairy farmer in the Buller district, in 1991 he published *Offcuts*, a slim volume of verse and short stories.
'38 Years', *Landfall*, No.143, 1982.

John Kneebone 1935-
A Waikato dairy farmer, farming leader, company director and former Nuffield Scholar, John Kneebone was national president of Federated Farmers in the 1970s and was awarded the CMG. During the early 1980s his column, 'The Land', was a regular in the *New Zealand Journal of Agriculture*.
'The Land: Call yourself a peasant', *New Zealand Journal of Agriculture*, May 1982.

Tom Landreth
Born in South Otago's Catlins district, he became an industrial chemist in the textile industry, and now lives in Cromwell. A member of the Cromwell writers' group, he is a successful and competitive limerick writer and his work has been published in the *Listener* and local publications.
'Sweet Dieseline', *Speaking in Tongues in the Wide Wilderness*, Parkburn Press, 1998.

William Langton
'With the Musterers', *Mark Anderson*, J. Wilkie & Co., 1889.

Jack Lasenby 1931-

A full-time writer, whose novels and short stories for young people appeal to many adults. After two years at Auckland University he spent 10 years in the Ureweras, deer culling. On returning to the city he became a schoolteacher, then a teachers' college lecturer. Now living in Wellington, Jack Lasenby has written several novels, four collections of short stories and other publications for children. Many of these have won major awards.

'Uncle Trev and the Howling Dog Service', *Uncle Trev*, Cape Catley, 1991. 'The Last of the Barn Dances', *Landfall*, No.141, March 1982.

Bob Linton

Born in Northland, he graduated from Massey University and worked as a Dairy Board consulting officer before taking over the family dairy farm at Waipu. He later moved to Fenland Farms in the Waikato. He wrote a regular *New Zealand Farmer* column, 'The View From Our Hill', and later worked on a World Bank dairy beef project in South Korea.

'The View From Our Hill: Presenting the Farmers' Case', *New Zealand Farmer*, 14 May 1970.

M.H. Linscott

'The Honey Tree', *The Honey Tree*, M.H. Linscott, 1975.

Heather McCrostie Little

Born in Balclutha and educated at Rangi Ruru, Heather McCrostie married Brian Little, a descendant of a founder of the Corriedale breed, and they ran Hui Hui Stud in Hawarden, North Canterbury. After his death she became involved in local body affairs and worked as a rural sociologist. The recipient of an MBE, Heather McCrostie Little has co-written several papers, a book on rural life and was a columnist for the *New Zealand Journal of Agriculture*.

'People: Drought is more than a physical battle', *New Zealand Journal of Agriculture*, June 1982.

Ralph Lowry 1900-

Born in Hawke's Bay and educated at Christ's College and Jesus College Cambridge, he was a double blue (rugby and tennis); he gained a BA in 1924 and in 1944, following war service, an MA. Ralph Lowry owned and lived on Ohinewairua Station on the Taihape-Napier Road and managed other family properties in Hawke's Bay, the Inland Patea and Australia.

'Representative Cricket', *Taihape: Be Happy, Die Happy*, Ralph Lowry, 1985.

Gordon Lucas

Born in Tarras and educated at Christ's College, Gordon Lucas mustered for some years, is a successful sheep dog triallist and judge and farms Nine Mile, a grazing property on the Otago side of the Lindis Pass.

'Fondest Memories', *On the Run*, Hawea-Wanaka Musterers' Reunion Committee, 1998.

Joan MacIntosh 1924-

Born Joan Dawson, in Wellington, she grew up in the South. After leaving Southland Girls' High School she worked in an Invercargill office, then the Tokanui General Store. Following marriage she became both a farmer and Southern Southland reporter for the *Southland Times*. Joan MacIntosh has written six regional histories and two books of autobiography and lives in retirement in Riverton.

'Getting to Know You', 'Isolation', *Never a Dull Moment*, John McIndoe, 1974.

Alice Mackenzie 1873-1963

Daughter and chronicler of the remarkable McKenzie family who settled on a 40-acre block at Martins Bay, 15 miles north of Milford Sound. In 1902 she married Peter Mackenzie of Glenorchy, where they farmed until retirement in Queenstown. Aged 71 she wrote her only book, *Pioneers of Martin's Bay*, though for many years she contributed jokes, verse and articles to farming magazines.

'The Women's Division of Farmers' Union', *Poems*, Mrs Peter Mackenzie, 1948.

Ross McMillan 1929-

Poet, musterer and small farmer, McMillan lives in the Naseby area of the Maniototo, his birthplace. For many years, as 'Blue Jeans', he has written verse and ballads, and four books of his work have been published, plus a recent volume of selected verse. Ross McMillan is an excellent example of a rural poet/balladeer, who reflects the life, work and landscape of his region.

'When Jean Deans Raced the Train', *The Country Bloke*, Ross 'Blue Jeans' McMillan, 2000. 'We Mustered Sheep Together', *In the Shade of the High Country*, *Central Otago News*, 1970.

Owen Marshall 1941-

Born in Te Kuiti, he was brought up in Blenheim and Timaru (where he now lives) and taught for many years at Waitaki Boys' High School. With over 150 of his stories published in nine volumes, Owen Marshall is regarded as the country's foremost exponent of short fiction. He has also published two novels. A full-time writer, he also teaches creative writing at Aoraki Polytechnic.

'Requiem in a Town House', *The Best of Owen Marshall's Short Stories*, Vintage, 1997.

Barry Mitcalfe 1930-1986

Journalist, schoolteacher, poet, peace activist and publisher, Barry Mitcalfe taught at country schools in Taranaki and Northland and lectured at Wellington Teachers' College. A published poet in both Maori and English, he wrote over 30 different publications, and established the Coromandel Press.

'Bobby Calf', *Uncle and Others*, Coromandel Press, 1978.

Jim Morris

Born in Christchurch, he worked as a high country shepherd and musterer and in time took up Manuka Point, on the 'other' side of the Rakaia, where he began to write poems and ballads. Now running Ben Avon Station, near Omarama, Jim has published one volume of verse – proceeds going to the Cancer Society – and is sought after as a commissioned poet and performer for rural occasions.

'Rajah', 'Sustainability', 'Different Worlds', *Different Worlds*, Jim Morris, 1997.

Yva Momatuik and John Eastcott

This wife and husband team write and photograph together. Yva, from Poland, has architectural qualifications and experience as a designer, cowhand and horse trainer. John, a New Zealander, was a photographer for *Salient*, then the *Evening Post*. They have worked on assignments throughout the world, often for *National Geographic*.

'High Country', *High Country*, A.H & A.W. Reed, 1980.

H.N. Munro

A North Canterbury farmer and horseman of repute, for many years Munro wrote 'Toprail Talk' for *New Zealand Farmer* readers with an interest in equestrian events and the pony club movement.

'Toprail Talk: Equine Psychology', *New Zealand Farmer*, 25 September 1969.

Bridget Musters

Born in England, she has worked around the world as a teacher, editor and journalist and now lives at Ironic in the Motueka Valley. Her work has been published in New Zealand and Britain.

'Love at First Sight', *Ten*, Nelson Writers Group, 1994.

New Zealand Free Lance 1900-1961

During the period that the three items appearing in this collection were published by the *Free Lance*, the magazine never identified their contributors. They hid behind 'Our Correspondent', 'Anon.' or their initials, as with 'J.J.' who, during the Second World War, penned a column for landgirls.

'Rounding Up Recalcitrant Cattle', 'J.J.', May 1943. 'Age-Old Right of Farmers', 'Anon.', July 1945. 'Killing a Bit of Beef in the Morning', 'Our Special Correspondent', August 1944, *New Zealand Free Lance*.

John Newton 1959-

Poet, critic and a member of Canterbury University's English department, John Newton was born in Blenheim, and brought up on a farm at Port Underwood in the Marlborough Sounds. He has had one book of verse published and contributed to several periodicals here and in Australia.

'Mutton', *Tales From the Angler's Eldorado*, Untold Books, 1985. 'Blood Poisoning', *Landfall*, No.169, March 1989.

Peter Newton 1906-1984

Although born in the North Island, Peter Newton became the South Island high country's most published voice. His first job was as cowboy on a sheep station; two years later he was mustering full time. Following war service Newton worked for the Valuation Department, managed two large stations, Mount White and Nokomai, and then took up a small run in the North Canterbury foothills. Twelve works of non-fiction and one novel followed his first book, the classic, *Wayleggo*.

'Sheepmen and their Dogs: Deals in Dogs', *New Zealand Farmer*, 14 September 1967. 'The Good Old Days', 23 December 1965, *New Zealand Farmer*.

William Owen 1925-

He is an author, illustrator, sailor and retired Great Barrier Island fisherman and farmer, whose book on navigating and enjoying the Hauraki Gulf has run to several editions, the latest in 1999. He has written one work of fiction and six of non-fiction.

'Loading the Bulls', *Tryphena's Summer*, William Collins, 1974.

Nancy Patulski

Another of her short stories, 'Finders Keepers', has been published for use in schools.
'Poles Apart', *Top Yarns From the New Zealand Farmer*, Shortland Publications, 1980.

Sean Pennycook

He was educated at Timaru Boys' High School and, after shepherding and mustering on several high country stations in the Mackenzie Country, became a partner with his brother Crawford on Makarora Station. From there, as 'Tussock-Jumper', he wrote 'High Country Diary' for the *New Zealand Farmer*. When a knee injury forced Pennycook to leave the high country he studied botany at Auckland University.

'High Country Diary: The Fall Muster Beats Them All', 27 January 1966, 'High Country Diary', 26 May 1966, *New Zealand Farmer*.

Katie Pye

Poet and songwriter, singer and musician in the group, Nettle Soup, Katie Pye is managing a dairy farm in the South Hokianga, while developing her own property. From a farming family in Poverty Bay, she has been a teacher, postie, truck driver and forestry worker and is a member of the South Hokianga Writers' Group.

'Busy', *Words of Whether, With Scattered Scowers*, The Rainbow Works Ink, 1985.

David Ray 1932-

While he was Professor of English at the University of Missouri Kansas City in 1987, David Ray spent a term on exchange at the University of Otago, and a collection of New Zealand poems was the result. In the United States he has published many books of fiction, poetry and essays.

'Scientific Management', *Wool Highways and Other Poems*, Helicon Nine Editions, 1993, Copyright c. David Ray. Reprinted by permission of Helicon Nine Editions, USA.

Nora Sanderson 1905-1975

Born in Opotiki, she grew up in the Hokianga, a member of a large and isolated pioneering family. A nurse, Mrs Sanderson trained under the legendary Dr G.M. Smith at Rawene Hospital. Married to a Methodist minister, she lived at Tai Tapu for many years, wrote some 20 novels of light romance and in 1974, an autobiography that remained unpublished for 25 years.

'Accident Prone', *One of the Family*, Steele Roberts, 1999.

Patricia M. Saunders

New Zealand-born, she went to London around the time of the outbreak of the Second World War. One collection of her verse has been published and between 1939 and 1946 five of her poems were included in *Art in New Zealand*.

'One of Our Aircraft Failed to Return', *Arena*, Hutchinson, 1948.

Mary Scott 1888-1979

Born Mary Clarke, of missionary parents in the Bay of Islands, she was brought up in Napier and educated in Auckland. After graduating MA (Hons) in English, teaching for two years and then marrying, she and her husband farmed in the Northern King Country for over 40 years. Mary Scott's writing career began with semi-autobiographical 'Barbara' stories for the *New Zealand Herald* supplement, and five collections of these appeared in book form. She then wrote 26 novels of light romance, and an autobiography.

'The Dipping', *Barbara on the Farm*, A.H. & A.W. Reed, 1953.

Glynellen Slater

'O'Reilly's Pig', *Province: New Nelson Writing*, Nelson Provincial Arts Council, 1987.

June Slee 1945-

She was brought up on the family property at Blackmount, Southland, and her brothers organised the Southland farmers' protest that she described in *Bloody Friday*. June Slee has an MA (Hons) in political science and a PhD in special education. Currently on the staff of the School of Education and Early Childhood Studies at the University of Western Sydney, she plans to become a grape grower in North Otago's Waitaki Valley.

Bloody Friday, John McIndoe, 1979.

Peter Stewart 1934-1990
Educated at Otago Boys' High School and Otago University, where he graduated with an MA in history, he was an adult education officer, teacher and freelance writer before he joined publisher John McIndoe as managing editor. From 1975 to 1978 he was editor of the Dunedin *Evening Star*, then worked in television until becoming editor of the *New Zealand Listener* from 1980 to 1983, a job to which he returned briefly in 1988. His last job was as senior lecturer in communications at Massey University.

'A Bitch Called Fly', *Short Stories From New Zealand*, Highgate/Price Milburn, 1988.

Amiria Manutahi Stirling, died 1983
A member of the Ngati Hinekehu sub-tribe of Ngati Porou, Amiria Stirling was born at Taumata-o-mihi near Ruatoria in the 1890s. In 1918 she married Eruera Stirling of Te Whanau-a-Maru in the Bay of Plenty, where farmed on two different properties until the death of their eldest son, when they moved to Auckland. There they became leaders of the Maori community and came in contact with the anthropologist, Dr (later Dame) Anne Salmond, to whom each told their life stories. Dame Anne published these as separate volumes, and is the author of other books on Maori history and customs.

'Life on the Farm', *Amiria: the Life Story of a Maori Woman*, A.H. & A.W. Reed, 1976.

J.H. Sutherland 1925-
A long-serving field librarian with the Country Library Service, J.H. Sutherland comes from Morrinsville. He has self-published two short story collections, two novellas and co-written two other publications.

'The Fifteenth Day', *This Earth and Other Stories*, J.H. Sutherland, 1977.

Brian Turner 1944-
This Dunedin born and educated poet has published six volumes of verse and, as an editor and writer, has been directly involved in many publications on conservation and the countryside and others in association with sporting figures. Turner represented New Zealand at hockey, still competes in triathlons and has cycled, climbed, tramped, fished and rambled over much of Southern New Zealand. He now lives in the Maniototo.

'The Hired Man', 'The Initiation', *Ladders of Rain*, John McIndoe, 1978. 'Abandoned Homestead', *All that Blue can be*, John McIndoe, 1989.

Elizabeth Underwood/Lyn McConchie 1946-
Elizabeth Underwood was the pseudonym Lyn McConchie used to write her first book, *Farming Daze*. She has had nine books and over 150 short stories published, many of them fantasy or science fiction for young adults and published in the United States. A former waitress, researcher and Probation Service administrator, some years ago Lyn McConchie took early retirement and bought a small farm at Norsewood in Southern Hawke's Bay.

'Quite a Lot of Bull', *Farming Daze*, GP Publications, 1980.

Becchi Watt
'A Day in the Life of a Farmer', *Herstory*, Rural Women's Network/New Women's Press, 1985.

M. Weatherall
'Follow Fellow', *New Zealand Farmer*, 14 May 1970.

Jackson Webb 1940-

Born in Denver Colorado, he first came to New Zealand to dodge the enlistment draft for the Vietnam War. Since then he has lived and worked around the world and been published here and overseas.

'My Landlord Peter', *Islands* 18, July 1977.

Pat White 1944-

Born on the South Island's West Coast, he was first a dairy farmer, against whom personal health and conditions conspired. He then became a librarian in Hokitika, Ashburton and, currently, Masterton, where he lives on a small farm at Gladstone. Pat White's poetry has appeared in *Landfall*, *Islands* and other periodicals, and has published four volumes of his work.

'Cats', 'Make a poem of this', '*Local farmers seek assistance – Wairarapa Times Age headline*', 'So easy', *Drought and other intimacies*, Steele Roberts, 1999.

May Williamson 1910-

Northland-based artist and short story writer whose work appeared in several magazines and local collections over many years.

'The Opener', *New Zealand Farmer*, 22 May 1969. 'The Winner', *When Women Write in Northland*, Whangarei Community Arts Council, 1985.

Vernice Wineera 1938-

Of Ngati Toa and Ngati Raukawa descent, Vernice Wineera grew up in Porirua and was educated at Wellington Technical College, Sydney Girls' High School and Brigham Young University in Hawaii. There she stayed, to teach English and creative writing. She has published one volume of verse and edited the anthology, *Ka Po'e La'ie*. She is currently Director of the Institute of Polynesian Studies at Brigham Young University in La'ie, Hawaii.

'Ao Tea Roa', 'The Farm-Boy Rides a Yamaha', *Mahanga*, Institute for Polynesian Studies Hawaii, 1978.